Lecture Notes
in Business Information Processing   **346**

More information about this series at http://www.springer.com/series/7911

Ewa Ziemba (Ed.)

Information Technology for Management

Emerging Research and Applications

15th Conference, AITM 2018
and 13th Conference, ISM 2018, Held as Part of FedCSIS
Poznan, Poland, September 9–12, 2018
Revised and Extended Selected Papers

 Springer

Editor
Ewa Ziemba 🔟
University of Economics in Katowice
Katowice, Poland

ISSN 1865-1348 ISSN 1865-1356 (electronic)
Lecture Notes in Business Information Processing
ISBN 978-3-030-15153-9 ISBN 978-3-030-15154-6 (eBook)
https://doi.org/10.1007/978-3-030-15154-6

Library of Congress Control Number: 2019933406

This Springer imprint is published by the registered company Springer Nature Switzerland AG
The registered company address is: Gewerbestrasse 11, 6330 Cham, Switzerland

Preface

Three editions of this book appeared in past three years: *Information Technology for Management* in 2016 (LNBIP 243), *Information Technology for Management: New Ideas or Real Solutions* in 2017 (LNBIP 277), and *Information Technology for Management: Ongoing Research and Development* in 2018 (LNBIP 311).

Given the rapid developments in information technology and its applications for improving management in business and public organizations, there was a clear need for an updated version.

The present book includes extended and revised versions of a set of selected papers submitted to the 13th Conference on Information Systems Management (ISM 2018) and 15th Conference on Advanced Information Technologies for Management (AITM 2018) held in Poznań, Poland, during September 9–12, 2018. These conferences were organized as part of the Federated Conference on Computer Science and Information Systems (FedCSIS 2018).

FedCSIS provides a forum for bringing together researchers, practitioners, and academics to present and discuss ideas, challenges, and potential solutions on established or emerging topics related to research and practice in computer science and information systems. Since 2012, the proceedings of the FedCSIS have been indexed in the Thomson Reuters Web of Science, Scopus, IEEE Xplore Digital Library, and other indexing services.

ISM is a forum for computer scientists, IT specialist, and business people to exchange ideas on management of information systems in organizations, and the usage of information systems for enhancing the decision-making process and empowering managers. It concentrates on various issues of planning, organizing, resourcing, coordinating, controlling, and leading the management functions to ensure a smooth operation of information systems in organizations.

AITM is a forum for all in the field of business informatics to present and discuss the current issues of IT in business applications. It is mainly focused on business process management, enterprise information systems, business intelligence methods and tools, decision support systems and data mining, intelligence and mobile IT, cloud computing, SOA, agent-based systems, and business-oriented ontologies.

For ISM 2018 and AITM 2018, we received 43 papers from 16 countries in all continents. After extensive reviews, only 10 papers were accepted as full papers and 12 as short papers. Finally, 12 papers of the highest quality were carefully reviewed and chosen by the Program Committee, and the authors were invited to extend their papers and submit them for the LNBIP publication. Our guiding criteria for including papers in the book were the excellence of publications indicated by the reviewers, the relevance of subject matter for the economy, and promising results. The selected papers reflect state-of-art research work that is often oriented toward real-world applications and highlight the benefits of information systems and technology for business and public administration, thus forming a bridge between theory and practice.

The papers selected to be included in this book contribute to the understanding of relevant trends of current research on information technology for management in business and public organizations. The first part of the book focuses on information technology and information systems for knowledge management, whereas the second part presents information technology and information systems for business and public administration transformation.

I would like to express my gratitude to all those people who helped create the success of the ISM 2018 and AITM 2018 research events. First of all, I want to thank the authors for extending their very interesting research and submitting new findings to be published in LNBIP. I express my appreciation to the reviewers for taking the time and effort necessary to provide insightful comments for the authors of papers. I am deeply grateful to the program chairs of ISM 2018 and AITM 2018, namely, Witold Chmielarz, Helena Dudycz, and Jerzy Korczak, for their substantive involvement in the conferences and efforts put into the evaluation of papers. I acknowledge the chairs of FedCSIS 2018, i.e., Maria Ganzha, Leszek A. Maciaszek, and Marcin Paprzycki, for building an active community around the FedCSIS conference. Last but not least, I am indebted to the team at Springer headed by Ralf Gerstner and Alfred Hofmann, without whom this book would not have been possible. Many thanks also to Christine Reiss and Mohamed Haja Moideen H for handling the production of this book.

Finally, the authors and I hope readers will find the content of this book useful and interesting for their own research activities. It is in this spirit and conviction we offer our monograph, which is the result of the intellectual effort of the authors, for the final judgment of readers. We are open to discussion on the issues raised in this book, we look forward to the readers' opinions, even critical, as to the content and form.

January 2019   Ewa Ziemba

Organizations

AITM 2018

Event Chairs

Frederic Andres	National Institute of Informatics, Tokyo, Japan
Helena Dudycz	Wrocław University of Economics, Poland
Mirosław Dyczkowski	Wrocław University of Economics, Poland
Frantisek Hunka	University of Ostrava, Czech Republic
Jerzy Korczak	Wrocław University of Economics, Poland

Program Committee

Witold Abramowicz	Poznan University of Economics, Poland
Frederik Ahlemann	University of Duisburg-Essen, Germany
Ghislain Atemezing	Mondeca, Paris, France
Agostino Cortesi	Università Ca' Foscari, Venezia, Italy
Beata Czarnacka-Chrobot	Warsaw School of Economics, Poland
Suparna De	University of Surrey, Guildford, UK
Jean-François Dufourd	University of Strasbourg, France
Bogdan Franczyk	University of Leipzig, Germany
Arkadiusz Januszewski	University of Science and Technology, Bydgoszcz, Poland
Rajkumar Kannan	Bishop Heber College (Autonomous), Tiruchirappalli, India
Grzegorz Kersten	Concordia University, Montreal, Canada
Ryszard Kowalczyk	Swinburne University of Technology, Melbourne, Australia
Karol Kozak	TUD, Germany
Marek Krótkiewicz	Wroclaw University of Science and Technology, Poland
Christian Leyh	University of Technology, Dresden, Germany
Antoni Ligęza	AGH University of Science and Technology, Poland
André Ludwig	Kühne Logistics University, Germany
Damien Magoni	University of Bordeaux – LaBRI, France
Krzysztof Michalak	Wroclaw University of Economics, Poland
Mieczyslaw Owoc	Wroclaw University of Economics, Poland
Malgorzata Pankowska	University of Economics in Katowice, Poland
Jose Miguel Pinto dos Santos	AESE Business School Lisboa, Portugal
Maurizio Proietti	IASI-CNR (the Institute for Systems Analysis and Computer Science), Italy
Artur Rot	Wroclaw University of Economics, Poland

Stanislaw Stanek   General Tadeusz Kosciuszko Military Academy
                              of Land Forces in Wroclaw, Poland
Jerzy Surma   Warsaw School of Economics, Poland
                              and University of Massachusetts Lowell, USA
El Bachir Tazi   Moulay Ismail University, Meknes, Morocco
Stephanie Teufel   University of Fribourg, Switzerland
Edward Tsang   University of Essex, UK
Jarosław Wątróbski   University of Szczecin, Poland
Tilo Wendler   Hochschule fur Technik und Wirtschaft Berlin,
                              Germany
Waldemar Wolski   University of Szczecin, Poland
Cecilia Zanni-Merk   INSA de Rouen, France
Ewa Ziemba   University of Economics in Katowice, Poland

ISM 2018

Event Chairs

Bernard Arogyaswami   Le Moyne University, USA
Witold Chmielarz   University of Warsaw, Poland
Dimitris Karagiannis   University of Vienna, Austria
Jerzy Kisielnicki   University of Warsaw, Poland
Ewa Ziemba   University of Economics in Katowice, Poland

Program Committee

Daniel Aguillar   Instituto de Pesquisas Tecnológicas de São Paulo,
                              Brazil
Saleh Alghamdi   King Abdulaziz City for Science and Technology,
                              Saudi Arabia
Boyan Bontchev   Sofia University St Kliment Ohridski, Bulgaria
Domagoj Cingula   Economic and Social Development Conference,
                              Croatia
Beata Czarnacka-Chrobot   Warsaw School of Economics, Poland
Robertas Damasevicius   Kaunas University of Technology, Lithuania
Yanqing Duan   University of Bedfordshire, UK
Ibrahim El Emary   King Abdulaziz University, Saudi Arabia
Susana de Juana Espinosa   University of Alicante, Spain
Christophe Feltus   Luxembourg Institute of Science and Technology,
                              Luxembourg
Aleksandra Gaweł   Poznan University of Economics and Business, Poland
Nitza Geri   The Open University of Israel, Israel
Leila Halawi   Embry-Riddle Aeronautical University, USA
Jarosław Jankowski   West Pomeranian University of Technology
                              in Szczecin, Poland
Krzysztof Kania   University of Economics in Katowice, Poland
Andrzej Kobyliński   Warsaw School of Economics, Poland

Contents

Information Technology and Systems for Knowledge Management

Enhancing Completion Time Prediction Through Attribute Selection

Claudio A. L. Amaral[1], Marcelo Fantinato[1](✉) ⓘ, Hajo A. Reijers[2] ⓘ,
and Sarajane M. Peres[1] ⓘ

[1] School of Arts, Sciences and Humanities, University of São Paulo,
1000 Arlindo Béttio St., Ermelino Matarazzo, São Paulo, SP 03828-000, Brazil
{claudio.amaral,m.fantinato,sarajane}@usp.br
[2] Department of Information and Computing Sciences, Utrecht University,
Princetonplein 5, 3584 CC Utrecht, The Netherlands
h.a.reijers@uu.nl
http://www.each.usp.br/fantinato, http://www.reijers.com,
http://www.each.usp.br/sarajane

Abstract. Approaches have been proposed in process mining to predict the completion time of process instances. However, the accuracy levels of the prediction models depend on how useful the log attributes used to build such models are. A canonical subset of attributes can also offer a better understanding of the underlying process. We describe the application of two automatic attribute selection methods to build prediction models for completion time. The filter was used with ranking whereas the wrapper was used with hill-climbing and best-first techniques. Annotated transition systems were used as the prediction model. Compared to decision-making by human experts, only the automatic attribute selectors using wrappers performed better. The filter-based attribute selector presented the lowest performance on generalization capacity. The semantic reasonability of the selected attributes in each case was analyzed in a real-world incident management process.

Keywords: Process mining · Attribute selection ·
Incident management · ITIL · Annotated transition systems

1 Introduction

Estimates for the completion time of business process instances are still precarious as they are usually calculated based on superficial and naïve abstractions of the process of interest [1]. Many organizations have been using Process-Aware Information Systems (PAIS), which record events about the activities carried out in the process involved, generating a large amount of data. Process mining can exploit these event logs to infer a more realistic process model [2], which can be used as a completion time predictor [3]. In fact, general data mining techniques and the similar have been applied for different purposes to improve the performance of organizations by making them intelligent [4–6].

© Springer Nature Switzerland AG 2019
E. Ziemba (Ed.): AITM 2018/ISM 2018, LNBIP 346, pp. 3–23, 2019.
https://doi.org/10.1007/978-3-030-15154-6_1

However, specifically in terms of distinct strategies addressing prediction of completion time for business processes, a common gap of is the lack of concern in choosing the input log configuration. It is not common to seek the best subset of descriptive attributes of the log to support constructing a more effective predictor, as happens in [3, 7–10]. For an incident management process, for example, some descriptive attributes for each instance process (i.e., for each incident) can be status, severity, symptom, category, impact, assignment group etc.

Two inputs are expected when building a process model as a completion time predictor – an event log and a set of descriptive attributes. Depending on the organizational settings, the number of existing descriptive attributes can be so large and complex that may be unfeasible to use all the attributes. In addition, studies have shown that the predictive accuracy of process models depends on which attributes have been chosen to create them [11]. Therefore, when building a prediction model, one needs to consider that not all attributes are necessarily useful. In fact, according to Kohavi and John [12], a predictor can degrade in performance (accuracy) when faced with many unnecessary features to predict the desired output. Thus, an ideal minimum subset of descriptive attributes should be selected that contains as much relevant information as necessary to build an accurate prediction model, i.e., a canonical subset of descriptive attributes should be selected.

However, a manual selection of a subset of descriptive attributes may be impracticable. In this sense, this paper details a proposal of how to apply two automatic attribute selection methods as the basis for building prediction models[1]. Consider here an event log e composed of a set of categorical descriptive attributes $\Delta = \{a_1, a_2, \cdots, a_m\}$ that characterize the events of a process instance. Consider Ω a set whose elements are all combinations of attributes in Δ; each combination of attributes $\omega_i \in \Omega$ can be used to generate a model $\theta_i \in \Theta$, where Θ is a set of models that represent a process under distinct aspects. Consider the process models $\theta_i \in \Theta$ as predictors of completion time, generated on samples e'_i of the event log e; each model $\theta(\omega, e')$ has a particular prediction performance. Consider the prediction error as the measure of performance. The problem of interest in this paper is formulated as

$$\operatorname*{argmin}_{\omega \in \Omega} \epsilon(\theta(\omega, e')),$$

where the minimization process looks for a $\omega \in \Omega$ such that $\epsilon(\theta_i(\omega_i, e'_i)) \leq \epsilon(\theta_j(\omega_j, e'_j)) \ \forall \ j$, where $i, j = \{1, \cdots, \#\Omega\}$, $i \neq j$ and $\#\cdot$ represents the number of elements in a set.

In this paper, the minimization process is implemented through a filter technique [14] and two wrapper techniques [12] as the attribute selection methods, using heuristic search techniques – a filter with ranking and the wrapper with hill-climbing and with best-first. These classical attribute selection methods are used to automatically determine a canonical subset of descriptive attributes to

---

[1] This paper details the approach and results published in a summarized preliminary version [13].

be subsequently supplied to the prediction model. Annotated Transition Systems (ATS) [3] were chosen as the prediction model to compare the different techniques used. ATSs are a good example of a prediction model in this context as they largely depend on the attributes used. For the experiments and analyzes reported herein, ϵ is the mean error on time prediction (in seconds), θ is implemented using ATS and e' are samples of an event log from a real-world incident management process.

The approach discussed herein was designed to address a real-world time prediction problem faced by an Information Technology (IT) organization. In this organization, the incident management process is supported by the ServiceNow^{TM} platform, which enables extraction of the event log and a series of descriptive incident attributes. Because it is an applied experiment, there is no prior initiative for comparison. To overcome this problem, the selection of attributes performed by human experts was used as the baseline. The semantic reasonability of the selected attributes in each case was analyzed in this real-world incident management process. The results show that only the wrapper-based solution could outperform human experts.

In summary, our goal is to discover an attribute subset that allows generating a model capable of minimizing the prediction error of the incident completion time during its resolution process. Fig. 1 presents an overview of the proposed strategy. The top of the figure shows the sequence of actions followed to build an enriched event log used to build the prediction models. The remaining part of the figure shows the three attribute selection methods explored in this paper: (i) expert-driven selection [used herein as our baseline for comparison], (ii) the filter with ranking and (iii) wrappers with two search techniques – hill-climbing and best-first.

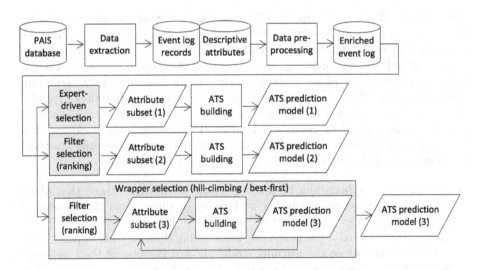

Fig. 1. Proposed strategy overview

The contribution of this work is threefold:

1. We present the feasibility of an automatic attribute selection approach used to improve the performance of prediction models that are sensitive to these attributes.
2. We confirm through experimental results that automatic methods can outperform human experts for a real-world incident management context even considering the own specific characteristics of such a context.
3. We provide the dataset used in our experiment, containing an event log enriched with data loaded from a relational database underlying the related PAIS, which can be used for replicability or other experiments.

The remainder of this paper shows: an overview of concepts related to attribute selection and annotated transition systems and some related work; the research method for experimentation, including the strategies for attribute selection, the application domain and the event log used; the findings of the experiments conducted; the discussion of such findings; and finally the conclusions.

2   Literature Review and Theoretical Background

This section presents the main concepts related to attribute selection and ATS as a theoretical basis for the rest of the paper and an analysis of the related works found in the literature review.

2.1   Attribute Selection

According to Blum and Langley [15], before undertaking automated learning activities, two tasks are needed to be carried out – deciding which features (or attributes) to use in describing the concept to be learned and deciding how to combine such features. Following this assumption, attribute selection is proposed herein as an essential phase to build prediction models capable of predicting completion time. The taxonomy of methods for selecting attributes typically uses three classes filters, wrappers and embedded [14]. A fourth class – heuristic search – is highlighted by Blum and Langley [15], however, one could say that this class is an extension of filter methods. In this paper, we apply the filter and wrapper methods [12,14,15], which are briefly described as follows:

- **Filter:** filter methods aim to select relevant attributes – those that alone or together can generate a better performing predictor than that generated from a set of irrelevant attributes – and remove irrelevant attributes. These methods are seen as a pre-processing step, seeing that they are applied independently and before the learning model chosen. Because of their independence, filter methods are often run-time competitive when compared to other attribute selection methods and can provide a generic attribute selection free from the behavior influence of learning models. In fact, using filters reduces the decision space dimensionality and has the potential to minimize the overfitting problem. In this paper, a filter method based on correlation analysis is applied. Each attribute is individually evaluated based on its correlation with the target attribute (i.e., the instance completion time).

- **Wrapper:** in wrapper methods, the attribute selection is carried out through an interaction with an interface of the learning model, which is seen as a black box. There is indeed a space of search states (i.e., combinations of attributes) that needs to be explored using some search technique. Such a search is driven by the accuracy got with the application of the learning model in each search state, considering the parameters (or, in the case of this paper, the attributes) that characterize that search state. In this paper, we apply: two well-known search techniques – hill-climbing and best-first (described below); ATSs as the learning model (cf. Sect. 2.2); and Mean Absolute Percentage Error (MAPE) [16,17] as the metric to evaluate the learning model accuracy, defined as

$$MAPE = \frac{1}{n} * \sum_{t=1}^{n} \frac{|F_t - A_t|}{A_t},$$

where n is the number of events in the log, F_t is the result got with the predictor for each event of the log and A_t is the expected/known prediction value, which represents the remaining time to complete the process instance and is calculated from the time the event was logged in until the instance is completed.

Hill-climbing is one of the simplest search techniques; it expands the current state, creating new ones, moves to the next state with the best evaluation, and stops when no child improves the current state. Best-first search differs from hill-climbing as it does not stop when no child improves the current state; instead, the search attempts to expand the next node with the best evaluation in the open list [12].

2.2   Annotated Transition Systems

Using transition systems in process mining was proposed by Aalst *et al.* [18], as part of an approach to discovering control-flows from event logs. Then, transition systems were extended with annotations (given rise to ATS), whose aim is to add statistical characteristics of a business process. ATSs can be applied as a predictor of the completion time of a process instance based on the annotated statistical data [3]. According to the authors, ATSs include alternatives for state representation, allowing to address over-fitting and under-fitting, which are frequent in prediction tasks.

Briefly, a transition system is defined as the triplet (S, E, T), in which S is a space of states, E is a set of labeled events and T is the transition relation such that $T \subseteq S \times E \times S$. A state is an abstraction of k events in the event log, which have occurred in a finite sequence σ that is called 'trace'. σ is represented by a string of symbols derived using abstraction strategies. Five strategies are presented by Aalst *et al.* [18], from which the following two are applied in the experiments presented herein:

1. *Maximal horizon*, which determines how many events must be considered in the knowledge representation of a state.
2. *Representation*, which defines three ways to represent knowledge about past and future at a trace momentum, i.e., per:
   - *Sequence*, recording the order of activities in each state.
   - *Multiset*, ignoring the order and considers the number of times each activity is performed.
   - *Set*, considering only the presence of activities.

To create the ATS, each state is annotated taking information collected from all traces that have visited it [3]. For time analysis, for example, this annotation considers information about the completion time of the instances related to each earlier trace, i.e., the annotation is carried out in a supervised way. The information is aggregated in each state producing statistics such as average times, standard deviation, median times etc. Such annotations allow using ATSs as a predictor. Thus, predicting the completion time for a running trace referring to some process instance can be carried out from its current state in the ATS flow.

Berti [7] also applied ATS for prediction, however, with partial and weighted traces aiming at dealing with changes during the running process. The ATS was extended through machine learning and enriched with date/time information and probability of occurrence of activities in the traces, by Polato *et al.* [8]. As several factors influence prediction, the view on the need to deal with information that enriches the ATS context is also used in the approach addressed herein.

2.3 Related Work

Only Hinkka *et al.* [11] presented a strategy with a purpose similar to the one presented herein, i.e., choosing the attribute configuration of the input log for building the predictor. The approach of these authors extracts structural features from an event log (i.e., activity counting, transitions counting, occurrence ordering), submits them to a selection process, and then uses the features selected to describe process instances. These process instances are used to create categorical prediction models. Different feature selection methods were applied, based on randomness, statistics, heuristic search and clustering. Among the strategies used by the authors, recursive elimination – a wrapper method – was the best performing selection method (84% of accuracy); however, it was one of the most expensive in terms of time response. Despite the similarity, this work is not directly comparable with ours since these authors work with a simple binary classification scenario whereas we work with numerical prediction, i.e., a continuous scenario. Moreover, our strategy does not use recursive elimination as them as our search method is a simple forward selection.

Alternatively, Evermann, Rehse and Fettke [19] and Tax *et al.* [20] also worked with the choice of the configuration of the predictor input log, but implicitly and automatically when using deep learning. Prediction is done directly from the descriptions of process instances, i.e., no process model is used or discovered as a basis for prediction. As a disadvantage of this type of approach, it is hard to explain the reasonableness of the predictions made when considering the process context, i.e., the implicit extraction of features does not allow easily interpreting the information leading to the results of the prediction. As a result, this type of solution hinders the use of the selected attributes for process improvement purposes.

3　Research Method

This section details the proposed solution and the basis for the experiments.

3.1　Attribute Selection Strategies

An overview of the proposed strategy for attribute selection is presented in Fig. 1 and detailed in this section.

For the **first strategy** – the expert-driven selection, no standard procedure was followed, since it fully depends on human judgment. This judgment highly depends on the application domain, among other factors. In the next section, the rationale specifically followed for the case used in our experiment is presented.

For the **second strategy** – the filter with ranking, stable concepts of specialized literature were followed [12,14,15]. Ranking was applied as pre-processing, as suggested by Kohavi and John [12], to create a baseline for attribute selection, regardless of the prediction model in use. The ranking should be created through a variance analysis by correlating the independent variables (i.e., the descriptive attributes) and the dependent variable (i.e., the prediction target attribute). Since most of the descriptive attributes are categorical in this context, the statistic η^2 (Eta squared) should be applied, as explained by Richardson [21]. From the ranking results, the filter method should be executed n times by combining the attributes as follows: $\{1^{st}\}; \{1^{st}, 2^{nd}\}; \ldots; \{1^{st}, 2^{nd}, \ldots, n^{th}\}$.

For the **third strategy** – the wrapper with hill-climbing and best-first [12], a forward selection mode[2] was applied. The search space is composed of all combinations of the attributes pre-selected by the filter with ranking strategy. Each one of the combinations represents a state in such a space, whose quality measure is calculated as the predictive power achieved by the predictor generated with the attribute subset associated with this model. For real problems, an exhaustive search procedure is probably unfeasible, and hence using heuristic search procedures is justified. Algorithms 1 and 2 show, respectively, how hill-climbing and best-first searches are carried out for our attribute selection strategy. The building function *build-ATS()* of an ATS and the evaluation function *eval()* of the ATS use, respectively, a training log excerpt (e_{train}) and a testing log excerpt (e_{test}), which represent disjoint subsets of the original event log (e) generated in

---

[2] In the forward selection, the search initial point is a singleton attribute subset to which one new attribute is incorporated at each new step in the search.

Algorithm 1. Hill-climbing technique

1: **input**: set of attributes l, event log e;
2: **output**: canonical subset of attributes l_{final};
3:
4: $l_{final} \leftarrow \emptyset$;
5: $\text{ATS}_{best} \leftarrow \emptyset$;
6: **repeat**
7:     $l_{expand} \leftarrow l - l_{final}$;
8:     $\text{ATS} \leftarrow \emptyset$;
9:     **for** $i = 1$ to $len(l_{expand})$ **do**   ▷ State expansion
10:         $att\text{-}set[i] \leftarrow concat\,(l_{final},\ l_{expand}[i])$;
11:         $\text{ATS}[i] \leftarrow build\text{-}ATS(att\text{-}set[i],\ e_{train})$;
12:     $i_{best} \leftarrow arg\text{-}min\,(eval\,(\text{ATS},\ e_{test}))$;
13:     **if** $(eval(\text{ATS}_{best}, e_{test}) > eval(\text{ATS}[i_{best}], e_{test}))$ **then**
14:         $\text{ATS}_{best} \leftarrow \text{ATS}[i_{best}]$;
15:         $l_{final} \leftarrow att\text{-}set[i_{best}]$;
16: **until** $(l_{final} \neq att\text{-}set[i_{best}])$ **or** $(l_{expand} = \emptyset)$
17: **return** l_{final}

---

the cross-validation procedure. The function *eval()* returns the MAPE for the ATS under evaluation and is used for a single ATS and a set of ATSs. The minimization function, *arg-min()*, applied to the ATS evaluation, returns the index of the model that produces the lowest MAPE when applied to the testing log. In Algorithm 2, there are two lists (open and closed) that maintain the states that represent the sets of attributes generated by the search and are used by the function *build-ATS()* to create the ATSs related to each state under evaluation. The search is interrupted when the maximum expansion counter is achieved.

For all selection methods, ATS is applied as the prediction model responsible for generating the estimates of the incident completion times, including to act as a state evaluator in the wrapper search spaces. For practical purposes, the ATS can be generated from an attribute subset which properly describes the currently completed incidents. From this point, ATS can be applied to predict the completion time of new incidents at run-time.

3.2 Application Domain

Operating areas in organizations are often complex, requiring a constant search for optimization to become more stable and predictable. In IT, this optimization is sought by adopting good practice frameworks such as the Information Technology Infrastructure Library (ITIL) [22]. ITIL covers several IT service management processes, from which incident management is the most commonly used one [23]. The incident management process addresses actions to correct failures and restore the normal operation of a service, as soon as possible, to minimize the impact on business operations [22]. Systematizing this business process allows defining monitoring indicators, including the completion time for

---

Algorithm 2. Best-first technique

1: **input**: set of attributes l, event log e, maximum # expansion movements with no improvement $max\_expcount$;
2: **output**: canonical subset of attributes l_{final};
3:
4: $l_{final} \leftarrow \emptyset$;
5: $l_{closed-states} \leftarrow \emptyset$;
6: $l_{open-states} \leftarrow expand\text{-}state(\ \emptyset, l_{closed-states}, l\ )$;
7: $ATS_{best} \leftarrow \emptyset$;
8: **repeat**
9:      $ATS \leftarrow build\text{-}ATS(l_{open-states}, e_{train})$;
10:      $i_{best} \leftarrow arg\text{-}min\ (eval\ (ATS, e_{test}))$;
11:      $currentstate \leftarrow l_{open-states}[i_{best}]$;
12:      $l_{open-states} \leftarrow l_{open-states} - currentstate$;
13:      $l_{closed-states} \leftarrow l_{closed-states} + currentstate$;
14:      **if** $(eval(ATS_{best}, e_{test}) > eval(ATS[i_{best}], e_{test}))$ **then**
15:          $ATS_{best} \leftarrow ATS[i_{best}]$;
16:          $l_{final} \leftarrow att\text{-}set(currentstate)$;
17:          $expcount \leftarrow 0$;
18:      **else**
19:          $inc(expcount)$;
20:      $l_{expand} \leftarrow expand\text{-}state(\ currentstate, l_{closed-states}, l\ )$;
21:      $l_{open-states} \leftarrow concat(\ l_{open-states}, l_{expand}\ )$;
22: **until** $(expcount \leq max\_expcount)$ **or** $(l_{open-states} = \emptyset)$
23: **return** l_{final}

---

incident resolution (also known as 'ticket completion time'), one of the most important indicators for this process [23].

When an incident occurs, it is identified and reported by a caller. Afterward, a primary expectation is to know the incident completion time. The usual estimates follow ITIL best practices, which are based on some specific incident attributes like urgency, category etc. This approach is general and inaccurate since it aggregates many situations and common target completion times. As the process evolves from the identification and classification stage to the initial support, investigation and diagnosis, some attributes are updated, and new ones are added. This can usually lead to a number close to 100 attributes, depending on the scope of the system implementation. Considering this whole scenario, there is an open issue related to providing assertive estimates on incident completion time that is not adequately solved by simple statistical methods. Incident management systems commonly store descriptive information of process instances and audit information about the history of updates of the process in progress. Combining both types of information allows executing a detailed step-by-step process evaluation and hence deriving estimates for each recorded event.

ServiceNow^{TM} is a proprietary platform in which IT process management is implemented regarding the ITIL framework. In this platform, the incident process management involves three actors in five basic process steps. The actors are: *caller*, affected by the unavailability or degradation of a service, caused by an incident; *service desk analyst*, responsible by registering and validating the data provided by the caller and executing the initial procedures to treat the incident; and *support analysts*, the group of agents responsible for further analyzing the incident and its causes and proposing workaround solutions to be applied until the service is reestablished or definitive solutions are found. The five basic process steps are: incident identification and classification, initial support, investigation and diagnosis, resolution and reestablishment, and closing.

3.3   Enriched Event Log

An enriched event log of the incident management process was extracted from an instance of the ServiceNow[TM] platform used by an IT company[3]. Information was anonymized for privacy reasons. This enriched event log is composed of data gathered from both the audit system and the platform's relational database:

- **Event log records:** ServiceNow[TM] offers an audit system that records data referring to events related to all data maintained by the system, including incident-related data. The main data recorded are event identifier, old data value, new data value, update timestamp and responsible user. Audit data was used to generate the main structure of the event log records to be mined. We considered 12 months (Mar-2016 to Feb-2017), totaling 24,918 traces and 141,712 events. Pre-processing was used to filter out the noise and organize audit records in an orderly sequence compatible with an event log format. Two audit log attributes were derived from this audit system *sys_updated_at* and *sys_updated_by*.
- **Incident descriptive attributes:** ServiceNow[TM] has 91 incident descriptive attributes. Some are worthless for process mining, have missing or inconsistent data, or represent unstructured information (i.e., text), whose use is outside our scope. After removing such unnecessary attributes, the final set of descriptive attributes comprised 34 attributes (27 categorical, 3 numeric and 4 timestamp ones). These attributes include the attribute *closed_at*, which is used as the basis for calculating the dependent variable for prediction.

An excerpt from the enriched event log is shown in Table 1. It refers to one incident (INC001) and contains: one audit attribute (*sys_updated_at*) and the other four are descriptive attributes (*number*, *incident_state*, *category* and *assignment_group*).

Statistical data on the enriched event log is presented in Table 2. A well-defined behavior for the incident management process is observed, as most incidents (75%) go through up seven updates, 50% go through up five updates and on average six updates are needed to the total of incidents. There are some outliers, with 58 as the maximum number of updates for one incident. Regarding time (in days), the behavior resembles an exponential distribution.

---

[3] Available at http://each.uspnet.usp.br/sarajane/?page_id=12.

Table 1. Incident enriched event log excerpt

Number	incident_state	sys_updated_at	Category	assig._group
INC001	New	3/2/2016 04:57	Internet	Field service
	New	3/2/2016 16:52	Internet	Field service
	Active	3/2/2016 18:13	Internet	Field service
	Active	3/2/2016 19:14	Internet	Field service
	Awaiting UI	3/2/2016 19:15	Internet	Field service
	Awaiting UI	3/3/2016 11:24	Internet	Field service
	Awaiting UI	3/3/2016 12:33	Internet	Field service
	Awaiting UI	3/3/2016 12:43	Internet	Field service
	Active	3/3/2016 12:43	Internet	Field service
	Active	3/3/2016 12:54	Internet	Field service
	Active	3/3/2016 12:57	Internet	Inf. security
	Active	3/3/2016 13:14	Internet	Inf. security
	Active	3/3/2016 13:16	Internet	Service desk
	Active	3/3/2016 19:57	Internet	Field service
	Active	3/4/2016 10:56	Internet	Field service
	Resolved	3/4/2016 11:02	Internet	Field service
	Closed	3/9/2016 12:00	Internet	Field service

Table 2. Enriched event log statistics: per incident/day

	1st Q.	2nd Q.	3rd Q.	Max	Mean	St. dev.
Per incident	3	5	7	58	6	3.67
Per day	0.01	0.40	5.29	336.21	6.67	21.20

4   Research Findings

This section presents the results of the experiments. The incident management process was used as the application domain. The enriched event log was split into 5 folds (i.e., 5 sublogs) to allow cross-validation on the ATS prediction models. The ATS accuracy is given in terms of the mean and the median MAPE [16] of the incident completion time taking all incidents in the test fold that are passing through the ATS states. Sojourn time is also considered. The ATS completeness (or non-fitting) was evaluated by accounting how many records do not have a corresponding state in the ATS. As a baseline for comparison, a prediction model based on human expertise-knowledge was first created.

Three experiments were conducted as described in Sect. 3. A set of ATSs was generated according to these parameter configurations:

- **Enriched event log:** the enriched event log was sampled by randomly creating two subsets, one with 8,000 (A) and another with 24,000 (B) incidents – with $A \subset B$.
- **Maximum horizon:** 1, 3, 5, 6, 7 and 'infinite' were used. The value 1 explores the simpler case with only the last event per incident trace; 3, 5, 6 and 7 explore the most frequent behaviors in this incident management process according to the statistics 'by incident' reported in Table 2; and, 'infinite' explores all events per incident trace.
- **State representation:** the three options described in Sect. 2.2 were used, i.e., *set*, *multiset* and *sequence* [18].

4.1   Experiment #1 – Expert-Driven Selection

First, attribute selection was driven by information about the domain held by human experts. According to ITIL best practices, to start the incident management, the caller should provide the initial incident information, which is complemented by the service desk agent, with information related to the incident category and priority (defined by impact and urgency). Additional information (attachments and textual descriptions) is also provided to help the support agents who need to act on the next stage, which is out of the scope of this work. Based on these practices, *incident_state*, *category* and *priority* were considered the most adequate attributes to correctly define the process model in ATS: *incident_state* reports the stage at which the incident is; *category* shows the type of service the incident belongs to; and *priority* determines the focus requested by the business. For this scenario, 18 ATSs were generated and used as completion time predictor, for the enriched event log sample with 24,000 incidents, varying the horizon and state representation parameters. The results are shown in Table 3. The best results were got with horizon 3 and state representation *sequence*.

Table 3. Experiment #1 – average prediction results. Used attributes: *incident_state*, *category* and *priority*. Log sample: 24,000 incidents. Metric: MAPE (Mean and Median). NF = % of non-fitting incidents. Bold: best results.

Max Hor	Set			Multiset			Sequence		
	Mean	*Med*	*NF*	*Mean*	*Med*	*NF*	*Mean*	*Med*	*NF*
1	113.93	88.29	0.22	113.93	88.29	0.22	113.93	88.29	0.22
3	106.93	77.46	0.98	91.35	75.87	1.23	**72.36**	**63.66**	**1.38**
5	119.18	109.28	1.64	177.05	162.08	2.95	126.12	104.67	3.38
6	183.52	115.59	1.83	122.54	98.74	3.72	102.73	84.01	4.41
7	93.22	75.11	1.95	1190.87	1184.75	4.44	107.58	98.04	5.48
Inf.	1146.57	1123.24	2.31	92.12	75.21	8.03	88.32	72.98	9.00

Table 4. The 15 descriptive attributes with the highest correlation with the dependent variable and respective η values. Attribute descriptions are provided in the appendix.

Order	Attribute	η	Order	Attribute	η
1st	Caller	0.54	9th	Active	0.25
2nd	Assigned_to	0.37	10th	Priority_confirmation	0.24
3rd	Assignment_group	0.35	11th	Created_by	0.21
4th	Symptom	0.33	12th	open_by	0.20
5th	Sys_updated_by	0.33	13th	Location	0.14
6th	Incident_state	0.32	14th	Made_SLA	0.14
7th	Subcategory	0.32	15th	Knowledge	0.12
8th	Category	0.27			

4.2 Experiment #2 – Filter with Ranking

Second, attribute selection was driven by filter using a ranking strategy. Following the strategy presented in Sect. 3, 15 attributes with the highest correlation with the dependent variable (i.e., the prediction target attribute, based on the attribute *closed_at*) were selected to compose the ranking. The variance analysis was carried out on the entire enriched event log. The attributes and correlation scores are listed in Table 4. These results showed that the descriptive attributes with the highest correlation with the dependent variable are those related with associated resources of the incident management process. Considering the ranking results, the filter method was executed by combining the attributes as follows: $\{Caller(1^{st})\}$; $\{Caller(1^{st}), Assigned\_to(2^{nd})\}$; ...; $\{Caller(1^{st}), Assigned\_to(2^{nd}), ..., Knowledge(15^{th})\}$. For this scenario, 18 ATSs were generated for each attribute subset and used as completion time predictor, for the enriched event log sample with 8,000 incidents, varying the maximum horizon and the state representation parameters. The results for each attribute subset are shown in Table 5. The best results were got with horizon 1 and the subsets $\{Caller, Assigned\_to\}$ and $\{Caller, Assigned\_to, Assignment\_group\}$, regardless of the state representation.

As a second part of experiment #2, aiming to compare the prediction results got through the ATS models generated using these two best ranked attribute subsets with the results got in experiment #1, two new set of ATSs were generated using as attributes those of best results in Table 5; however, using in this case the enriched event log sample with 24,000 incidents. The results are shown in Table 6. The results with the ranked attribute subsets were slightly worse than those got in experiment #1. By checking these results, one can notice that resource-related attributes often impair generating the prediction model, i.e., such attributes do not reflect the process behavior with the same fidelity that the control attribute do (i.e., the incident state). Regarding non-fitting, an explanation for the poor results could be the frequent changes in the values of the human resource assigned to solve different incidents.

Table 5. Experiment #2 – average prediction results. Used attributes: selected by filter. Log sample: 8,000 incidents. Metric: MAPE (Mean and Median). NF = % of non-fitting incidents. Bold: best results.

Att	Max Hor	Set			Multiset			Sequence		
		Mean	*Med*	*NF*	*Mean*	*Med*	*NF*	*Mean*	*Med*	*NF*
1	Inf.	160.22	140.99	20.77	114.62	109.79	30.95	114.62	109.79	30.95
2	**1**	**110.98**	**90.81**	**59.89**	**110.98**	**90.81**	**59.89**	**110.98**	**90.81**	**59.89**
3	**1**	**112.27**	**88.99**	**63.92**	**112.27**	**88.99**	**63.92**	**112.27**	**88.99**	**63.92**
4	6	129.41	98.90	72.22	123.72	96.08	72.72	122.83	95.11	72.73
5	4	128.71	98.52	72.89	128.36	98.11	73.08	128.49	98.15	73.08
6	Inf.	129.25	100.28	73.39	133.72	102.29	73.51	133.72	102.29	73.51
7	Inf.	146.08	117.20	73.58	129.63	98.36	73.70	129.63	98.36	73.70
8	Inf.	143.84	114.87	73.66	129.42	98.06	73.77	129.42	98.06	73.77
9	Inf.	143.84	114.87	73.66	129.42	98.06	73.77	129.42	98.06	73.77
10	Inf.	130.46	101.07	73.67	133.72	101.61	73.72	139.35	107.19	73.72
11	3	135.57	103.93	73.65	133.30	101.25	73.67	134.97	102.96	73.67
12	Inf.	147.31	118.41	73.76	130.57	99.36	73.86	130.57	99.36	73.86
13	7	127.16	97.58	73.78	128.37	98.20	73.87	128.28	98.16	73.87
14	Inf.	124.96	96.09	73.78	126.14	96.85	73.88	126.14	96.85	73.88
15	Inf.	125.70	96.75	73.78	130.25	98.98	73.88	130.25	98.98	73.88

Table 6. Experiment #2 – average prediction results. Used attributes: best attribute subsets selected by filter. Log sample: 24,000 incidents. Metric: MAPE (Mean and Median). NF = % of non-fitting incidents. Bold: best results.

Max Hor	Set			Multiset			Sequence		
	Mean	*Med*	*NF*	*Mean*	*Med*	*NF*	*Mean*	*Med*	*NF*
Attribute subset: {*caller, assigned_to*}									
1	208.61	196.42	30.10	208.61	196.42	30.10	208.61	196.42	30.10
3	102.09	89.17	32.48	86.41	72.50	33.87	98.69	84.37	33.90
5	90.73	76.30	33.31	**69.69**	**57.85**	**35.67**	80.97	69.10	35.73
6	292.51	280.42	33.44	77.53	65.66	36.15	82.78	70.92	36.20
7	171.55	159.95	33.51	91.22	79.66	36.41	103.14	90.27	36.46
Inf.	249.06	238.05	33.60	96.66	85.85	36.73	78.82	67.97	36.76
Attribute subset: {*caller, assigned_to, assignment_group*}									
1	80.17	67.87	34.04	80.17	67.87	34.04	80.17	67.87	34.04
3	93.16	80.65	37.48	102.64	86.15	38.58	131.73	118.08	38.67
5	91.34	80.96	39.22	**76.21**	**64.98**	**40.67**	86.20	74.89	40.75
6	85.55	74.76	39.58	94.38	83.01	41.04	78.05	66.67	41.11
7	96.99	85.00	39.76	102.01	86.35	41.19	105.66	94.33	41.25
Inf.	85.96	74.00	40.03	81.33	70.36	41.33	79.76	68.76	41.36

Table 7. Experiment #3 – average prediction results. Used attributes: Best attributes selected by wrapper (*incident_state, location*). Log sample: 8,000 incidents. Metric: MAPE (Mean and Median). NF = % of non-fitting incidents. Bold: best results.

Max Hor	Set			Multiset			Sequence		
	Mean	*Med*	*NF*	*Mean*	*Med*	*NF*	*Mean*	*Med*	*NF*
1	501.18	450.23	0.88	501.18	450.23	0.88	501.18	450.23	0.88
3	528.98	522.63	1.92	497.56	475.72	2.70	92.71	64.01	2.96
5	185.12	66.39	2.51	113.64	84.77	5.71	143.45	72.07	6.60
6	33.90	19.51	2.58	43.02	23.74	6.91	33.85	22.87	8.19
7	**17.82**	**10.13**	**2.69**	21.36	15.19	8.07	25.07	15.46	9.74
Inf.	60.69	42.95	2.92	251.79	230.73	14.01	239.53	218.17	15.50

4.3 Experiment #3 – Wrappers with Hill-Climbing and Best-First

Last, the attribute selection was driven by the wrapper method using a forward selection mode with the hill-climbing and best-first search techniques [12] (cf. Sect. 3). The search space is composed of all combinations of the 15 attributes pre-selected by the filter with ranking strategy, i.e., the attributes in Table 4. Thus, the search space had $2^{15} = 32,768$ states, taking the 18 ATSs generated for each state, the range of the horizon and the state representation parameters. As stated before, using heuristic search procedures is justified in this case. The wrapper method was carried out on the enriched event log sample with 8,000 incidents. For the best-first search technique, the maximum number of expansion movements with no improvement was set to 15. The prediction results for the ATSs generated for this scenario are listed in Table 7. Both search techniques resulted in selecting the same best attribute subset, which are {*incident_state, location*}. Despite the high agreement between the two search techniques, some information can be extracted from their execution processes:

- **Hill-climbing:** the stopping criterion was reached after the third expansion movement; 42 states of the search space were explored; the mean and median for all ATSs generated in the state representation *set* were on average 146.80 and 103.76, respectively; and the average for non-fitting was 8.97.
- **Best-first:** 17 expansion movements were done; 172 states of the search space were explored; in average, the mean and median statistics for all ATSs generated in the state representation *set* were 114.96 and 89.68, respectively; the average for non-fitting was 36.27.

The best results were got with horizon 7 and the state representation *set*; however, the results got with the other state representations for the same horizon are good as well. These results are significantly better than those results got by the filter and better in terms of mean and median than those got by the expert-driven selection. Overall, the low non-fitting results are promising.

As a second part of experiment #3, with the purpose of comparing the prediction results got with the ATS models generated with these attribute subsets selected by wrapper with the results got in experiments #1 and #2, a new set of ATSs was generated using as parameters those of best results in Table 7, however using now the enriched event log sample with 24,000 incidents. The results are shown in Table 8 and it is noticed that the best results (maximum horizon set to 5) overcome the best results got in the previous experiments considering the MAPE evaluations. The results for MAPE are less than half of those measures got by expert-driven selection keeping non-fitting values at the lowest level.

4.4   Summarized View

Table 9 shows information detailing the average number of states on each set of ATSs created in experiment instances. One can check that best results (experiments #1 and #3) for MAPE also have the small number of states when compared with experiment #2.

Table 8. Experiment #3 – average prediction results. Used attributes: best attribute subsets selected by wrapper. Log sample: 24,000 incidents. Metric: MAPE (Mean and Median). NF = % of non-fitting incidents. Bold: best results.

Max Hor	Set			Multiset			Sequence		
	Mean	*Med*	*NF*	*Mean*	*Med*	*NF*	*Mean*	*Med*	*NF*
1	138.60	97.59	0.35	138.60	97.59	0.35	138.60	97.59	0.35
3	107.69	52.48	0.85	69.02	47.17	1.09	65.57	37.25	1.22
5	**50.45**	**24.49**	**1.11**	**41.90**	**29.35**	**2.30**	**35.09**	**27.28**	**2.74**
6	69.32	48.98	1.13	59.71	52.16	2.95	57.13	47.21	3.57
7	132.81	110.51	1.16	153.96	114.83	3.57	68.53	56.39	4.36
Inf.	66.75	46.16	1.24	43.02	35.86	6.51	70.54	38.26	7.43

Table 9. Consolidated view of the numbers of ATSs' states. Log sample: 24,000 incidents. Metrics: AVGS = AVErage number of States in the ATS; SD = Standard Deviation. Bold: refers to the set of ATSs with the best performances.

Max Hor	Set		Multiset		Sequence	
	AVGS	SD	AVGS	SD	AVGS	SD
Attribute subset: {incident_state, category, priority} – Exp. #1						
1	648.8	3.11	648.8	3.11	648.8	3.11
3	2428.0	13.01	3734.0	24.44	**4139.6**	**28.89**
5	3273.0	16.30	7895.4	50.66	9071.2	57.39
6	3456.8	15.27	9853.2	63.19	11501.4	65.77
7	3535.0	14.10	11678.0	73.84	13711.4	65.17
Inf.	3660.6	20.69	18423.4	115.99	19653.4	84.88
Attribute subset: {caller, assigned_to} – Exp. #2						
1	15297.4	67.56	15297.4	67.56	15297.4	67.56
3	18814.4	92.89	40474.4	142.09	41558.0	147
5	17658.6	76.79	**52537.2**	**150.95**	54034.4	157.18
6	17343.0	72.94	56218.4	160.01	57671.0	166.91
7	17062.6	69.26	58919.6	169.46	60287.6	173.83
Inf.	16205.6	62.87	66131.8	171.75	66151.2	170.66
Attribute subset: {caller, assigned_to, assignment_group} – Exp. #2						
1	24305.6	58.72	24305.6	58.72	24305.6	58.72
3	34664.4	68.94	54123.0	135.33	55942.2	141.48
5	31740.2	65.22	**64243.8**	**166.85**	66125.2	173.65
6	30425.0	70.68	66610.8	175.79	68193.4	189.58
7	29282.6	58.83	68037.2	179.03	69336.0	191.92
Inf.	26093.6	49.53	70795.0	197.57	70820.6	201.09
Attribute subset: {incident_state, location} – Exp. #3						
1	901.2	14.13	901.2	14.13	901.2	14.13
3	2322.6	25.16	3586.0	34.62	3939.0	36.61
5	**2675.2**	**27.10**	**6950.4**	**44.95**	**7972.6**	**52.66**
6	2697.4	25.54	8481.2	41.61	9881.6	47.67
7	2706.2	27.88	9838.8	36.38	11590.0	39.82
Inf.	2634.8	26.03	15901.8	78.16	17259.6	69.63

5   Discussion of Findings

With the analysis of the results, we could verify that the expert-driven and the filter with ranking strategies allow us building models with similar predictive power. However, when checking the model fitting capabilities, some differences (1.38 and 35.67, respectively) are observed between them for the best results.

Such differences were caused because of the different process perspectives represented by the attribute subset used in each case. For the first case, the ATS generation was driven by incident descriptive attributes recommended by ITIL best practices suggested by human experts for incident clustering and routing; then, the resulting model could accurately represent the process. For the second case, the set of attributes automatically selected to build the ATS represents organizational and resource perspectives of the incident management process; what means that, in this case, the ATS captured how teams (i.e., people) act to support user requests and became highly specialized and incapable of generalizing the real process behavior. This happens because the attributes selected represent information that presumably changes frequently ('caller' and 'technical people' in charge of the incident). The MAPE results for experiment #1 were compared to those got for experiment #2, using the paired Wilcoxon test. This test showed that there is no statistical difference among the distributions of the MAPE values as with $p_{value} = 0.3125$ the null hypothesis for equal distributions cannot be rejected.

The wrapper-based experiment achieved an average MAPE measure (24.49) that is 38.47% of the average MAPE achieved in the expert-driven experiment. The model non-fitting continued in an even lowest level (1.11%) as that got in the first one. The paired Wilcoxon statistical test was applied to compare the MAPE results got for experiment #1 with those got for experiment #3. The null hypothesis for equal distributions was rejected with $p_{value} = 0.0312$. This result allows affirming that the attribute selection got with the wrapper is better than the expert's choice in terms of accuracy and generalization (i.e., low non-fitting) in this incident management process.

The attribute subset selected by wrapper unifies expert knowledge with an organizational perspective, which produced a completion time predictor with high accuracy and low non-fitting rates. The results were similar for hill-climbing and best-first search techniques. This behavior has already been observed in experiments executed by Kohavi and John [12], in which, for diverse types of datasets, additional search effort did not produce better results.

6   Conclusions

Using the wrapper method could select a set of attributes that supported a significant improvement in the accuracy of ATS as a prediction model when compared to both the filter and the expert knowledge. Furthermore, such a search process points out that the maximum horizon and distinct types of state representations have a high influence on the prediction model results. This approach has the potential as a useful pre-processing step before applying other prediction methods besides the ATS method used in this study. These results are important when considering a business process scenario in which different actors need to collaborate for its execution, generating complexity and unpredictability of the completion time, for example.

This paper focuses on a specific application domain to illustrate that the proposed strategy is a way to solve a generic problem. However, while it is a promising heuristic procedure, there is no guarantee that the search will yield satisfactory results for all applications in similar scenarios. As the proposed approach performs a search in the event log derived from a specific process, it implements an inductive reasoning mechanism dependent on the properties of such an underlying process, regardless of the chosen prediction technique. As a result, for each specific case of application, different results are likely to be got.

In addition, it is still necessary to verify the influence of outliers throughout the process (search and prediction) as the results got in the experiments presented some varying degree. Using other search methods (such as genetic algorithms) or other options to build process model-based predictors (such as Petri nets or variations of ATSs), applied on benchmark event logs for comparison, are points for exploration.

Acknowledgments. This work was funded by the São Paulo Research Foundation (Fapesp), Brazil; grants 2017/26491-1 and 2017/26487-4.

Appendix

A brief description of the 15 attributes listed in Table 4 is presented in Table 10.

Table 10. Description of the 15 attributes used in the experiment

ID	Attribute	Description
1	*caller*	Identifier of the user affected
2	*incident_state*	Eighth levels controlling the incident management process transitions from opening until closing the case
3	*assigned_to*	Identifier of the user in charge of the incident
4	*assignment_group*	Identifier of the support group in charge of the incident
5	*symptom*	Description of the user perception about the service availability
6	*sys_updated_by*	Identifier of the user who updated the incident and generated the current log record
7	*subcategory*	Second level description of the affected service (related to the first level description, i.e., to *category*)
8	*category*	First level description of the affected service
9	*active*	Boolean attribute indicating if the record is active or closed/canceled
10	*priority_confirmation*	Boolean attribute indicating whether the *priority* field has been double-checked
11	*created*	Incident creation date and time
12	*open_by*	Identifier of the user who reported the incident
13	*location*	Identifier of the location of the place affected
14	*made_SLA*	Boolean attribute that shows whether the incident exceeded the target SLA
15	*knowledge*	Boolean attribute that shows whether a knowledge base document was used to resolve the incident

References

1. de Leoni, M., van der Aalst, W.M., Dees, M.: A general process mining framework for correlating, predicting and clustering dynamic behavior based on event logs. Inf. Syst. **56**, 235–257 (2016). https://doi.org/10.1016/j.is.2015.07.003
2. van der Aalst, W.M.P.: Process Mining - Discovery, Conformance and Enhancement of Business Processes, 2nd edn. Springer, Heidelberg (2016). https://doi.org/10.1007/978-3-642-19345-3
3. van der Aalst, W., Schonenberg, M., Song, M.: Time prediction based on process mining. Inf. Syst. **36**(2), 450–475 (2011). https://doi.org/10.1016/j.is.2010.09.001
4. Boonjing, V., Pimchangthong, D.: Data mining for positive customer reaction to advertising in social media. In: Ziemba, E. (ed.) AITM/ISM-2017. LNBIP, vol. 311, pp. 83–95. Springer, Cham (2018). https://doi.org/10.1007/978-3-319-77721-4_5
5. Łobaziewicz, M.: The role of ICT solutions in the intelligent enterprise performance. In: Ziemba, E. (ed.) AITM/ISM-2016. LNBIP, vol. 277, pp. 120–136. Springer, Cham (2017). https://doi.org/10.1007/978-3-319-53076-5_7
6. Pawełoszek, I.: Data mining approach to assessment of the ERP system from the vendor's perspective. In: Ziemba, E. (ed.) Information Technology for Management. LNBIP, vol. 243, pp. 125–143. Springer, Cham (2016). https://doi.org/10.1007/978-3-319-30528-8_8
7. Berti, A.: Improving process mining prediction results in processes that change over time. In: Proceedings of the 5th International Conference on Data Analytics, pp. 37–42. IARIA (2016)
8. Polato, M., Sperduti, A., Burattin, A., de Leoni, M.: Data-aware remaining time prediction of business process instances. In: Proceedings of the 2014 International Joint Conference on Neural Networks, pp. 816–823. IEEE, July 2014. https://doi.org/10.1109/IJCNN.2014.6889360
9. Rogge-Solti, A., Vana, L., Mendling, J.: Time series Petri net models - enrichment and prediction. In: Proceedings of the 5th International Symposium on Data-driven Process Discovery and Analysis (SIMPDA), pp. 109–123 (2015). https://doi.org/10.1007/978-3-319-53435-0_6
10. Rogge-Solti, A., Weske, M.: Prediction of business process durations using non-Markovian stochastic Petri nets. Inf. Syst. **54**, 1–14 (2015). https://doi.org/10.1016/j.is.2015.04.004
11. Hinkka, M., Lehto, T., Heljanko, K., Jung, A.: Structural feature selection for event logs. In: Teniente, E., Weidlich, M. (eds.) BPM 2017. LNBIP, vol. 308, pp. 20–35. Springer, Cham (2018). https://doi.org/10.1007/978-3-319-74030-0_2
12. Kohavi, R., John, G.H.: Wrappers for feature subset selection. Artif. Intell. **97**(1), 273–324 (1997). https://doi.org/10.1016/S0004-3702(97)00043-X
13. do Amaral, C.A.L., Fantinato, M., Peres, S.M.: Attribute selection with filter and wrapper: an application on incident management process. In: Proceedings of the 15th Conference on Advanced Information Technologies for Management (AITM) in Federated Conference on Computer Science and Information Systems (FedCSIS), vol. 15, pp. 679–682 (2018). https://doi.org/10.15439/2018F126
14. Guyon, I., Elisseeff, A.: An introduction to variable and feature selection. J. Mach. Learn. Res. **3**, 1157–1182 (2003). https://doi.org/10.1162/153244303322753616
15. Blum, A.L., Langley, P.: Selection of relevant features and examples in machine learning. Artif. Intell. **97**(1–2), 245–271 (1997). https://doi.org/10.1016/S0004-3702(97)00063-5

16. Armstrong, J.S., Collopy, F.: Error measures for generalizing about forecasting methods: empirical comparisons. Int. J. Forecast. **8**(1), 69–80 (1992). https://doi. org/10.1016/0169-2070(92)90008-W
17. de Myttenaere, A., Golden, B., Grand, B.L., Rossi, F.: Mean absolute percentage error for regression models. Neurocomputing **192**, 38–48 (2016). https://doi.org/ 10.1016/j.neucom.2015.12.114
18. van der Aalst, W.M.P., Rubin, V., Verbeek, H.M.W., van Dongen, B.F., Kindler, E., Günther, C.W.: Process mining: a two-step approach to balance between under-fitting and overfitting. Softw. Syst. Model. **9**(1) (2008). https://doi.org/10.1007/ s10270-008-0106-z
19. Evermann, J., Rehse, J.R., Fettke, P.: Predicting process behaviour using deep learning. Decis. Support Syst. **100**, 129–140 (2017). https://doi.org/10.1016/j.dss. 2017.04.003
20. Tax, N., Verenich, I., La Rosa, M., Dumas, M.: Predictive business process mon-itoring with LSTM neural networks. In: Dubois, E., Pohl, K. (eds.) CAiSE 2017. LNCS, vol. 10253, pp. 477–492. Springer, Cham (2017). https://doi.org/10.1007/ 978-3-319-59536-8_30
21. Richardson, J.T.E.: Eta squared and partial eta squared as measures of effect size in educational research. Educ. Res. Rev. **6**(2), 135–147 (2011). https://doi.org/10. 1016/j.edurev.2010.12.001
22. itSMF: Global survey on IT service management. http://www.itil.co.il
23. Marrone, M., Gacenga, F., Cater-Steel, A., Kolbe, L.: IT service management: a cross-national study of ITIL adoption. Commun. Assoc. Inf. Syst. **34**, 49.1–49.30 (2014). https://doi.org/10.17705/1CAIS.03449

Application of Ontology in Financial Assessment Based on Real Options in Small and Medium-Sized Companies

Helena Dudycz[✉] ⓘ, Bartłomiej Nita ⓘ, and Piotr Oleksyk ⓘ

Wrocław University of Economics, Wrocław, Poland
{helena.dudycz,bartlomiej.nita,
piotr.oleksyk}@ue.wroc.pl

Abstract. The paper entitled "Attempt to Extend the Knowledge of Decision Support Systems for Small and Medium-Sized Enterprises" [1] presented a prototype of an intelligent business forecasting system based on the real option approach to the prospective financial assessment of Small and Medium-Sized Enterprises (SME). This prototype integrates real options, financial knowledge, and predictive models. The content of the knowledge is focused on essential financial concepts and relationships connected with risk assessment, taking into consideration internal and external economic and financial information. In this project, the ontology is used to create the necessary financial knowledge model. The aim of this paper is to present the application of ontology in financial assessment based on real options approach to support financial assessment in an Early Warning System. In the paper, the process of creating a financial assessment ontology is described. The use created ontology in financial assessment based on the real options approach is discussed.

Keywords: Ontology · Financial ontologies · Financial analysis · Real options · Early Warning Systems

1 Introduction

Small and Medium-Sized Enterprises (SMEs) are forced to operate under the constraints and pressures of the rapidly changing and highly volatile market, which adds to the uncertainty of their everyday activities. Under such conditions, the manager can be seen as a future-oriented process of making informed decisions. From a manager's viewpoint, making decisions in business is a process of identifying and selecting a course of action to solve a specific problem or to make good use of a business opportunity. The SME's manager needs innovative methods combined with advanced financial analysis tools, which are required to correctly assess the economic situation of their company as well as the required investments.

In general, an enterprise works better on the competitive space if it tries to identify development opportunities and threats of disruption to its leading activity. This requires the implementation of prospective financial assessment in a SME. Examination of most of the future changes provides the signals (so-called weak signals) that facilitate

© Springer Nature Switzerland AG 2019
E. Ziemba (Ed.): AITM 2018/ISM 2018, LNBIP 346, pp. 24–40, 2019.
https://doi.org/10.1007/978-3-030-15154-6_2

anticipating their approach. However, the main hurdle is connected with choosing and properly identifying the relationships between them. Moreover, the moment in which they are identified constitutes critical information.

Most of SME managers are not skilled enough to understand and respond to threats coming from the business environment. Proper integration of signals coming from the environment with the performance achieved by an enterprise constitutes the basis for making good decisions involving corporate change. Managers who keep postponing making investment decisions expose their company to a risk of bankruptcy or a loss of continuity. This is especially important if such threats relate to a loss of competitive advantage due to technological backwardness. Failure to consider new investments could trigger off negative effects. These could provide the first signs of impending company bankruptcy since they are observable in the long-term perspective. The large variability of the environment demands companies' flexible adjustment to prevailing external conditions.

In the literature, [1] the proposal of a prototype based on the real option approach that integrates financial knowledge, predictive models, and business reasoning to support financial assessment in Early Warning Systems was presented. In this project, it is assumed that financial knowledge is formally defined by the domain ontology, which is one of the commonly used methods of representing knowledge in information systems.

The aim of the paper is to present the application of ontology in financial assessment based on the real options approach to support financial assessment in an Early Warning System. The paper has been structured as follows. In the next section we describe Early Warning Systems in the context of financial assessment, the use of real options for the purposes of investment appraisal, and an ontological approach to the representation of financial and business knowledge. In section three, we present the proposal of smart EWS for SMEs and the process of creating a financial assessment ontology. Next, we present a case study analysis that refers to prospective financial assessment based on the real option approach. Finally, in the last section, some conclusions are drawn.

2   Theoretical Background

2.1   Critical Analysis of Early Warning Systems in the Context of Financial Analysis

The manager should analyze diverse information from external and internal sources (Fig. 1). Depending on this information, there is a number of possible scenarios, each of them associated with some opportunities and threats. When identifying threats, enterprises often have to analyze various potential investments that can minimize the risk to the company's operations.

Early warning is a process which allows an organization to consistently anticipate and address competitive threats. As far back as the early seventies, managers of firms started thinking about methods that would allow early identification of opportunities and threats present in their business environment. It led to the emergence of Early Warning Systems, which were to forewarn of approaching threats and opportunities as early as possible and explore their weak signals.

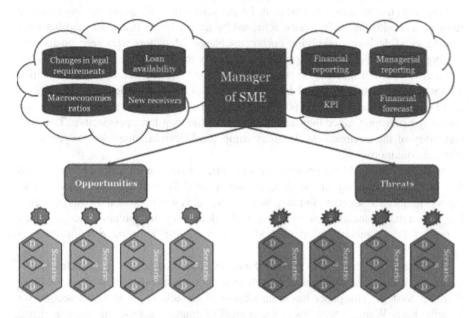

Fig. 1. A number of possible scenarios of opportunities and threats depending on external and internal sources

The first Early Warning Systems were focused on the performance indicators (KPIs), which are a business metric used to evaluate factors crucial to the success of an organization and to help an enterprise assess progress toward declared goals. An Early Warning System supports continuous monitoring, collecting, and processing of information needed by strategic management to effectively run the business, even in real time.

Regardless of the area of application, the main functions of Early Warning Systems do not change: it is early information about approaching threats and/or opportunities. This requires the development of solutions to help and enable warning signs. Many methods have been developed to analyze SME performance aimed at creating an Early Warning System [2]. Unfortunately, they are more often based on past data, and this, at present, is simply not enough. The essential requirement for an SME to survive in a competitive market is the development of mechanisms allowing the generation of revenues from core operations in the future. In planning future activities, companies' managers emphasize the need to maintain existing customers. If this is not possible, attempts are made to search for new customers. It is also necessary to analyze competitive actions, which in the near future could lead to a significant decrease in market share.

The loss of the company's competitive potential constitutes one of the most common threats to maintaining the forecasted sales revenues. This loss may occur due to various factors, including:

- a drop in the quality of manufactured products or delivered services,
- technological backwardness, which is the reason for the inability to meet customers' expectations,
- a low level of corporate capacity that significantly reduces the time necessary for delivery,
- a lack of ability to cooperate with other entities in order to execute orders exceeding the production capacity.

Of course, the listed reasons do not represent all the problems related to the loss of companies' ability to compete effectively. These are factors that cannot be registered by means of typical Early Warning Systems. Implementation of innovations and other changes in the structure of fixed assets should be considered as the first approach solution. The basic problem of conducting a development project is the lack of equity funds and a limited possibility of obtaining external financing. If the owners of a company are not able to increase equity, then debt financing is required. While taking bank loans or issuing bonds to finance innovations are possible solutions, they generate a high risk of insolvency. The managers should make multi-faceted analyses when making investment decisions. These analyses should take a contingent approach to financial forecasting and analysis in the long-term perspective.

One of the main weaknesses of existing Early Warning Systems is the lack of a formal representation of the knowledge and analytical models that take into consideration both internal and external information. Internal information refers to resource consumption, cost structure, etc., whereas external information takes into account market conditions, competitive actions, legal requirements, etc. In consequence, the reasoning tasks and computation are very limited.

The traditional Early Warning Systems are oriented towards identifying threats based mainly on the past information, and the design of such systems in an SME refers usually to internal reporting. Managers using simple Early Warning Systems receive various alerts, but they do not know which problems should be addressed first. Moreover, these systems do not indicate for managers which suggestions are to be implemented, hence managers have to rely solely on their managerial intuition. It is, therefore, necessary to extend the EWS functionality.

2.2 Using Real Options for Assessment Investment

The standard approach to investment appraisal is based on the discounted cash flow methodology, and NPV (Net Present Value) analysis in particular. This approach is currently insufficient mainly due to the high volatility of external factors affecting a company [3, 4]. The commonly used net present value criterion is currently considered as static mainly because it is calculated at a given moment and does not anticipate changes that may occur in the future. Moreover, while computing NPV, managers assume in advance that they know all factors affecting the investment's effectiveness. As a result, the NPV criterion does not take into account the opportunity to react to new circumstances, such as [5]:

- an unexpected collapse of the market, which leads to a reduction in the business size,
- significant changes in prices, which may have a significant impact on the profitability of the project,
- an exceptionally favourable situation that allows expanding the scope of activities.

Summarizing, the disadvantage of NPV is that it is based only on internal data and past data. Thus, the NPV calculated in this way is often referred to as passive or static.. The use of NPV for the assessment of investment project does not take into account external information, which may have both a negative (e.g. an unexpected collapse of the market, significant changes in prices) and a positive (e.g. an exceptionally favourable situation) impact on the implementation of an investment. Taking into account the limitations of the NPV criterion, the concept of real options should be applied.

The term "real option" was initially used in 1977 by Myers [6]. This concept was further developed by Dixit and Pindyck [7]. The term "real option" can be defined using an analogy to the financial option. Real option, therefore, means the right of its holder to buy or sell some underlying assets (basic instrument, which is usually an investment project) in specified sizes, at a fixed price and at a given time [8, p. 172]. Generally, it can be said that the real option is the right to modify an investment project in an enterprise [9, p. 269]. It helps managers create value, for if everything goes well, a project can be expanded; however, if the environment was to turn out to be unfavourable, then implementation of the project could be postponed. Projects that can be easily modified are much more valuable than those that do not provide for such flexibility. The more uncertain the future is and the more risk factors associated with the project, the more valuable is the flexibility of the project. Thus, real options can serve as a very helpful solution in making decisions on launching development projects as well as they are useful tools for managers looking for means to deal with their company's financial problems.

Techniques based on the net present value are still necessary and valuable, hence they should not be underestimated in any case. However, real options allow for a deeper analysis of the investment appraisal issue and somehow expand the traditional methods due to the identification of various investment possibilities embedded in the investment projects. Jahanshahi et al. [10] argues the role that real options can play in an SME to increase market orientation and organizational learning, consequently providing a firm with the ability to both attain and sustain competitive advantage, particularly in a volatile environment.

The value of this flexibility is reflected in the option price (option premium); it increases if the probability of receiving new information increases and ability to bear risk increases. The value of this flexibility is the difference between the value of the investment project with the right of managers to modify the project embedded and the value of the project in the absence of managerial discretionary to modify the project. This relationship can be described as follows [11]:

$$S\text{-}NPV = NPV + OV$$

where S-NPV – a strategic net present value, NPV – a standard (static, passive, direct) net present value, OV – an Option value.

The lack of flexibility is especially the main factor preventing managers from taking risks. They are often afraid of launching a new investment project and are not aware of the existence of a flexibility option. This is the reason why the development project is rejected. In addition, this kind of risk aversion may trigger off the company's bankruptcy process. Power and Reid [12] test empirically whether real options logic applies to small firms implementing significant changes (e.g. in technology). Their research findings imply that strategic flexibility in investment decisions is necessary for good long-run performance of small companies.

The value of real options is very useful information for managers of small companies in the decision-making process related to undertaking an investment project. If a manager obtains information about the negative NPV of a project, then the project is usually rejected. Were a manager to adjust the static NPV with regard to the value of the real option, the final strategic value of the project could significantly change. This kind of financial projection prompts a manager to undertake the development project. Real options are treated as risk management instruments used to assess the financial risk of high-risk development projects as well as to influence the company's ability to continue as a going concern in the future [13, 14].

The valuation of real options takes into account the scenario analysis prepared by managers before making the decision on the implementation of the development project. Very often, standard methods of investment appraisal do not take into account the possibilities that will occur during the implementation stage. Such omission may result in a loss of the ability to offer products with features similar to or exceeding those provided by competitors, and finally in the company's bankruptcy.

The valuation of real options is a difficult task – very often impossible to be carried out by the manager of an SME. It should be noted that the value of real options is closely linked with high risk. A manager without advanced financial knowledge can increase the level of risk associated with running a business. Thus, it is necessary to use an information system that will guide the manager through all the risks associated with the investment project taking into account contingency factors.

2.3   Ontology of Financial and Business Knowledge

In the literature, we can find many definitions of ontology. A wide review of this issue is presented in [15, 16]. Most often, the term refers to the definition given by Gruber [17, p. 907], who describes it as "an explicit specification of a conceptualization". Therefore, ontology is a model that defines formally the concepts of a specific area and the semantic relations between them. Constructing ontology always denotes analysis and organizing knowledge concerning a specific field noted in a formalized structure.

In general, the ontology is used to create the necessary knowledge models for defining functionalities in analytical tools. Using ontologies supporting an information search in an information system may help to reduce the following weaknesses of management information systems: (1) a lack of support in defining business rules for getting proactive information and support with respect to consulting in the process of decision making, and (2) a lack of a semantic layer describing relations between different economic concepts [18]. Ontology can be used to create the necessary knowledge (especially financial knowledge) models in analytical tools. The created financial ontologies, which contain experts' knowledge, may serve as a strong support for decision makers in SMEs. The domain knowledge about relations between economic and financial ratios will make the analysis and interpretation of contextual connections easier. This is very important in the case of SMEs, where a company does not employ experts in economic-financial analysis, and using external consulting is too costly. Reproducing knowledge with the use of visualization of semantic network contributes inter alia to a better understanding of economic concepts and the interpretation of specific economic and financial indicators.

Ontology can be presented by visualization of a semantic network, which is a multifaceted, interactive presentation tool, also allowing interactive visual searches for information [19]. This solution can contribute to a better understanding of economic concepts and the interpretation of specific economic and financial indicators, among other things. In this approach, special attention is paid to the role of the visualization of a semantic network which is not only a tool for presenting data but also one providing an interface allowing interactive visual information searching [20, 21].

In the relevant literature, many research projects show that creating an ontology of economic and financial indicators is advantageous in decision making [22–26].

3 Research Methodology

3.1 Proposal of Smart Early Warning Systems

A proposal of a smart Early Warning System for SMEs is presented in the paper [1]. This solution integrates financial knowledge, predictive models, and business reasoning to support the financial assessment of an enterprise and assess the profitability of an investment project. This EWS has introduced several new solutions. Figure 2 presents a functional schema of a smart EWS. There are four important elements:

- using real options to calculate strategic NPV,
- analysis of internal and external information,
- using ontology of business knowledge,
- integration of financial knowledge and predictive models.

The presented smart EWS can facilitate automated analysis of information available in financial databases and external data. In this solution, real options are used to calculate the strategic net present value. The valuation of real options is a difficult task and very often impossible to be carried out by the manager of an SME, so financial knowledge is formally defined by the domain ontology. This proposal of a smart ESM is based on the introduction of financial ontology, containing internal and external variables related to real options. A manager can browse the hierarchy of concepts, relationships, and annotations. They can also define conditions such as positive and negative effects of decision process execution.

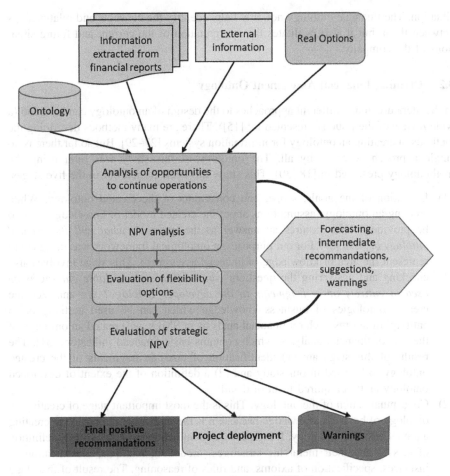

Fig. 2. Functional schema of a smart EWS (Source: [1])

This smart EWS includes also extended analytical methods, which aims at integrating data from internal reporting with external information. The internal and external information and information about real options is interpreted by the decision rules, for example [1]:

if fi threshold f

then message f-warning else message f-positive

where ® denotes a specific relationship between the values of fi and the threshold.

The system processes selected information from financial reports and the business environment, subsequently forecasting a company's economic and financial situation. In a situation of a negative forecast, in addition to warning messages, it indicates the possibility of using the real options that would allow a manager to exit a critical situation. The financial ontology not only helps identify the concepts and relationships between them, but it also facilitates the interpretation of the current and future situations of the company.

3.2 Creating Financial Assessment Ontology

In the literature, many different approaches to the design of an ontology can be found (a wide review of the issue is presented in: [15]). There are many methods describing the methods of creating an ontology for information systems [27–29]. But so far there is no single approach accepted by all. The ontology of this study was built using the methodology presented in [18, 30]. This study has been carried out in the five stages:

(1) Definition of the goals, scope, and constraints of the created ontology. While creating an ontology, assumptions about the created model of knowledge have to be provided. That requires an answer to the question: *what will the created ontology be used for?* For our purpose, an ontological framework was designed to represent the area of knowledge of financial assessment. This stage involves also checking and answering the question: *can existing and available ontologies be used in entirety or in fragments in the developed ontology?* We analyzed the created ontologies of business knowledge which can be used partially or in entirety. In our research on financial analysis in SMEs, we created an ontology of the part of financial analysis, which contains basic financial indicators [31]. The results of this stage are (1) identification of possible fragments of the created ontology to be used in our study and (2) a definition of the extent of developed ontology and its required level of detail.

(2) Conceptualization of the ontology. This is the most important stage of creating an ontology of business knowledge because it is the most important stage in creating a model based on ontology. It includes the identification of all concepts, definition of classes and their hierarchic structures, modelling relations, identification of instances, specification of axioms, and rules of reasoning. The result of this stage is a constructed model of an ontology of the defined field of business knowledge with respect to financial assessment (Fig. 3).

(3) Verification of the ontology's correctness by experts. The aim of this stage is to answer the question: *is it necessary to modify the ontology model developed for the chosen part of business knowledge?* The created ontology was verified in the following way: (1) a formal verification of the specified ontology (e.g. incorrect relations were indicated) and (2) a content verification (e.g. correctness of taxonomic concepts, and correctness of relational dependencies between concepts).

(4) Encoding the ontology is described in the formal language or editor of ontology. We encoded the ontology using Protégé, which is a free, open-source platform (http://protege.stanford.edu/), which can be extended with many plug-ins for ontology visualization (http://protegewiki.stanford.edu/wiki/Visualization).

(5) Validation and evaluation of the built ontology. In this stage, the encoded ontology is checked to ensure that it meets the needs of the users (e.g. the managers). Validation is carried out in two areas. Firstly, validation of usefulness and correctness of the created ontology is carried out by experts. Secondly,

validation of predefined use cases is carried out. That requires an answer to the questions: *(1) will the created ontology be useful for the users (the managers) who will use it?* and *(2) is it necessary to modify the encoded ontology for the selected part of business knowledge?* We prepared use cases of financial assessment scenarios and validated the created ontology. In our study, evaluation of semantic network visualization as they pertained to contextual dependencies was conducted using the OntoGraf module in the Protégé 4.1 program.

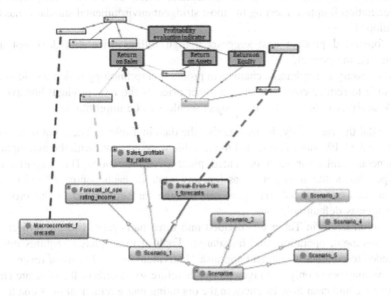

Fig. 3. The example of the part of the created ontology

The presented process of the created ontology is characterized by iterative design. The iterative design of ontology is important because the created ontology should be useful to the managers. The use of ontologies within analytical tools can help you solve the following problem: support in defining business rules in order to obtain proactive information and advice in the decision-making process. The use of the created ontology in financial assessment based on the real options approach to support financial assessment in EWS will be discussed in the next section.

4   Case Study

To illustrate the need for real option valuation, we present the case of a project that would be rejected on the basis of traditional analytical methods. Based on the valuation of flexible option to expand, we have shown that to avoid going bankrupt, the management should choose to implement the project.

Assumptions of the case study [see also: 1]:

- managers of a manufacturing company producing water heaters and wood fire-places, while preparing sales forecasts, identify a significant problem with the company's ability to continue its operations,
- managers, based on their expertise and experience, foresee that if they decide to abandon development projects, the company will lose the ability to continue its operations within 5–7 years,
- when planning innovations in the enterprise, a new design of a fully ecological cogeneration fireplace meeting the most stringent environmental standards has been developed,
- the forecasted product cost suggests a high selling price that does not allow launching the project,
- it is necessary to implement changes in production technology which would make it possible to reduce costs and offer a lower price of the new product; however, the NPV analysis indicates that the project would still be unprofitable.

To detail the case study, let us examine the data in Table 1. The input data needed to estimate the NPV values presented in this table were prepared with the assumption of homogeneous ranks for each presented piece of information. The prepared EWS prototype allows the manager to assign any rank to each source of information. However, less experienced managers can use the hint embedded in the prototype, which suggests default solutions.

The information in Table 1 is divided into three parts related to the project's life cycle: investment, operation, and liquidation. Each of these phases requires different data needed to conduct investment appraisal. Individual items of costs of revenues and cash flows may occur only in a given phase, therefore some cells of the table are empty. Sales revenue and cash flow balances in the operating phase remain at the same level in the period 2025–2027, as the company, without taking advantage of embedded real options, is not in a position to develop.

Based on the above assumptions and data, managers should not make any decision to implement any development project in the company. The data presented in the table clearly show that the analyzed development project is not profitable, as the NPV is negative and equals − 2.2 million PLN. The financial prospect of this company is bad. However, the lack of profitability has been projected based on traditional measures. Relying on the additional external information, a manager may apply the flexibility option, and all of a sudden the project becomes profitable.

However, it is clear that the rejection of the investment may lead to the company's bankruptcy. It is necessary to apply advanced analyses that take into account the option of developing business in the future. The valuation of such an option is based on the following premises:

- high social pressure on promoting environmentally-friendly solutions,
- anticipated changes in law indicate that in the future it will not be possible to build houses meeting high ecological standards without the modern heaters and fireplaces,

Table 1. Financial forecast (in thousands PLN)

	2018	2019	2020	2021	2022	2023	2024	2025	2026	2027
Investment launch phase										
Expenditure on investments in fixed assets	982	364	1 425							
Expenditure on investments in net working capital			988							
Total expenditure in the investment launch phase	982	364	2 413							
Operation phase										
Sales revenues				1 998	2 353	2 772	3 249	3 249	3 249	3 249
Variable costs				1 499	1 765	2 079	2 437	2 437	2 437	2 437
Fixed costs without depreciation				720	720	720	720	720	720	720
Depreciation				615	565	465	415	265	265	265
Profit before tax				−836	−697	−492	−323	−173	−173	−173
Income tax				−167	−139	−98	−65	−35	−35	−35
Net profit				−668	−557	−394	−258	−138	−138	−138
Depreciation				615	565	465	415	265	265	265
Expenditure on investments in net working capital				150	167	71	0	0	0	0
Total balance of cash flows in the operating phase				−204	−159	0.509	157	127	127	127
Project liquidation phase										
Proceeds from the sale of fixed assets										772
Recovery of investments in net working capital										1 376
The balance of cash flows in the liquidation phase										2 148
Total cash flow balance	−982	−364	−2 413	−204	−159	0.509	157	127	127	2 275
Discounting factor	0.8621	0.7432	0.6407	0.5523	0.4761	0.4104	0.3538	0.3050	0.2630	0.2267
Current value	−847	−271	−1 546	−113	−76	0.209	55	39	33	0.516
NPV	**−2 208**									

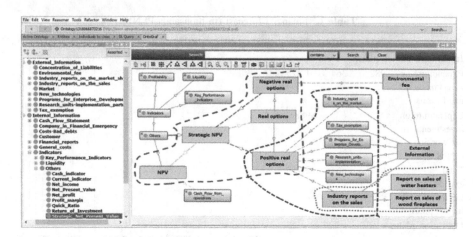

Fig. 4. An example of visualization of a semantic network of *Strategic NPV* (Source: own elaboration using Protégé editor)

- the design of the new technological solution allows its use in other products because, along with favourable external conditions and small expenditures, it will be possible to expand the range of new environmentally-friendly products,
- governmental research agencies plan to subsidize new solutions that meet high environmental standards in the future,
- within the national entrepreneurship development strategy, there are various aid programs for innovative entrepreneurs.

At this moment, the manager can use the module of the created ontology in the smart EWS. Figure 4 presents important concepts in rectangles for the analysis of the strategic NPV. There are two panels on the screenshot. The panel to the left shows taxonomic relations, while the one to the right allows for visualization of taxonomic and semantic relations between defined concepts (semantic network visualization). The presented part of the ontology shows that Strategic NPV depends on standard NPV and Real options, which contain Positive real options and Negative real options. Positive real options increase Strategic NPV, while negative real options decrease Strategic NPV. Instances of positive and negative real options are External information (for example Industry reports on the sales and Environmental fee). This part of the ontology shows to the manager that if they want to calculate Strategic NPV, they should estimate Real options. The manager can see that they should analyze External information affecting the calculation of the positive and negative values of real options. The manager can add, modify, as well as retrieve concepts related to the problem at hand.

The above market conditions based on external information serve as the basis for valuation of the flexible development option, which extends the traditional investment appraisal analysis. The sales forecast of the company indicates the clear signal of significant operating losses. Among the most important causes of the significant decrease in the ROS ratio were: a declining demand for the company's products and high operating leverage, i.e. a significant share of fixed costs in the total cost of production.

Thus, in order to survive, it is necessary to implement new products as well as to modify the current manufacturing technology. This is why the manager requests the profitability analysis of the investment project. The basis for this analysis is future sales revenues from new products and funds allocated for the acquisition of new technologies. The future cash flows obviously should be discounted to the present, taking into account the time value of money. The net present value is negative, thus the static analysis indicates that the project implementation is not profitable and the project should not be undertaken.

The Early Warning System based on the created ontology and in-depth analysis of the extended (strategic) version of NPV estimated using stochastic models [32] suggests extending the decision-making context. This extension takes into account the valuation of the flexibility option. For the purposes of the valuation of flexibility options, the system uses the following external information that involves the following:

- an opportunity to obtain additional external financing for an investment project involving the implementation of low-carbon technology (the amount of up to PLN 200,000) dedicated for Polish enterprises from the SME sector,
- a possibility of financing innovative environmentally-friendly technologies with amounts of up to 80% of eligible costs for enterprises from the SME sector,
- a possibility of receiving a tax relief for SME enterprises investing in reconstruction and implementation of environmentally-friendly production solutions.

The ontology built into the EWS (Fig. 2) explains to the manager the basic concepts and problems associated with the sales profitability. The ontology also presents the knowledge that combines the profitability issue with the investment project appraisal. Information transformed by the system indicates the possibility of a comprehensive profitability analysis. The system triggers off a signal that informs the manager of the option of analyzing the strategic NPV. This signal contains the suggestion that it is necessary to obtain additional information. After processing the available data for the purposes of the analyzed company, the system returns the value of the flexibility option that exceeds the negative NPV. In the analyzed company, the situation allows initiating preparatory activities to launch the project.

5   Conclusion and Future Works

The main objective of the paper was to present the application of ontology in smart Early Warning Systems. The created ontology contains knowledge about internal and external variables related to real options. The knowledge contained in the ontology explains to the manager the essence of valuating the flexibility option. The ontology also indicates the necessary external data that would make valuation possible. A manager who does not have detailed financial knowledge – is able to learn – thanks to the ontology – the relation between the flexibility option and the investment project profitability. The system presents a set of fundamental information needed to evaluate the flexibility option, but the information should be verified by the manager.

The example discussed in the paper is based on real data extracted from a small company. A risk of bankruptcy could be avoided by making decisions based on intelligent in-depth analysis of external information combined with the analysis of financial situation that allows the implementation of corrective solutions. From a financial perspective, the presented case study supports the conclusion that the decision to undertake any investment cannot be based solely on the estimation of standard NPV. It also requires an analysis of various external factors determining the decision-making process. Managers of SMEs may take advantage of the smart EWS that integrates the created ontology of financial knowledge and predictive models. Therefore, the system provides knowledge not only on the required internal information from various reports but also from external information (which consists in weak signals). The proposed ontology seems to be a promising extension to Early Warning Systems. It not only improves the quality of analysis but also enhances the managerial ability to better understand relations between financial data (internal information) and various factors affecting the development of SMEs (external information).

The presented process of designing an ontology in this paper requires further work verifying its usefulness in creating an ontology of financial knowledge. The use of an ontology of business knowledge seems to be a promising extension of EWS for SMEs. It not only should improve the efficiency of analysis, but also increase SMEs managers' capacity of understanding economic and financial data.

Further work should be focused on a global process-oriented approach to financial assessment, which will not be possible without large databases of real case studies and the use of knowledge possessed by experienced managers and financial analysts. For a company, the multidisciplinary approach to developing the prospective analysis in an Early Warning System could contribute to the attainment of a competitive advantage and increasing its financial stability.

Acknowledgement. The authors would like to thank Jerzy Korczak from the International University of Logistics and Transport, Wrocław, Poland, for his significant contribution to the development of the concept and prototype of the smart EWS as well as cooperation on the development of methods for automating inference rules.

References

1. Nita, B., Oleksyk, P., Korczak, J., Dudycz, H.: Prospective financial assessment based on real options in small and medium-sized company. In: Ganzha, M., Maciaszek, L., Paprzycki, M. (eds.) Proceedings of the 2018 Federated Conference on Computer Science and Information Systems, Annals of Computer Science and Information Systems, vol. 15, pp. 789–793 (2018). https://doi.org/10.15439/2018f161
2. Koyuncugil, A.S., Ozgulbas, N. (eds.) Surveillance Technologies and Early Warning Systems: Data Mining Applications for Risk Detection. IGI Global (2009). https://doi.org/10.4018/978-1-61692-865-0
3. Adelaja, T.: Capital Budgeting: Capital Investment Decision Paperback. CreateSpace Independent Publishing Platform (2016)
4. Götze, U., Northcott, D., Schuster, P.: Investment Appraisal: Methods and Models. Springer, Heidelberg (2015). https://doi.org/10.1007/978-3-662-45851-8

5. Damodaran, A.: The promise of real option. In: Stern, J.M., Chew, D.H. (eds.) The Revolution in Corporate Finance. Blackwell Publishing (2003). https://doi.org/10.1111/j.1745-6622.2000.tb00052.x
6. Myers, S.C.: Determinants of capital borrowing. J. Financ. Econ. **5**, 147–175 (1977)
7. Dixit, A., Pindyck, R.S.: Investment Under Uncertainty. Princeton University Press, Princeton (1994)
8. Nita, B.: Metody wyceny i kształtowania wartości przedsiębiorstwa [Methods of Corporate Valuation and Value-Based Management]. PWE, Warszawa (2007)
9. Brealey, R.A., Myers, S.C.: Principles of Corporate Finance. Mc-Graw Hill, New York City (2003)
10. Jahanshahi, A., Nawaser, K., Eizi, N., Etemadi, M.: The role of real options thinking in achieving sustainable competitive advantage for SMEs. Global Bus. Organ. Excell. **35**(1), 35–44 (2015). https://doi.org/10.1002/joe.21643
11. Trigeorgis, L.: Real Options. Managerial Flexibility and Strategy in Resource Allocation. The MIT Press, Cambridge (1998)
12. Power, B., Reid, G.: Organisational change and performance in long-lived small firms: a real options approach. Eur. J. Finance **19**(7/8), 791–809 (2013). https://doi.org/10.1080/1351847X.2012.670124
13. Benaroch, M., Lichtenstein, Y., Robinson, K.: Real options in information technology risk management: an empirical validation of risk-option relationships. MIS Q. **30**(40), 827–864 (2006)
14. Favato, G., Vecchiato, R.: Embedding real options in scenario planning: a new methodological approach. Technol. Forecast. Soc. Chang. **124**(C), 135–149 (2017). https://doi.org/10.1016/j.techfore.2016.05.016
15. Smith, B.: Ontology and information systems (2010). http://ontology.buffalo.edu/ontology%28PIC%29.pdf
16. Arp, R., Smith, B., Spear, A.D.: Building Ontologies with Basic Formal Ontology. MIT Press, Cambridge (2015)
17. Gruber, T.R.: Toward principles for the design of ontologies used for knowledge sharing. Technical report KSL, Knowledge Systems Laboratory, Stanford University (1993). http://tomgruber.org/writing/onto-design.pdf
18. Dudycz, H., Korczak, J.: Conceptual design of financial ontology. In: Ganzha, M., Maciaszek, L., Paprzycki, M. (eds.) Proceedings of the 2016 Federated Conference on Computer Science and Information Systems. Annals of Computer Science and Information Systems, vol. 5, pp. 1505–1511 (2015). https://doi.org/10.15439/978-83-60810-66-8
19. Ertek, G., Tokdemir, G., Sevinç, M., Tunç, M.M.: New knowledge in strategic management through visually mining semantic networks. Inf. Syst. Front. **19**, 165–185 (2015). https://doi.org/10.1007/s10796-015-9591-0
20. Grand, B.L., Soto, M.: Topic maps, RDF graphs, and ontologies visualization. In: Geroimenko, V., Chen, C. (eds.) Visualizing the Semantic Web. XML-Based Internet and Information Visualization, pp. 59–79. Springer, London (2010). https://doi.org/10.1007/1-84628-290-X_4
21. Wienhofen, L.W.M.: Using graphically represented ontologies for searching content on the semantic web. In: Geroimenko, V., Chen, C. (eds.) Visualizing the Semantic Web. XML-Based Internet and Information Visualization, pp. 137–153. Springer, London (2010). https://doi.org/10.1007/1-84628-290-x
22. Aruldoss, M., Maladhy, D., Venkatesan, V.P.: A framework for business intelligence application using ontological classification. Int. J. Eng. Sci. Technol. **3**(2), 1213–1221 (2011)

23. Cheng, A., Lu, Y.-C., Sheu, C.: An ontology-based business intelligence application in financial knowledge management system. Expert Syst. Appl. **36**(2), part 2, 3614–3622 (2009). https://doi.org/10.1016/j.eswa.2008.02.047

24. Korczak, J., Dudycz, H., Dyczkowski, M.: Design of financial knowledge in dashboard for SME managers. In: Ganzha, M., Maciaszek, L., Paprzycki, M. (eds.) Proceedings of the 2013 Federated Conference on Computer Science and Information Systems. Annals of Computer Science and Information Systems, vol. 1, pp. 1111–1118 (2013)

25. Korczak, J., Dudycz, H., Nita, B., Oleksyk, P., Kaźmierczak, A.: Extension of intelligence of decision support systems: manager perspective. In: Ziemba, E. (ed.) AITM/ISM-2016. LNBIP, vol. 277, pp. 35–48. Springer, Cham (2017). https://doi.org/10.1007/978-3-319-53076-5_3

26. Neumayr, B., Schrefl, M., Linner, K.: Semantic cockpit: an ontology-driven, interactive business intelligence tool for comparative data analysis. In: De Troyer, O., Bauzer Medeiros, C., Billen, R., Hallot, P., Simitsis, A., Van Mingroot, H. (eds.) ER 2011. LNCS, vol. 6999, pp. 55–64. Springer, Heidelberg (2011). https://doi.org/10.1007/978-3-642-24574-9_9

27. Dudycz, H.: Mapa pojęć jako wizualna reprezentacja wiedzy [The topic map as a visual representation of economic knowledge] (in Polish). Wydawnictwo Uniwersytetu Ekonomicznego we Wrocławiu, Wrocław (2013)

28. Gomez-Perez, A., Corcho, O., Fernandez-Lopez, M.: Ontological Engineering: with Examples from the Areas of Knowledge Management, e-Commerce and the Semantic Web. Springer, London (2004). https://doi.org/10.1007/b97353

29. Noy, F.N., McGuinness, D.L.: Ontology development 101: a guide to creating your first ontology (2005). http://www.ksl.stanford.edu/people/dlm/papers/ontology101/ontology101-noy-mcguinness.html

30. Dudycz, H., Korczak, J.: Process of ontology design for business intelligence system. In: Ziemba, E. (ed.) Information Technology for Management. LNBIP, vol. 243, pp. 17–28. Springer, Cham (2016). https://doi.org/10.1007/978-3-319-30528-8_2

31. Korczak, J., Dudycz, H., Nita, B., Oleksyk, P.: Semantic approach to financial knowledge specification - case of emergency policy workflow. In: Ziemba, E. (ed.) AITM/ISM-2017. LNBIP, vol. 311, pp. 24–40. Springer, Cham (2018). https://doi.org/10.1007/978-3-319-77721-4_2

32. Schulmerich, M.: Real Options Valuation: The Importance of Interest Rate Modelling in Theory and Practice. Springer, Heidelberg (2010). https://doi.org/10.1007/978-3-642-12662-8

Increasing Credibility of Teachers in e-Assessment Management Systems Using Multiple Security Features

Jaroslav Majerník[✉] [iD]

Faculty of Medicine, Pavol Jozef Šafárik University in Košice,
Trieda SNP 1, 040 11 Košice, Slovakia
jaroslav.majernik@upjs.sk

Abstract. Assessment of students' knowledge and skills, not only in medical education, has been conducted as a combination of paper based tests followed by oral examination for many years. Thanks to the development of modern technologies and advances achieved in learning management systems almost each education institution operates more or less effectively, the teachers obtained various sophisticated and fully electronic assessment tools. However, many of the teachers still prefer to spend incomparably more time using traditional pen-and-paper approach, as they are afraid of a time-consuming and technically challenging change, but most of all they do not trust the security and reliability of such tools can be high enough to minimize the wide range of potential risks related to frauds in the assessment processes. In this paper, we describe the approach we used in implementation of an e-assessment management system at our faculty as well as the security related features integrated into the individual assessment forms to guarantee the highest possible safety levels. The results of our work convinced us this approach was set as very good compromise, because of continuously increasing number of active examiners, i.e. our teachers and because of their satisfaction after initial work and time investment.

Keywords: Electronic assessment · Management system ·
Knowledge evaluation · Education · Security

1 Introduction

The pedagogical aspects of higher education curriculum integrate not only teaching and learning, but also assessment that judge the results of teaching and learning. Assessment itself can significantly influence the process of helping and encouraging the students to learn and understand their progresses in learning [1, 2]. From that point of view, the evaluation of students' knowledge, skills and performance represents an inseparable part of education process. In the same way, as the history brought various teaching and learning approaches, it also brought various, more or less effective assessment methods and tools [3–5]. These methods and tools tried to offer teachers the most objective ways to evaluate students' knowledge as well as to prove the importance of involved questions and feedback that can be adapted to the particular performance of students [6]. During the history, the assessment processes were gradually

© Springer Nature Switzerland AG 2019
E. Ziemba (Ed.): AITM 2018/ISM 2018, LNBIP 346, pp. 41–52, 2019.
https://doi.org/10.1007/978-3-030-15154-6_3

moved from traditional hand written assessments, through semi and/or fully automated evaluation of papers using scanning devices and support to fully automated electronic assessment management systems (Fig. 1).

Fig. 1. Historical milestones in assessment of learners' knowledge.

Nowadays, thanks to various e-learning platforms, e-portfolio solutions and learning management systems (LMS), the e-assessment methods become more available and more widespread across individual levels of education system [7]. However, the major problem we have to overcome during integration of such systems is to convince the traditionally thinking teachers that the security levels can be high enough to ensure the assessment will be as or more reliable than their paper passed alternatives.

The heterogeneity in usage of various assessment methods at our faculty, as well as involvement of naturally existing subjective factors, forced us to search for the solutions that can be applicable in our medical and health care study programs, courses and examinations and also acceptable by our teachers. The most frequently mentioned requirements, while discussing the assessment needs of our teachers stated the systems should be secure, intuitive to use and available only for authorized users i.e. teachers and their students. Therefore, we searched for the most optimal principles and methodologies of e-Assessment management systems (AMS) that were subsequently implemented into the medical education at our faculty to automatically assess of students' knowledge and competences.

This paper comprises of six sections. The current section i.e. the introduction, is followed by the section explaining the theoretical background of AMS and their practical utilization in assessment of students' knowledge. The research methodology, scenarios and motivation to solve the problem are described in the third section of the paper. Fourth section explains the results we obtained as well as the experiences based on two years of practical application. The fifth section discusses advantages, and benefits we reached in relation to the recent state of AMS implementation. This section is followed by the conclusions of the paper summarized in the sixth section.

2 Literature Review

Combination of paper based tests and oral examinations have been used as the main forms to evaluate students' knowledge and skills for many years. Teachers and examiners used the papers in examinations to evaluate learners' knowledge obtained during educational periods. Some forms of written tests were also involved in course requirements to measure concept assimilation presented in lectures or practical exercises [8, 9]. Various clinical performance assessment tools are also used in practice medical education [10–12]. However, there is still no generally accepted framework of competency assessment in medicine and health care [13, 14]. A well-organized alternative can be found in Objective Structured Clinical Examinations (OSCE) that are exams in which the learners have to demonstrate their practical abilities together with communication skills by completing different tasks at several separated workplaces or stations [15].

Nowadays, thanks to the advances in information and communication technologies (ICT), the needs of papers and the time the teachers spent by evaluation of individual tests were significantly reduced. Universities as well as other educational institutions discovered advantages of innovative technologies and adopted various types of smart tools to facilitate their assessment needs. Simulations and work-based assessments methods for specific purposes and clinical performance, including medical history taking, physical examination skills, procedural skills, clinical judgment etc. have also been used and involved in medical education systems [16, 17].

The common electronic assessment tools were integrated either in LMS that offer complex modules for teaching, learning and assessment within education institution [18, 19], or they are designed as independent systems to fully manage all assessment needs, and are generally known as AMS. In both cases, assessment practices serve teachers and students as a part of continual teaching and learning. AMS can be classified as systems based either on client-server architecture or as web-based services [20]. The most of the administrators prefer to adopt online available AMS, where everything can be organized through networks and without the needs to use any pen-and-paper based approach. Except of the environmental factors, there is also no need to install any clients on students' devices. Thus, the tests can be accessed anytime and anywhere, no matter which platform is used to manage assessment procedures.

A well implemented AMS and understood by the teachers can save the time required to organize and evaluate exams. In this point of view, their performance is also positively affected as the marking load is significantly reduced and the results are available immediately after the exam is completed [21]. On the other hand, the assessment itself should have clear purpose and has to match both the educational programmes and learning outcomes. Thus, any assessment method must be reproducible to show similar results on different occasions and valid to reflect appropriate representation of educational content. AMS are considered comfortable in all assessment related tasks, including measurement and documentation of knowledge, skills, and attitudes of individual learner and/or learning community [22, 23]. AMS principles should be based on methodology that, except of others, allow examiners to create a bank of questions, to generate different types of tests, to mix questions and/or answers in the tests, to specify exact dates and times when the learners must take the exams and to automatically score and share test results to learners. Furthermore, the capabilities of AMS should be also focused on the ways how the users interact with the systems and how it is adopted to their needs.

3   Research Methodology

Aiming to solve the assessment related issues in a complex and comprehensive way, we had to consider various factors and questions. Is there any system that will meet the requirements of our teachers and that can be integrated at institutional level? Do the systems allow specifying assessment plans in relation to the learning outcomes? How to grant the permissions of different groups of users to access the system? These and many other similar questions were solved and discussed during our initiatives leading to the satisfying solution that was accepted very well by both the teachers as well as by the learners [24].

As first, a survey among our teachers was conducted to identify the needs and requirements on assessment processes. The purpose was to discover what kind of assessment methods are currently used, what are the most preferred forms to evaluate students' knowledge during diagnostic, formative and summative examinations, and what are/should be the most preferred features of AMS. The survey was realized online using Google forms, and 65 teachers of our faculty participated on it. The findings illustrated wide usage of ICT in everyday praxis, however, the engagement with e-Assessment was only 12.3%, i.e. only 8 of 65 respondents actively utilized some electronic form to evaluate students' knowledge. The responses resulted in the list of features our teachers require from AMS. Not surprisingly, these features included possibilities to test large number of students at the same time; place/room independence; protected access and high security of all exams related data; repository of questions and tests; multimedia support in tests; limited access to registered students only; easy to use interface in national language; reporting per examination; and low or no financial expenses. Except of the above mentioned features, the technicians had to consider numerous technical and administrative related aspects too. Thus, the fully functional AMS required to solve the tasks related to the safe and reliable servers, wide and secure network infrastructure, large computer rooms, and professional administrative staff support.

Comparing the features, technical requirements and supporting documentation of various commercial (AEFIS, beSocratic, Blackboard Learn, Digication AMS, eLumen, LiveText, rGrade, Taskstream) and open-source (openIGOR, Rogō, Unicon, TAO) assessment systems, we decided to test the Rogō system that was developed at the University of Nottingham in cooperation with their partner institutions, now involved in development community. The results of the tests and the functionalities offered in AMS Rogō convinced us to integrate it into the ICT infrastructure of the faculty, including Slovak language pack developed during testing phase. Our decision was supported also by abilities to integrate third party systems, LDAP authentication, functionalities allowing VLE or other LMS to launch and single sign into Rogō.

4 Research Findings

The integration of AMS was fully adopted to the faculty infrastructure and requirements. The hierarchic structure reflects the faculty teaching units, study fields, courses with learning objectives, different assessment methods and of course the users with different roles in the system (Fig. 2).

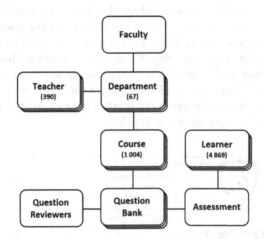

Fig. 2. The structure of e-Assessment management system integrated at Pavol Jozef Safarik University in Kosice, Faculty of Medicine.

All authorised users of the system (examiners, teachers, question reviewers and learners) were connected to the accounts of faculty's LMS. Thus, 390 teachers and 4,869 learners were able to use the system without any registration procedures. Similarly, the full list of all courses (1,004) was imported to the system. Information related to the course registration lists ensured the teachers create questions and examination papers only within their courses and the learners do the exams only in courses they are enrolled in.

Considering various purposes for which the students are assessed and relations to in-course or end of course teaching activities, there was a need to organise different types of assessments. The most frequent types included summative, formative and diagnostic exams. In summative assessment, the learner performance against the standard knowledge is awarded by grades. Then, the grade can either be a part of in-course assessment, or assessment at the end of a course. Formative assessment is organized during the course, and provides feedback to learners. While the summative assessment is used for certification, the formative assessment helps students improve their learning as the failure rate can be reduced and the performance can be increased. Diagnostic assessment is used to evaluate the level of learning that has been achieved by learners. In general, it can be used at the beginning of the course to determine the level of knowledge, or at the end of the lessons to know how the learners understood the topics. However, diagnostic assessment does not provide tools of feedback as it is in formative assessment. The questions for various assessments can be chosen from the same Question Bank of the course or group of courses.

The system holds the large amount of highly important data which must be kept safe at all times. Therefore, the users' data, question banks, exam tests, results as well as all the information stored in AMS are secured using multiple protection levels. From the security point of view, it is very important that the summative exams are not available anytime and anywhere. The students should not find/access the tests before the exam dates and the results must be delivered to them securely. On the other hand, the security issues are not necessary to be so strict in formative assessments.

Summative assessments can only be taken by learners assigned to the course during the time allocated to the exam in specific allocated room or place. Thus, the summative tests are not accessible to the students anywhere and at any other time. To increase security, the tests and all questions are locked and cannot be amended to ensure that the questions in the bank accurately match the results of the exam. The protection levels used in summative exams are shown in Fig. 3.

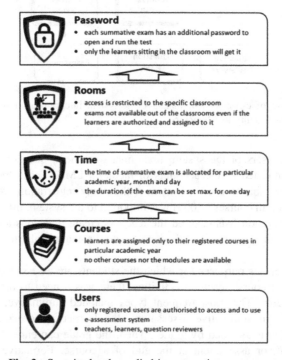

Fig. 3. Security levels applied in summative assessment.

Despite of combination of various security levels there were still some doubts of teachers related to the personal authentication of learners to be sure that the learner completing the assessment is learner that confirmed its identity. Regarding the importance of particular type of assessment, the summative types have to be delivered under invigilated conditions using secure systems. Other assessment forms, where no grading of the results is required, need not to be additionally secured. Thus, for example the formative assessments can be opened to be completed anytime, anywhere and even using learners own devices connected either to the faculty or commercial network. On the other hand, all summative exams at the faculty are organized using advanced mechanisms for personal as well as for equipment identification. Figure 4 shows the main concept of additional summative assessment security mechanism we implemented to ensure the summative exams are performed personally by the learners.

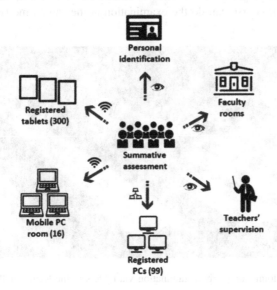

Fig. 4. Additional security related mechanisms incorporated into the summative assessments.

All summative exams are organized only in designated faculty computer classrooms and/or lecture halls depending on the size of tested group of learners. The learners are identified by the teacher(s) before they will enter the examination room. Learners' personal identification cards can be used in all lecture halls to register their attendance electronically. One or more teachers supervise the summative examination and offer the support to the learners if they have some technical problems during examination. Six computer classrooms with 99 PCs all together are used to test smaller groups of learners. All computers are protected and the internet connection is blocked. The e-Assessment is the only available service during the exams. If the test is restricted to the particular room, then it is not possible to see and open it in another room even if the learner is authorized to perform the examination. Small groups of learners can be also tested everywhere at the faculty using mobile computer classroom (16 laptops) where the connection to the e-Assessment system is realized through protected and hidden WiFi network that is a part of that mobile computer classroom.

However, the biggest challenge was to assess the mass groups of learners in particular study fields. Therefore, we built a separate network of secured wireless hotspots across main lecture halls (12 all together) of the faculty. This network has also protected access and the services are limited to allow usage of AMS functions and features. In these lecture halls, the learners are doing the summative exams using registered tablets (300 learners can do the exam in one lecture hall at the same time). The tablets are set to access the exam papers only and everything is preloaded when the students start to do examination. In this manner, the learners are only asked to sign into the system, to enter the exam's password that is announced by the teacher once the exam will start and to do the exam. The most preferred way is to organize the examinations for large groups of students in lecture halls, where all the students registered in particular course can do the examination at the same time (Fig. 5).

Fig. 5. Learners doing summative examination via tablets in the lecture hall of the faculty.

5 Discussion of Findings

Despite of naturally existing situations in which the traditional pen-and-paper approach cannot be replaced by electronic methods or it is not time and financially effective, the e-assessment methods brought modern and effective tools to evaluate learners' knowledge, performance and skills. The higher education benefits from the e-assessment as it assists learning and determines the effectiveness of the education system. AMS allow examiners development and managing of various types of questions and tests; creation of huge question banks; assigning of registered students to the tests/exams; setting of dates, times and places/rooms for the tests/exams; summarizing and sharing of the tests results; analysing of questions' quality and many others.

Depending on the course management, the Question Banks of particular courses can be created by guarantors or by the team of teachers associated with these courses. Naturally, the questions can be imported and/or added manually if there is no previously created electronic list of questions. Implementing the AMS system into the faculty's ICT infrastructure we offered our teachers to use one system in which almost any type of questions is supported. This did the assessment processes easily adjustable to various types of courses as well as their learning objectives. Except of commonly used Multiple Choice Questions (MCQ) the teachers are allowed to create questions including Area, Calculation, Dichotomous, Extended Matching, Fill-in-the-Blank, Image Hotspot, Labelling, Likert Scale, Matrix, Multiple Response, Random Question Block, Ranking, Script Concordance Test (SCT), Textbox or True-False. All of these question types can be combined in Random Question Blocks if there is a requirement to organize exams with randomly generated questions. Once the questions are stored in the Question Bank, it is possible to export them to external QTI or Rogō files and use them in other systems or in other Rogō instances.

The credibility of our teachers in electronic assessment was increased by implementation of multiple security features and after the first summative examinations were realized. The positive reactions were noticed also when they discovered the AMS is flexible and ready to solve potential problems in the case of unexpected events. The most frequently mentioned doubts of the teachers, noticed during their first exams, related to the network failures or to the technical problems with computer equipment. As the system continuously registers each activity of the learner during the exam, any network failures or computer related problems, will not affect the result of the examination. The assignment can be extended until the problem is solved or the learner can be logged into the system again and continues to solve the exam with all previously marked answers. However, during two years' experience we noticed only one problem related to WiFi failure and no problems with PCs in computer classrooms. So, the likelihood of such failures is very low.

The teachers have variety of reasons to use assessment tools, including to pass or fail students, to grade students, to select best ones for future courses, to prove what students have learnt, to reveal strengths and weaknesses of both students and courses, and many others. When implementing an AMS, it is necessary to clarify requirements and needs of particular educational institutions and staff working at these institutions. Only the well fitted system can be accepted across whole institution, can satisfy the need of users and may have positive effect on overall performance.

The AMS was successfully implemented into the faculty's infrastructure and is available to all departments and staff. The number of involved examiners and teachers is continuously growing as the newly recruited ones are positively motivated by those who already discovered the advantages of e-assessment. During the period of almost two academic years, the teachers generated more than 1,400 summative exams with more than 9,200 tests and more than 56,500 questions in their question banks.

6 Conclusions

6.1 Research Contribution

Implementation of AMS into the education process at our faculty minimized the subjective assessment factors and saved the significant portion of time and energy of our teachers. Of course, many of them disagreed when they started to use it. Initially, they were loaded by the similar tasks and problems as it is in paper-based assessment forms. Mainly, it was because they had to spend their time by preparing questions and organizing of all assessment related issues. However, the teachers mind was changed once they understood this is a long-term investment, in which the lifecycle of e-assessment materials will save considerable development and supporting workload. Integration and adaptation of AMS brought also many other advantages, as reported by the teachers. These advantages include, but are not limited to possibilities to generate both the summative and formative exams with various types of tasks and questions; to follow continuous progress in individual learners through their stored and archived results; to obtain course overall feedback or to identify problematic parts in taught topics via detailed analysis of collected answers.

6.2 Implications for Research and Practice

Integration of the AMS into to the ICT infrastructure of the faculty showed the great potential of modern technologies through which both the continuous and the summative assessments can be administered easily even in the case of large learner groups. The teachers and examiners got equipment and electronic tools that offers functions and features that cannot be used in traditional paper-based examinations. Furthermore, the combination of different security levels minimized their worries about assessment safety and increased the credibility in such assessment approach. The complex and unique way we used to reach our objectives was innovative for most of them as there was no system covering such wide range of assessment needs used at our faculty until now. The research methodology was applied in the field of medicine, but in the same way, it can be universally applied in any study branch, at any education level and in any country.

6.3 Limitations and Future Works

We understand there exist various ways to organize evaluation of students' knowledge and skills in pedagogical processes. In addition, the rapidly growing market with either assessment management systems or learning management systems offers new and/or improved products that may be equipped by better features or functions then those mentioned in our research. Therefore, we will continuously follow the trends in this area and we will adopt our approach accordingly together with our teachers' requirements that may change in time.

In the next stage of our research work, we plan to increase the awareness of formative assessment benefits among our teachers to be utilized more frequently in their curricula. The great potential of formative assessment is in instant feedback and continuous monitoring of learners' progress through which they can identify areas of their weakness and are motivated to study for better understanding of particular topics before final summative exams will take place.

Acknowledgment. Results presented in this paper were obtained with the support of the national agency's grants KEGA 017UPJS-4/2016 "Visualization of education in human anatomy using video records of dissections and multimedia teaching materials" and KEGA 011UPJS-4/2019 "Increasing of competences and critical thinking level in students of medical study programs using simulation tools of Problem-Based Learning and Evidence-Based Medicine".

References

1. Barrio, M.I.P., Escamilla, A.C., García, M.N.G., Fernández, E.M., García, P.R.: Influence of assessment in the teaching-learning process in the higher education. Proc.-Soc. Behav. Sci. **176**, 458–465 (2015). https://doi.org/10.1016/j.sbspro.2015.01.497
2. McSherry, R., Duggan, S.: Involving carers in the teaching, learning and assessment of masters students. Nurse Educ. Pract. **16**(1), 156–159 (2016). https://doi.org/10.1016/j.nepr. 2015.08.015
3. McDonald, E.W., Boulton, J.L., Davis, J.L.: E-learning and nursing assessment skills and knowledge – an integrative review. Nurse Educ. Today **66**, 166–174 (2018). https://doi.org/ 10.1016/j.nedt.2018.03.011
4. Burke, E., Kelly, M., Byrne, E., Chiardha, T.U., Mc Nicholas, M., Montgomery, A.: Preceptors' experiences of using a competence assessment tool to assess undergraduate nursing students. Nurse Educ. Pract. **17**, 8–14 (2016). https://doi.org/10.1016/j.nepr.2016. 01.004
5. Pezzino, M.: Online assessment, adaptive feedback and the importance of visual learning for students. The advantages, with a few caveats, of using MapleTA. Int. Rev. Econ. Educ. **28**, 11–28 (2018). https://doi.org/10.1016/j.iree.2018.03.002
6. Jimaa, S.: The impact of assessment on students learning. Proc.-Soc. Behav. Sci. **28**, 718–721 (2011). https://doi.org/10.1016/j.sbspro.2011.11.133
7. Bolat, E., Bobeva, M.: Using tablets for e-assessment of project-based learning. In: Proceedings of the European Conference on E-Learning, vol. 108962, pp. 56–64 (2014)
8. Pachler, N., Daly, C., Mor, Y., Mellar, H.: Formative e-assessment: practitioner cases. Comput. Educ. **54**, 715–721 (2010). https://doi.org/10.1016/j.compedu.2009.09.032
9. Lee, C., Wang, M.H., Huang, C.: Performance verification mechanism for adaptive assessment e-platform and e-navigation application. Int. J. e-Navig. Marit. Econ. **2**, 47–62 (2015). https://doi.org/10.1016/j.enavi.2015.06.005
10. Thorne, C.J., et al.: E-learning in advanced life support – what factors influence assessment outcome? Resuscitation **114**, 83–91 (2017). https://doi.org/10.1016/j.resuscitation.2017.02. 014
11. O'Connor, A., McGarr, O., Cantillon, P., McCurtin, A., Clifford, A.: Clinical performance assessment tools in physiotherapy practice education: a systematic review. Physiotherapy **104**(1), 46–53 (2018). https://doi.org/10.1016/j.physio.2017.01.005
12. Kubicek, J., Rehacek, T., Penhaker, M., Bryjova, I.: Software simulation of CT reconstructions and artifacts. Lecture Notes of the Institute for Computer Sciences, Social-Informatics and Telecommunications Engineering, LNICST, vol. 165, pp. 428–437 (2016). https://doi.org/10.1007/978-3-319-29236-6_41
13. Sureda-Demeulemeester, E., Ramis-Palmer, C., Sesé-Abad, A.: The assessment of medical competencies. Rev. Clin. Esp. **217**(9), 534–542 (2017)
14. Komenda, M., Karolyi, M., Vyškovský, R., Ježová, K., Ščavnický, J.: Towards a keyword extraction in medical and healthcare education. In: Federated Conference on Computer Science and Information Systems 2017, FedCSIS 2017, pp. 173–176 (2017). https://doi.org/ 10.15439/2017F351
15. Graf, J., et al.: Communication skills of medical students during the OSCE: gender-specific differences in a longitudinal trend study. BMC Med. Educ. **17**(1), 75 (2017). https://doi.org/ 10.1186/s12909-017-0913-4
16. Norcini, J.J., McKinley, D.W.: Assessment methods in medical education. Teach. Teach. Educ. **23**(3), 239–250 (2007). https://doi.org/10.1016/j.tate.2006.12.021

17. Daly, S.C., et al.: A subjective assessment of medical student perceptions on animal models in medical education. J. Surg. Educ. **71**(1), 61–64 (2014). https://doi.org/10.1016/j.jsurg. 2013.06.017

18. Chmielarz, W., Szumski, O.: Analysis of selected internet platforms of distributors of computer games in the assessment of users. In: Federated Conference on Computer Science and Information Systems 2018, FedCSIS 2018, pp. 691–695 (2018). https://doi.org/10. 15439/2018F67

19. Moura, J.G., Brandão, L.O., Brandão, A.A.F.: A web-based learning management system with automatic assessment resources. In: 37th Annual of Frontiers in Education Conference-Global Engineering: Knowledge Without Borders, Opportunities Without Passports, FIE 2007. IEEE (2007). https://doi.org/10.1109/FIE.2007.4418100

20. Bukie, O.F.: Understanding technologies for e-assessment: a systematic review approach. J. Emer. Trends Comput. Inf. Sci. **5**(12), 936–947 (2014)

21. Lee, Y.: Assessment management system based on IMS QTI 2.1. Int. J. Softw. Eng. Appl. **8** (1), 159–166 (2014). https://doi.org/10.14257/ijseia.2014.8.1.14

22. Amelung, M., Krieger, K., Rosner, D.: E-assessment as a service. IEEE Trans. Learn. Technol. **4**(2), 162–174 (2011)

23. Živčák, J., Hudák, R., Tóth, T.: Rat skin wounds tensile strength measurements in the process of healing. In: Proceedings of IEEE 10th Jubilee International Symposium on Applied Machine Intelligence and Informatics, SAMI 2012, pp. 389–392. https://doi.org/10. 1109/SAMI.2012.6208996

24. Majerník, J.: E-assessment management system for comprehensive assessment of medical students knowledge. In: Federated Conference on Computer Science and Information Systems, FedCSIS 2018, pp. 795–799 (2018). https://doi.org/10.15439/2018F138

Quantitative Comparison of Big Data Analytics and Business Intelligence Project Success Factors

Gloria J. Miller[✉] [iD]

maxmetrics, Heidelberg, Germany
g.j.m@ieee.org

Abstract. Decision support systems such as big data, business intelligence (BI), and analytics offer firms capabilities to generate new revenue sources, increase productivity and outputs, and gain strategic benefits. However, the field is crowded with terminology that makes it difficult to establish reasonable project scopes and to staff and manage projects. This study clarifies the terminology around data science, computational social science, big data, business intelligence, and analytics, and defines decision support projects. The study uses quantitative methods to empirically classify the project scopes, investigate the similarities and differences between the project types, and identify the critical success factors. The results suggest BI and big data analytics projects are differentiated based on analytics competence, proprietary algorithms, and distinctive business processes. They are significantly different for 19 of the 52 items evaluated. For big data analytics projects, many of the items are correlated with strategic benefits, while for BI projects they are associated with the operational benefits of cost and revenue performance. Project complexity is driven by the project characteristics for BI projects, while the external market drives the complexity of big data analytics projects. These results should inform project sponsors and project managers of the contingency factors to consider when preparing project plans.

Keywords: Big data · Analytics · Data science · Business intelligence · Success factors · Project management

1 Introduction

Data science and computational social science are emerging interdisciplinary fields that overlap in content with big data (BD), business intelligence (BI), and analytics [1, 2]. As more data have become available on the internet, social media, and from other sources, organizations have begun to collect it in growing volumes, new business models and algorithms have emerged, and data sales have become potential revenue sources [1, 3]. Deriving organizational benefits from the new technologies requires a unique set of organizational and technical implementation activities, i.e., a project [4]. However, despite the increased attention to big data, the critical success factors for decision support projects have received little attention in the project management literature. Decision support projects are implementation projects that deliver data,

© Springer Nature Switzerland AG 2019
E. Ziemba (Ed.): AITM 2018/ISM 2018, LNBIP 346, pp. 53–72, 2019.
https://doi.org/10.1007/978-3-030-15154-6_4

analytical models, or analytical competence, or all three, for unstructured decision-making and problem-solving. They include subspecialties such as big data, advanced analytics, business intelligence, or artificial intelligence. The context of the project matters to defining its success factors and criteria [4, 5]. Without insights into the project's critical success factors, it can be challenging for project sponsors and managers to establish a reasonable project strategy and to achieve the desired benefits [6].

The emerging status of these fields means that scant research exists about the scientific and commercial implications of these domains to managing projects. This paper empirically investigates the critical success factors for decision support projects and provides a comparative analysis of big data analytics and BI projects. This analysis provides unique results on the structural factors that contribute to decision support project success. The findings of this study add to technology and project management practices and, in particular, provide in-depth insights into what factors influence the success of big data analytics and BI projects. Furthermore, they provide information on the similarities and differences in the factors contributing to success. These results should inform project sponsors and project managers of the contingency factors to consider when preparing project charters and plans.

Section two defines the decision support terminology and project success factors through a review of the literature. In addition, it establishes the research questions. Section three describes the research methodology including the operationalization of the measurement instrument and the data analysis techniques. Section four presents the research findings, and section five discusses the findings. The final section provides the conclusions including the implications to practice and the limitations of the study.

2 Literature Review

2.1 Decision Support Success Factors

Decision support systems are information systems that provide data and models to support decision-makers with the effectiveness of unstructured decision-making and problem-solving [1]. The domain includes multiple information systems disciplines with divergent definitions but common uses and purposes. The following section describes the decision support subspecialties and their success factors.

Business intelligence refers to the technology, processes, and software used to transform raw data into intelligence for computer-aided decision-making. The BI process includes the collection, evaluation, analysis, and storage of data and the production and dissemination of intelligence [2]. Olbrich et al. [3] identified 25 success factors that define the conditions necessary to use and exploit BI. At a high level, BI strategy, top management support, user involvement, specialized skills, data concerns, and Information Technology (IT) infrastructure were identified as success factors. Implementation time and financial resources were described as constraints. Other researchers have identified similar BI success factors; Yeoh and Koronios [4] and Dawson and Van Belle [5] deepened the discussion by justifying specific BI success factors from a project perspective.

Davenport and Harris [2] define *analytics* as a sub-category of BI that includes *"the extensive use of data, statistical and quantitative analysis, explanatory and predictive models, and fact-based management to drive decisions and actions"* [2, p. 7]. Otherwise, the term analytics is not standardized in literature. Lucas Jr. [6] argues that implementation success of operations research models (i.e., statistical and quantitative models) is a factor of quality, user attitudes, user decision-style, management support, and personal situational factors. Thomas and Kielman [7] reported success factors for visual analytics that are similar to those of other decision support systems. Specifically, the need for robust, interdependent, and performant technical infrastructure, a data architecture to support multiple types, forms, and sources of data and information, and useful tools for real-time data collection, data validity, security, and privacy.

As data volumes have grown and computing requirements have increased, the technologies and tools used to manage, manipulate, and understand data have evolved [8, 9]. On the one hand, there is a consensus that *"big data"* refers to the attributes of data—velocity, variety, validity, and volume—and on the other hand, it refers to innovative technologies and processes that allow for the use of data in novel ways [10]. Géczy [10] refers to the "Big Data problem," which is attributed to the: *"digitization of business processes and accompanying data, accumulation of extra data, extraction of actionable knowledge from data, and monetization of data"* [10, p. 23]. The success factors for big data include making the data trustworthy and understandable for employees; training the employees; the active role of top management; clear goals and technology strategy; changing business practices (e.g., marketing, production or operations management); integrating talent, technology and information; data quality; safe data handling, including privacy and data security; cybersecurity; skills including technical, analytical, and governance; networked resources; and having a business strategy/blueprint [11–13].

Data science is an interdisciplinary field that includes data analysis, statistics, data mining, and models with the goal of transforming data into knowledge by finding patterns and trends in the data [8, 14]. The terminology originated as a role description for a single person who could act as a Business Analyst, Statistician, Engineer, or Research Scientist [8]. Davenport and Patil [14] popularized the data scientist's role in their Harvard Business Review article; they described it as *"a high-ranking professional with the training and curiosity to make discoveries in the world of big data"* [14, p. 72].

Computational social science can reveal patterns related to group and individual behavior and encompasses data collection and intelligence. It is based on the emergence of scientific research methods that can leverage big datasets [15]. Data collection includes the ability to collect and analyze data at a scale that may reveal patterns. Computational intelligence refers to approaches where algorithms imitate human information processes and reasoning [16].

2.2 Project Success Factors

Projects are a form of temporary organization for introducing transitions into organizations; the transition is the change or transformation expected as a consequence of the temporary organization's tasks. *Project success* refers to the project delivering its expected output and achieving its intended objective [17, 18], the main elements of which are the success criteria and success factors. *Success criteria* are used to judge the outcome of the project, and *success factors* influence the likelihood of achieving a successful outcome. That is, the success criteria determine measures or indicators for success, while the success factors refer to the circumstances, conditions, and events that support the project in achieving its objectives [17, 18].

Pinto and Slevin [19] define ten *project success factors* that are under the control of the project team and four factors that influence project success but are not under the control of the project team. The ten controllable success factors are project mission, top management support, schedule and plans, client consultation, personnel, client acceptance, technical tasks, monitoring and feedback, communication, and troubleshooting. The four external factors comprise the competence of the project leader, the political activity and perception of the project in the organization, external environmental factors, and the perception of the importance of and need for the project. Rather than identifying specific project success factors, Belassi and Tukel [20] identified four groups of interrelated factors that could be analyzed across any type of project. They include factors related to the project, the project manager and team members, the organization, and the external environment. Ziemba and Kolasa [21] identified 10 interrelated risk factors grouped in five dimensions (structure, technology, individuals and roles, management process, project strategy) that can be used as a planning guide for information systems critical success factors.

2.3 Summary

The study performed a comprehensive review of information systems literature to clarify the definition of the decision support subspecialties and to identify the corresponding critical success factors. There is significant overlap in the implementation processes, technologies, and success factors used between big data, analytics, BI, data science, and computational social science. We can summarize the terminology as follows for further use in this paper. BI, big data, and computational social science have similar technical processes and techniques but differ in use cases. They use technology and analytic techniques to transform raw data into intelligence. BI focuses on the platforms, architectures, and tools for the provision of data and intelligence and has an enterprise orientation. Big data seeks to monetize data directly through its sale or indirectly through data-driven business models or algorithms. Computational social science has a scientific research focus in leveraging big datasets for learning. Data science refers to the responsibilities of the people who use BI, big data, or analytical techniques; it describes a role or job. Projects are used to execute the implementation and transformation tasks needed to benefit from the technologies, and projects have success factors and criteria that differ from the technologies.

2.4 Research Questions

A significant number of studies have investigated the implementation success of information systems, including enterprise resource planning systems [22], business intelligence [3–5], big data [11, 12], and analytics [2, 6]. However, the author could find no studies that provide a guide to classifying or differentiating the types of decision support projects. Thus, the goal of this research was to identify the structural factors that contribute to decision support project success. It asks the research questions:

- What are the critical success factors for decision support projects?
- Are there significant differences between big data analytics and BI projects?
- What factors influence the success of big data analytics and BI projects?

This literature review answers the first research question: What are the critical success factors for decision support projects? The project critical success areas are based on Pinto and Slevin [19], the dominant critical success framework in project management literature [18]. The project and decision support critical success factors are summarized in Table 1. Next, the study defines a measurement instrument to analyze the similarities and differences between decision support subspecialty project critical success factors. The measurement instrument was used to collect data for answering the remaining research questions. Finally, the study will empirically classify the decision support project domains and compare the critical success factors.

3 Research Methodology

3.1 Procedure

The research used a literature review to define the critical success factors, a web-based survey to collect data on decision support projects, and quantitative analysis methods to explore the difference in project characteristics between BI and big data analytics. In the literature review, peer-reviewed journal publications from 2006 to 2017 were evaluated to identify the decision support system characteristics and critical success factors. Table 1 maps the decision support critical success categories and success factors to the project management success factors.

The measurement instrument was developed based upon a combination of existing constructs, with some modifications, following an extensive literature review. Pre-existing constructs were used where possible. Since information on the dependent and independent variables was collected from a single informant in a single measurement instrument, steps were taken to design the survey instrument to avoid common method bias. Prior to executing the survey, a two-stage peer review was conducted with a panel of five specialists familiar with the project management or decision support domains. The survey operations were tested using three different devices (i.e., PC, iPad, smartphone) to ensure proper technical functioning.

The survey collected the data over a ten-week period (September 2017 to December 2017) from a single informant. The respondents that participated provided their consent and were promised confidentiality and anonymity. One hundred and forty-two people responded to the survey, from which 102 responses provided complete details on the project characteristics used in the classification model and 82 responses included data on all measurement items. The true response rates cannot be determined due to the use of multiple sampling techniques.

3.2 Measurement Instrument

This section describes how the measurement items were derived. This study uses measurement items and composite variables based on a review of the literature and quantitative analysis conducted by Miller [23]. Most of the items are based on a five-point Likert scale (1 = Not at all; 5 = To a great extent). To ensure completeness of data, "Don't know" or "Not Applicable" was added to the Likert scale. Items that used different scales are described in the relevant sections.

Project Mission. The project mission represents the clarity of goals and directions [19]. The following deliverables proposed by Davenport and Harris [2] as valuable components of analytics projects were used in the analysis to define the project strategy and classify the project types: *Proprietary algorithms* or business models, *new data* that was not previously available in the company, deliverables embedded into *distinctive business processes*, and data science or *analytic competence*. These deliverables are consistent with the definition of decision support systems as information systems that use data and models to support decision-makers with unstructured decision-making and problem-solving [1]. The measurement instrument did not directly ask a question on the project objectives. The organizational impacts of the project were used as proxies for defining the business strategy and vision. The impacts include the cost and effort-saving or increases in productivity as *cost performance*, increases in revenue as *revenue performance*, and outcomes such as providing new or reusable learning, improving forecast and prediction accuracy, or preparing for the future as *strategic benefits*.

Top Management Support. Top management support is needed to authorize the project and to provide the resources and authority to execute the project [19]. Barki and Hartwick [24] divide user contribution into user participation and user involvement. Participation represents an active role in the development process and involvement represents the importance and personal relevance an individual place on the system or project. Top management support was measured based on *top management* and *senior manager involvement* according to the scales provided by Barki and Hartwick [24].

Project Schedule/Plan. The project plan represents the steps needed to reach the project goal [19]. The Shenhar and Dvir [25] project classification model was used to define the plan attributes of the project. Three levels of *technological uncertainty* refer to the degree to which technology existed before the project start: no new technology, some new, almost all new, or all new technology. *Complexity* is described on three levels: assembly, system, and an array. *Pace* describes the sense of urgency as regular, fast/competitive, time-critical, and blitz. *Product novelty* represents the uncertainty of the project goals and its position in the market: derivative, platform, and breakthrough.

Client Consultation. Client consultation involves engaging the internal and external stakeholders to give them the opportunity to air their views, influence the project plans, and know what has been decided [17]. Top management, senior manager, and business user involvement in *steering* (establishing criteria), *directing* (steering and solving conflicts), *acceptance* (evaluating outcomes), and *participation* (in project tasks, specifically setting requirements and building models) were evaluated.

Personnel. Having the correct personnel for the project is a critical success factor [19]. Competency attributes were used to evaluate the specialized skills required for the staff [3, 8, 14]. The items measure the effort required to deliver quality services during the project for competencies highlighted by Debortoli, Müller and Vom Brocke [26] as being relevant to BI and big data, including *technical, business, data, and analytical competence*. The technical competence for big data was in the form of statistics, programming knowledge, quantitative analysis, and machine learning. For BI, the technical competence was for specific software vendor packages. The *data scientist* item considers the involvement of an analytically competent person or persons on the team.

Client Acceptance. Lucas Jr. [6] suggests that the decision-making style of the users is a factor in their ability to comprehend and accept the results of analytical systems. Thus, *system use* is a measure of client acceptance. System use covers mandatory and voluntary use as a measure of system success [27]. Top management and senior manager participation include their usage of system results in *decision-making* and *acting* on the analytical outcomes of the delivered system.

Technical Tasks. This success factor covers the ability to accomplish the technical actions needed by having the necessary technology and expertise [19]. Success factors for technical tasks are addressed from multiple perspectives such as data sources and IT infrastructure, which includes the availability and quality of data, as well as the heterogeneity and sophistication of IT infrastructure [3]. New items and existing items from the DeLone and McLean information systems success model [28] were used by Miller [23] to create factors and evaluate the technical tasks. The subcategories were derived based on critical success factors for decision support systems [2–7, 9, 11, 12].

Monitoring and Feedback, Communication, Troubleshooting. The project manager and team members, the organization, and the external environment are four interrelated groups of project success factors [19, 20]. The management of information occurs at each phase of the implementation process to control the outcome, communicate all relevant factors, and resolve unexpected events. Debortoli, Müller and Vom Brocke [26] found that project management was one of the business competencies requested in business intelligence jobs; it was not a requirement in big data advertisements. *Project management competency* is a quality measure for change management, planning, or agile competency [26].

Other Contingency Factors. Project success is also dependent upon factors external to the project such as organizational and environmental factors [19, 20]. Thus, project and organizational characteristics were included in the data collection and analyzed for variance between project types. Environmental factors evaluated include project demographics such as budget, duration, number of departments involved, number of organizations involved, and team size. Organizational demographics include revenue, number of employees, and market share position and revenue position relative to competitors.

3.3 Data Analysis

Project managers, team members, and sponsors from completed decision support projects were asked to take the survey. The survey sample was comprised of 82 usable responses as follows: 76% of the respondents had a master's degree or higher; 38% performed IT roles; 18% were from a project management office; 48% were project or program managers; 5% agile coaches; 22% project team members; and 5% were project sponsors. The organizations sponsoring the projects were mostly publicly traded (51%) and were large, with more than 249 employees (83%) and US$50 million in revenue (78%). They were spread throughout 22 different industries and 24 countries. The majority of the participants were from Europe (74%).

The responses were checked for scope, completeness, consistency, ambiguity, missing data, extreme responses, outliers, and leverage. Validity checks for common method bias, response bias, and reliability were conducted. No bias was found, and the data were considered to be reliable and valid. Latent Class Analysis (LCA) was used to classify the types of projects. Descriptive statistics, mean ranking, Wilcoxon score, and correlation analysis were used to explore the characteristics, establish the validity and reliability, and explain the relationship between the variables.

Latent Class Clustering. The latent class clustering technique was used to identify the homogeneous clusters. The dimensions were modeled in RStudio 1.0.153 using poLCA for the analysis. LCA offers the ability to analyze relationships in categorical data and to characterize latent variables. The technique is similar to factor analysis in that it identifies latent classes but differs in that the observed and latent variables can be categorical. It can be distinguished from other cluster analysis techniques as being based on a statistical model derived from the data population. The four items for the BI/BD strategy in Table 1 were specified as indicators in the models. They were executed with 50,000 iterations for 1 to 10 classes, and 10 repetitions each per model. The analysis was performed with 102 observations that included complete data for the four variables. The data sample and number of indicators met the minimal recommendation for such models; 70 observations using high-quality indicators [29]. Each observation was assigned to a latent class based on having the highest a posteriori probability (modal assignment).

Rank Analysis. SAS Studio Release: 3.6 (Basic Edition) was used to perform the mean score ranking. The means were computed and ranked. The Wilcoxon test was used to compare the means of variables between the two classes of projects and to provide the significance of the comparison. The Wilcoxon scores with a p-value of less than 0.05 indicate that there are significant differences in the project types. The rank indicates the relative position—equated to importance—of the item for that project type.

Correlation Analysis. Kendall's tau-b correlation coefficient was used to evaluate the strength, direction, and significance of the relationship between measurement items. Kendall's tau-b was chosen because of the non-normal structure of the data and the small sample size. The correlation coefficient does not indicate which variable causes the change in the other variable and does not explain causality. The correlations should help increase understanding of the relationships between measurement items and to expected project outcomes in order to identify important success factors. Correlations with a p-value of less than 0.05 were significant with a 95% confidence interval. SAS Studio Release: 3.6 (Basic Edition) was used to perform the correlation analysis.

4 Research Findings

In the latent class analysis, the two-cluster model was selected, given that it had the lowest Bayesian Information Criterion measures and the highest maximum likelihood. Figure 1 includes the mean distribution for the two-cluster solution. The delivery of algorithms and analytic competence provide the most differentiation between clusters. Thus, each cluster has a strong differentiating feature. Cluster 1 was named *Big Data Analytics*, and Cluster 2 was named *Business Intelligence*.

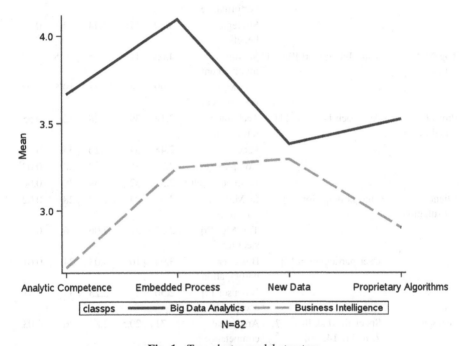

Fig. 1. Two-cluster model structure

The mean ranking and Wilcoxon score and significance for the variables for the two project classes are shown in Table 1. Nineteen of the 52 characteristics are significantly different between the two project types. The 13 items for project and organizational attributes and demographics are excluded from Table 1 for space reasons.

Table 1. Mean ranking and Kruskal-Wallis test of critical success factors (n = 82)

Critical success factor			BD analytics		BI		KW
Project [19]	BI & BD	Measurement item	Mean	Rank	Mean	Rank	p
Project mission	BI/BD strategy [3, 4, 11, 30]	New data	3.38	29	3.30	21	0.67
		Distinctive bus process	4.1	8.5	3.25	22	0.00
		Proprietary algorithms	3.52	26.5	2.90	25	0.02
		Analytic competence	3.67	22.5	2.67	29	0.00
	Bus strategy/vision [3, 4, 9, 11]	Cost performance	3.46	28	3.56	11	0.90
		Revenue performance	3.67	22.5	3.62	9.5	0.80
		Strategic benefits	3.89	17	3.44	14	0.12
Top Mgt support	Top Mgt support [9, 11]	Sr Mgr involvement	4.05	11	3.35	16.5	0.09
		Top Mgt involvement	3.99	14	3.31	19.5	0.07
Project schedule/plans	Approach [4, 7, 9, 11]	Technological uncertainty	2.14	39	2.28	32	0.55
		Pace	2.48	34	2.10	35	0.19
		Complexity	2.33	35	1.92	38	0.03
		Product novelty	2.52	32	1.69	39	0.00
Client consultation	Mgt participation [2]	Sr Mgt Prj directing	3.60	24	2.78	28	0.02
		Top Mgt Prj steering	2.57	31	2.06	36	0.11
	User participation [3]	Bus user participation	3.94	16	3.08	24	0.01
		Bus user Prj acceptance	2.50	33	2.23	33	0.41
Personnel	Specialized skills [2, 3, 7, 8, 11, 14, 26]	Analytical competence	3.71	20.5	2.84	26	0.03
		Bus competence	4.05	11	3.62	9.5	0.19
		Data competence	3.95	15	3.31	19.5	0.03
		Data scientist in team	4.10	8.5	2.79	27	0.00
		Technical competence	4.19	3.5	3.77	2	0.01

(continued)

Table 1. (continued)

Critical success factor			BD analytics		BI		KW
Project [19]	BI & BD	Measurement item	Mean	Rank	Mean	Rank	p
Client acceptance	Mgt participation [2, 11]	Sr Mgt fact-based decision	2.24	36.5	2.17	34	0.93
		Top Mgt data driven acting	2.14	38	1.99	37	0.81
	User [24, 27]	System use	3.81	18	3.86	1	0.67
Technical tasks	Analytic tools [6, 11]	Analytical sophistication	3.33	30	3.33	18	0.79
	Data architecture [3, 12]	Data availability	4.14	5.5	3.63	8	0.03
		Data privacy	3.81	19	3.20	23	0.03
		Data quality	4.21	2	3.66	5	0.02
		System security	4.00	13	3.64	6.5	0.16
	Data [3, 12]	Data velocity	2.24	36.5	2.44	31	0.72
		Data volume	4.38	1	3.64	6.5	0.01
		Data variety	3.52	26.5	2.64	30	0.01
	IT infrastructure [2, 12]	Ease of operations	3.54	25	3.37	15	0.50
		Performance quality	4.19	3.5	3.73	3	0.03
	Service quality [11, 28]	Bus support quality	4.05	11	3.50	13	0.03
		Personal qualities	3.71	20.5	3.35	16.5	0.14
		Technical service quality	4.13	7	3.72	4	0.05
Monitoring and feedback	Prj Mgt [3, 4, 26]	Prj Mgt competence	4.14	5.5	3.54	12	0.10

Abbreviations: BI - Bus Intelligence, Bus - Business, BD - Big data analytics, Prj - Project, Mgr - Manager, Mgt - Management, Sr - Senior, KW - Kruskal Wallis

Table 2 includes the correlation between the measurement items and the cost, revenue, and strategic benefits performance measures for both project classifications. The remaining correlation tables are not included for space reasons. Where relevant, their results are given in the discussion. The Kendall's tau-b correlation coefficient is represented by the symbol τ and the probability is represented by the symbol ρ.

5 Discussion of Findings

In the comparative analysis, many of the results were expected based on the findings from the literature review. However, there were also some unexpected results. The results are evaluated for each of the project success factor categories.

Project Mission. The rank analysis results suggest BI and big data analytics projects are differentiated based on *analytic competence, proprietary algorithms,* and distinc*tive business processes.* Analytic competence and distinctive business processes were ranked higher for big data analytics than for BI. The organizational performance measures for revenue performance, cost performance, and strategic benefits were not significantly different between the two classes. However, BI was correlated with cost and revenue performance for distinctive business processes and with cost and strategic benefits for proprietary algorithms.

Table 2. Kendall's tau-b correlation coefficients (τ)

Critical success factor		Organizational performance					
		BD analytics (N = 21)			BI (N = 61)		
Project	Item	Cost Perf	Strategy benefits	Revenue Perf	Cost Perf	Strategy benefits	Revenue Perf
Project mission	New data	−0.05	0.28	0.18	0.14	0.2	0.03
	Bus processes	0.08	−0.27	−0.38	0.33**	0.16	0.31**
	Prop algorithms	−0.05	−0.07	−0.09	0.32**	0.21*	0.05
	Analytic Comp	−0.14	0.36	0.2	0.02	0.14	−0.15
	Cost performance		0.24	0.33		0.35***	0.46***
	Revenue Perf	0.33	0.60***		0.46***	0.17	
	Strategic benefits	0.24		0.60***	0.35***		0.17
Top Mgt support	Sr Mgr involve	−0.1	0.26	0.06	0.39***	0.31**	0.26*
	Top Mgt Involve	−0.2	0.15	−0.06	0.30**	0.15	0.24*
Project schedule/plans	Tech uncertainty	0.12	0.31	0.34	0.15	0.15	0.07
	Pace	−0.07	−0.01	−0.04	0.03	−0.01	0.06
	Complexity	0.09	−0.14	−0.11	0.08	0.05	0
	Product novelty	0.09	0.08	0	0.28**	0.18	0.2
Client consultation	Sr Mgt Prj directing	−0.05	0.2	0.07	0.40***	0.26**	0.37***
	Top Mgt Prj steering	0.09	0.12	−0.1	0.32***	0.25**	0.24*
	Bus user participation	−0.05	0.1	0.1	0.31***	0.30**	0.28**
	Bus user Prj accept	−0.31	−0.04	−0.02	0.17	0.06	0.13

(continued)

Table 2. (*continued*)

Critical success factor		Organizational performance					
		BD analytics (N = 21)			BI (N = 61)		
Project	Item	Cost Perf	Strategy benefits	Revenue Perf	Cost Perf	Strategy benefits	Revenue Perf
Personnel	Analytical Comp	−0.08	0.38*	0.33	0.1	0.19*	0.14
	Bus Comp	−0.01	0.32	0.12	0.35***	0.21*	0.51***
	Data Comp	0.11	0.08	−0.12	0.29**	0.16	0.26*
	Data scientist in team	−0.16	0.18	0.09	0.19	0.29**	0.09
	Technical Comp	0.06	0.29	0.2	0.13	−0.02	0.36**
Client accept	Sr Mgt FB Dec	−0.31	−0.1	−0.09	0.30**	0.29**	0.18
	Top Mgt DD act	−0.29	0.05	−0.18	0.34***	0.18	0.20*
	System use	0.52**	0.24	0.3	0.39***	0.17	0.24*
Technical tasks	Analytical Soph	−0.02	0.48**	0.3	0.08	0.17	0.27*
	Data availability	0.35*	0.05	−0.02	0.36***	0.15	0.37***
	Data privacy	0.26	0.33	0.06	0.14	0.14	0.13
	Data Qual	0.41*	0.32	0.09	0.43***	0.23*	0.43***
	System security	−0.22	0.15	−0.03	0.28**	0.12	0.40***
	Ease of operations	0.43*	0.59***	0.49**	0.35***	0.11	0.39***
	Performance Qual	0.12	0.22	0.2	0.29**	0.03	0.46***
	Bus support Qual	0.24	0.25	0.06	0.37***	0.23*	0.40***
	Personal Qual	0.3	0.19	−0.05	0.37***	0.09	0.43***
	Tech service Qual	0.35*	0.46**	0.45*	0.24*	0.05	0.43***
	Data velocity	0.04	−0.01	−0.01	−0.04	0.11	0.07
	Data volume	0.33	0.37*	0.3	0.36***	0.16	0.37***
	Data variety	0.17	0.16	0.23	0.06	0.14	0.09
Mon	Prj Mgt Comp	0.31	0.57**	0.32	0.31**	0.1	0.30**

Abbreviations: Accept - Acceptance, BI - Bus Intelligence, Bus - Business, BD - Big Data analytics, Comp - Competence, DD - Data Driven, Dec - Decision, FB - Fact-based, Involve - Involvement, Perf - Performance, Prj - Project, Mgr - Manager, Mgt - Management, Mon - Monitoring, Qual - Quality, Sr - Senior, Soph - Sophistication, Tech - Technical

***p < .001, **p < .01, *p < .05

Top Management Support. The importance that senior managers and top management gave to the project was equally significant in both classes. However, the involvement was ranked higher for both roles, meaning more important, for big data analytics than BI. Interestingly, senior manager involvement was correlated to all performance variables for BI.

Project Schedule/Plans. Both project types have a similar level of *technological uncertainty* and *pace* but significantly different *product novelty* and *complexity*. For big data analytics projects, technological uncertainty was correlated with the number of organizations involved ($\tau = 0.40$, $\rho = .04$) and team size ($\tau = 0.43$, $\rho = .03$) and for BI projects it was correlated with the number of internal departments involved ($\tau = 0.36$, $\rho < .001$) and team size ($\tau = 0.39$, $\rho = .0002$) as well as the project duration ($\tau = 0.46$, $\rho < .0001$) and project budget ($\tau = 0.25$, $\rho = .03$). This points to an internal staffing strategy for BI projects while big data analytic projects rely on multiple organizations. This finding is consistent with Olbrich, Pöppelbuß and Niehaves [3] that IT literacy of staff and the technical and in-house capabilities are critical success factors to implement and maintain BI systems.

For big data analytics projects, the market share ($\tau = -0.42$, $\rho = .03$) of the organizations was negatively correlated with the pace. This inverse relationship suggests that projects undertaken by market leaders may have a slower pace and those undertaken by market laggards require a faster pace. These measures were not significantly correlated with pace for BI projects.

While complexity was significantly different between the classes, the project demographics for project duration, team size, budget, number of organizations, and number of departments were not significantly correlated to complexity for big data analytics projects but were for BI projects. Conversely, complexity was correlated with the revenue size of the organization ($\tau = 0.51$, $\rho = .03$) for big data analytics, but not for BI. Thus, the complexity is most likely driven by the interplay with the business environment for big data analytics and by project characteristics for BI.

Product novelty for big data analytics projects was not significantly correlated with any organization or project characteristics, but it was correlated with the technical tasks of analytical sophistication ($\tau = 0.49$, $\rho = .01$). For BI projects, cost performance, budget, duration, and team size, the involvement of top management ($\tau = 0.27$, $\rho = .01$) and senior managers ($\tau = 0.37$, $\rho = .001$), top management steering ($\tau = 0.27$, $\rho = .01$), senior manager directing ($\tau = 0.22$, $\rho = .03$), business user participation ($\tau = 0.23$, $\rho = .02$), and the technical tasks of performance quality ($\tau = 0.28$, $\rho = .03$), data volumes ($\tau = 0.23$, $\rho = .04$), data availability ($\tau = 0.20$, $\rho = .05$), business support quality ($\tau = 0.27$, $\rho = .01$), and personal qualities ($\tau = 0.32$, $\rho = .003$) were correlated with product novelty.

Client Consultations. Both types of projects showed similar client consultation for top management steering and business user project acceptance. However, the differences in senior manager project directing and business user participation between classes were significant. In both cases, the ranks for big data analytics indicate their participation is more important than for BI. Meanwhile, the correlations for these measures to performance were not significant for big data analytics. Conversely, the same correlations were significant for BI. Furthermore, there were significant correlations between business user participation and ease of operations ($\tau = 0.21$, $\rho = .03$), data quality ($\tau = 0.21$, $\rho = .03$), and data variety ($\tau = 0.24$, $\rho = .01$) for BI projects. The same correlations for big data analytics projects were not significant. Thus, consistent with Olbrich, Pöppelbuß and Niehaves [3] and with Halaweh and El Massry [12], the results identify senior manager support as a success factor. However, these finding additionally identify a correlation between their participation and the quality objectives for BI projects. This finding was similar to that found by Chatzoglou, Chatzoudes and Apostolopoulou [22] for enterprise resource planning systems. In that study, end-user involvement and skills development were the most important factor that predicted implementation success.

Personnel. *Analytical, technical,* and *data competence* and *data scientist in the team* are significantly different between the two classes. A data scientist in the team and analytical and data competence are ranked higher for big data analytics than BI, and technical and business competence is ranked higher for BI than for big data analytics. Furthermore, there is a correlation between having a data scientist in the team and analytical competence in both types of projects, and in data variety in BI projects ($\tau = 0.24$, $\rho = .01$).

For BI projects, the data ($\tau = 0.28$, $\rho = .005$) and business competence ($\tau = 0.26$, $\rho = .01$) are correlated with system use. No significant correlations between competence and system use exist for big data analytics projects. Analytic competence is correlated with strategic benefits in both classes. Otherwise, there are no significant correlations to performance for big data projects in these classes. For BI projects technical, data and business competence are correlated to revenue performance; analytic and business competence and having a data scientist in the team are correlated to strategic benefits; data and business competence are correlated to cost performance. Like Davenport and Harris [2], this study finds a correlation between analytical competence and organizational performance. However, previously unreported is the finding that technical and data competence are critical factors for succeeding with analytics.

Client Acceptance. *System use,* in general, and by top management and senior managers in *decision-making* and *acting* was not significantly different between the classes. However, system use was ranked much higher for BI, suggesting that usage by all types of end-user is an important success criterion. System use was correlated with top management steering ($\tau = 0.19$, $\rho = .04$), senior manager directing ($\tau = 0.20$, $\rho = .04$), and business user participation ($\tau = 0.20$, $\rho = .04$) for BI; no such significant correlation existed for big data analytics. Furthermore, for BI system use was correlated with cost and revenue performance while for big data analytics, it was only correlated with cost performance. For senior manager engagement in fact-based decision-making, there is also a correlation to strategic benefits for BI projects. The correlation between analytical sophistication and system use was not significant for BI nor for big data analytics.

These findings support statements that experts and fully automated solutions are the decision-makers for big data analytic systems. Hammerbacher [8] and Davenport and Harris [2] describe it as the job of the data scientist to carry out the end-to-end process from designing, refining, and deploying the models. Furthermore, Davenport and

Harris [2] attribute decision making to fully automated applications: "*Fully automated applications are configured to translate high-volume or routine decisions into action quickly, accurately, and efficiently because they are embedded into the normal flow of work*" [2, p. 150]. In addition, the finding confirms the Davenport and Harris [2] assertion that there is a correlation between management using an analytical system to make decisions and take actions and organizational performance.

Technical Tasks. The technical tasks are where the most difference between the two project classes can be found. The sophistication of the analytics was not a differentiator, while items from data architecture, data, IT infrastructure, and service quality were differentiators. Oddly, *analytical sophistication* and *data velocity* were ranked higher for BI than for big data analytics. Innovative technologies such as MapReduce- and Apache Hadoop-based systems exist specifically to process significant amounts of data and store structured and unstructured data such as text, sound, images, video, etc. [9]. Thus, that *data variety* and *data volume* were more highly associated with big data analytics, is as expected. However, an unexpected result was that *data quality* was higher for big data analytics than BI. Data validity, equated to data quality, is one of the attributes of big data. Nevertheless, given the novelty of big data analytics and its innovative uses, it is unusual that data quality would rank higher.

As expected, *data privacy* is a differentiator, with big data analytics giving the topic more importance. Technical and project management competencies are significantly correlated with data privacy for both project types. On the other hand, system security was not significantly different and was not ranked higher for big data analytics.

That *performance quality* is a significant differentiator underscores the need for big data analytic solutions to offer efficient methods and algorithms to secure high volumes of data [13]. However, that *performance quality* and *ease of operations* (which includes ease of use) are ranked higher for BI defines them as BI critical success factors.

Personal qualities were not significantly different between the two project types. As expected, they were ranked as more important in BI projects than in big data analytic projects.

The technical tasks for BI projects are mostly correlated with the cost and revenue aspects of performance, while those for big data analytics projects are more correlated with strategic performance than for BI projects.

Monitoring and Feedback, Communication, Troubleshooting. The *project management competence* and project efficiency against time, budget, and requirements were not significantly different between the project classes. However, project management competence was ranked higher for big data projects signaling that it may be more important in those engagements than in BI projects. Project management competence was not significantly correlated with the project efficiency measures of budget or requirements for either class. However, for big data analytics project management competence was correlated with strategic benefits and overall project success ($\tau = 0.43$, $\rho = .03$) and for BI with cost and revenue performance and delivery time ($\tau = 0.26$, $\rho = .01$).

Other Contingency Factors. The 13 items for project and organizational attributes and demographics were not significant in the mean ranking and are excluded from the tables for space reasons. Nevertheless, organizational market and revenue position, organizational revenue, number of departments and organizations involved, project duration, delivery time, and overall project success were correlated with one or more of the other measurement items as described in the previous sections.

Summary. For big data analytics projects, many of the measurement items are correlated with strategic benefits, while for BI projects they are associated with the operational benefits of cost and revenue performance. Project complexity is driven by the project characteristics for BI projects, while external market factors drive the complexity of big data analytics projects. Based on the analysis, we can further summarize the factors that influence the likelihood of achieving a successful project outcome as shown in Table 3.

Table 3. Summarized differentiating critical success factors

Business intelligence projects	Big data analytics projects
• Staff through competent in-house people from multiple departments	• Staff through a network of organizations
• Include technical, data, and business competence in the team	• Include analytical competence especially a Data Scientist in the team
• Involve business users in system performance, data quality, and data variability	• Include business users in the project acceptance
• Define system use as a success criterion	• Senior managers should provide project direction
• Include project management competence; it is associated with cost and revenue performance	• Include project management competence; it is associated with strategic benefit
• Analytical competency is associated with strategic benefits	
• Technical competence is important	
• Analytics can be monetized for both project types	

6 Conclusions

This study collected project success criteria across many types of decision support systems specifically business intelligence, analytics, and big data. It then offered a multidimensional analysis of big data analytics and BI projects by using latent class analysis, rank mean scoring, and correlation analysis to classify and describe the differences and similarities between the two project types. The results suggest BI and big data analytics projects are differentiated based on analytics competence, proprietary algorithms, and distinctive business processes. For big data analytics projects, many of the items are correlated with strategic benefits, while for BI projects they are associated with the operational benefits of cost and revenue performance. Project complexity is driven by the project characteristics for BI projects, while the external market drives the complexity of big data analytics projects.

The practical implication is that sponsors and project managers should use this information to plan projects, establish success criteria, and manage risks. Based on the literature review, the results establish the contingency factors for BI and big data analytics projects. That is, the measurement items offer a guide for defining the infrastructure, personnel, technical tasks, and governance for a project. Consequently, the items can be used to facilitate discussions to assign accountable human and financial resources to the project goals. Furthermore, they can be used as a template for risk identification as the success factors are the inverse of risk factors [21]. Secondly, the results can be used to formulate success criteria that can be measured and monitored during the project. For example, leading indicators could be defined around important aspects of personal quality and system use. The final contribution of this study is to add clarity on the differences between BI and big data analytics projects, which could be used by the project manager, project sponsors, and portfolio managers to prioritize and evaluate project expectations against organizational objectives.

The majority of organizations undertaking the projects analyzed in the study were large in terms of revenue and number of employees. Thus, these findings may not be relevant for small or midsized organizations. Furthermore, the results of this study are not generalizable beyond decision support projects, and the findings are limited due to the small sample size. Future research could focus on defining system criteria and going beyond identifying correlations to identifying predictors of success.

References

1. Eom, S.B.: The contributions of systems science to the development of the decision support system subspecialties: an empirical investigation. Syst. Res. Behav. Sci. **17**, 117 (2000). https://doi.org/10.1002/(SICI)1099-1743(200003/04)17:2<117:AID-SRES288>3.0.CO;2-E
2. Davenport, T.H., Harris, J.: Competing on Analytics: The New Science of Winning. Harvard Business School Press, Boston (2007)
3. Olbrich, S., Pöppelbuß, J., Niehaves, B.: Critical contextual success factors for business intelligence: a Delphi study on their relevance, variability, and controllability. In: 45th Hawaii International Conference on System Sciences, pp. 4148–4157 (2012). https://doi.org/10.1109/HICSS.2012.187
4. Yeoh, W., Koronios, A.: Critical success factors for business intelligence systems. J. Comput. Inf. Syst. **50**, 23–32 (2010). https://doi.org/10.1080/08874417.2010.11645404
5. Dawson, L., Van Belle, J.-P.: Critical success factors for business intelligence in the South African financial services sector. S. Afr. J. Inf. Manag. **15**, 1–12 (2013). https://doi.org/10.4102/sajim.v15i1.545
6. Lucas Jr., H.C.: Empirical evidence for a descriptive model of implementation. MIS Q. 27–42 (1978). https://doi.org/10.2307/248939
7. Thomas, J., Kielman, J.: Challenges for visual analytics. Inf. Vis. **8**, 309–314 (2009). https://doi.org/10.1057/ivs.2009.26
8. Hammerbacher, J.: Information platforms and the rise of the data scientist. In: Segaran, T., Hammerbacher, J. (eds.) Beautiful Data: The Stories Behind Elegant Data Solutions, pp. 73–84. O'Reilly Media Inc., Sebastopol (2009)

9. Sun, S., Cegielski, C.G., Li, Z.: Amassing and analyzing customer data in the age of big data: a case study of Haier's online-to-offline (O2O) business model. J. Inf. Technol. Case Appl. Res. **17**, 156–165 (2015). https://doi.org/10.1080/15228053.2015.1095017
10. Géczy, P.: Big data management: relational framework. Rev. Bus. Financ. Stud. **6**, 21–30 (2015)
11. Akter, S., Wamba, S.F.: Big data analytics in E-commerce: a systematic review and agenda for future research. Electron. Markets **26**, 173–194 (2016). https://doi.org/10.1007/s12525-016-0219-0
12. Halaweh, M., El Massry, A.: Conceptual model for successful implementation of big data in organizations. J. Int. Technol. Inf. Manag. **24**, 21–34 (2015)
13. Siddiqa, A., et al.: A survey of big data management: taxonomy and state-of-the-art. J. Netw. Comput. Appl. **71**, 151–166 (2016). https://doi.org/10.1016/j.jnca.2016.04.008
14. Davenport, T.H., Patil, D.J.: Data scientist: the sexiest job of the 21st Century. Harv. Bus. Rev. **90**, 70–76 (2012)
15. Chang, R.M., Kauffman, R.J., Kwon, Y.: Understanding the paradigm shift to computational social science in the presence of big data. Decis. Support Syst. **63**, 67 (2014). https://doi.org/10.1016/j.dss.2013.08.008
16. Iqbal, R., Doctor, F., More, B., Mahmud, S., Yousuf, U.: Big data analytics and computational intelligence for cyber-physical systems: recent trends and state of the art applications. Future Gener. Comput. Syst. (2017). https://doi.org/10.1016/j.future.2017.10.021
17. Turner, R.J., Zolin, R.: Forecasting success on large projects: developing reliable scales to predict multiple perspectives by multiple stakeholders over multiple time frames. Proj. Manag. J. **43**, 87–99 (2012). https://doi.org/10.1002/pmj.21289
18. Ika, L.A.: Project success as a topic in project management journals. Proj. Manag. J. **40**, 6–19 (2009). https://doi.org/10.1002/pmj.20137
19. Pinto, J.K., Slevin, D.P.: Critical success factors across the project life cycle. Proj. Manag. J. **19**, 67 (1988)
20. Belassi, W., Tukel, O.I.: A new framework for determining critical success/failure factors in projects. Int. J. Proj. Manag. **14**, 141–151 (1996). https://doi.org/10.1016/0263-7863(95)00064-X
21. Ziemba, E., Kolasa, I.: Risk factors relationships for information systems projects – insight from Polish public organizations. In: Ziemba, E. (ed.) Information Technology for Management. LNBIP, vol. 243, pp. 55–76. Springer, Cham (2016). https://doi.org/10.1007/978-3-319-30528-8_4
22. Chatzoglou, P., Chatzoudes, D., Apostolopoulou, G.: Examining the antecedents and outcomes of ERP implementation success: an explanatory study. In: Ziemba, E. (ed.) AITM/ISM-2016. LNBIP, vol. 277, pp. 157–178. Springer, Cham (2017). https://doi.org/10.1007/978-3-319-53076-5_9
23. Miller, G.J.: Decision support project: project success and organizational performance. Project and program management. DBA thesis, p. 465. SKEMA Business School, Lille, France (2018)
24. Barki, H., Hartwick, J.: Measuring user participation, user involvement, and user attitude. MIS Q. **18**, 59–82 (1994). https://doi.org/10.2307/249610
25. Shenhar, A., Dvir, D.: Reinventing Project Management: The Diamond Approach to Successful Growth and Innovation. Harvard Business School Press, Boston (2007)
26. Debortoli, S., Müller, O., Vom Brocke, J.P.D.: Comparing business intelligence and big data skills. Bus. Inform. Syst. Eng. **6**, 289–300 (2014). https://doi.org/10.1007/s12599-014-0344-2
27. Barki, H., Huff, S.L.: Change, attitude to change, and decision support system success. Inf. Manag. **9**, 261–268 (1985). https://doi.org/10.1016/0378-7206(85)90050-3

28. DeLone, W.H., McLean, E.R.: Information systems success: the quest for the dependent variable. Inf. Syst. Res. **3**, 60–95 (1992). https://doi.org/10.1287/isre.3.1.60
29. Wurpts, I.C., Geiser, C.: Is adding more indicators to a latent class analysis beneficial or detrimental? Results of a Monte-Carlo study. Front. Psychol. **5**, 920 (2014). https://doi.org/10.3389/fpsyg.2014.00920
30. Eom, S.B., Lee, S.M., Ayaz, A.: Expert systems applications development research in business: a selected bibliography (1975–1989). Eur. J. Oper. Res. **68**, 278–290 (1993). https://doi.org/10.1016/0377-2217(93)90309-B

Recommendations Based on Collective Intelligence – Case of Customer Segmentation

Maciej Pondel[1]([✉]) [iD] and Jerzy Korczak[2]([✉]) [iD]

[1] Wrocław University of Economics, Komandorska 118/120, Wrocław, Poland
maciej.pondel@ue.wroc.pl
[2] International School of Logistics and Transport,
Sołtysowicka St. 19 B, 51-168 Wrocław, Poland
jerzy.korczak@ue.wroc.pl

Abstract. The article discusses the usage and benefits of the recommendation systems based on data mining mechanisms targeting e-commerce industry. In particular the article focuses on the idea of collective clustering to perform customer segmentation. Results of many clustering algorithms in segmentation inspired by the RFM method are presented. The positive business-oriented outcomes of collective clustering are demonstrated on real-live marketing databases.

Keywords: Clustering · Collective intelligence · Recommendation systems

1 Introduction

The first seminars and conferences of the 90 s on advisory systems [1–3] provided a significant stimulus for the rapid interest in the methods and techniques of automation of recommendations not only in practice, but also by research. In recent years, under the influence of IT development, social networks, and artificial intelligence methods, the concept of the recommendation system and the scope of its main functionalities have significantly expanded. Today, a recommendation system constitutes a complex interactive platform allowing one to determine a rank of a product or the preferences that the customer would assign to a given product or group of products [4].

The specific economic benefits of a personalized recommendation achieved by e-commerce tycoons (Amazon, Alibaba, eBay, Booking, etc.) have shown the increasing effectiveness of recommendations systems. It has resulted not only in increased sales and marketing effectiveness, but also in significant analytical and decision support for marketing managers. Modern recommendation systems are no longer limited to giving such recommendation as, you bought this product, but others who bought it bought/watched X, Y, Z products. Many of them have based their recommendations on customer profile, and product characteristics as well as on behavioral and psychological analysis of customers.

© Springer Nature Switzerland AG 2019
E. Ziemba (Ed.): AITM 2018/ISM 2018, LNBIP 346, pp. 73–92, 2019.
https://doi.org/10.1007/978-3-030-15154-6_5

The aim of the article is to present methods of analysis and profiling of customers available in the Upsaily[1] recommendation system targeting online internet stores. It is a hybrid system combining recommendation techniques through collaborative filtering and contextual analysis. In the development of recommendations, in addition to transactional data, the system also uses geo-location and social network data. The data is a source of information for many clustering algorithms in the system. These algorithms can work autonomously or collectively, cooperating with each other in order to achieve semantically rich segmentation of interesting business interpretations. This second approach is the subject of the article. Although the source data set is the same, the innovativeness of the solution manifests itself in the selection of algorithms; each of them was selected from a different computing class and applies different similarity criteria. Among the algorithms, in addition to the commonly used k-means that uses Euclidean distance measure, we have chosen the Gaussian Mixture Model based on probability distributions, the DBSCAN algorithm taking into account the density of observation and the RMF involving the manager engagement. The unification of clustering results in our application is specific to the e-commerce applications – not all the clusters are used, but only one or several clusters. Cluster selection criteria include both statistical metrics as well as external, mainly economic, criteria.

The structure of the article is as follows: the next section describes the categories of advisory mechanisms used in recommendation systems. The third section sketches functional architecture of the recommendation system Upsaily and defines the problem of data mining in marketing. The fourth section presents the algorithms used in collective clustering together with unification principles of clustering results. The last section of the article describes the experiments carried out and the advantages of collective clustering on real marketing data.

2   Theoretical Background

In the literature, these systems are considered in three main perspectives: from the managerial perspective, the recommendation system is a decision support system that uses large, heterogeneous data and mechanisms generating recommendations related to the sales strategy and promotion of the products offered; from the client's perspective, it is an advisory system facilitating selection of products in accordance with one's interests, needs, and preferences; from an IT perspective, the recommendation system is an interactive computing platform containing a number of data analysis and exploration models, integrated with transactional systems of the online store and the environment. This platform must guarantee not only access to various information resources, but also scalability of applications operating on a large number of information collections.

Currently, the recommendation systems are founded on one of the four categories of advisory mechanisms: recommendation by collaborative filtering of information,

---

[1] Upsaily system was developed by the Unity S.A., Wrocław, in the framework of the Real-Time Omnichannel Marketing (RTOM) project, RPO WD 2014-2020.

content-based recommendation, knowledge-based recommendation, and hybrid recommendation [5–10]. Recommendation by collaborative filtering is the most common method, it is based on recommending products highly rated by customers with similar profile and preferences [11–13]. Here the key issues are as follows: designation of the similarity between clients and choosing the customer segmentation method. These issues will be discussed in more detail later in the article. The content-based recommendation is founded on analysis and data mining of products purchased by the customer [1, 14]. In contrast to the previous method, the key issue is to analyze a customer's purchase history and determine the similarity of the products. The third group of methods builds recommendations based on analysis of product features with reference to its usefulness for the client [15]. In order to take advantage and reduce the negative features of the aforementioned methods, hybrid recommendation systems are increasingly being designed [9, 16].

Additionally, for a number of years now, we have been observing a growing interest in recommendation systems by owners and managers of online internet shops in Poland. In 2010, every third online shop used a recommendation based on a simple analysis of CBR and Business Intelligence systems [17]. In recent years in Poland, artificial intelligence, personalized recommendation, and digital marketing have dominated the orientation of developers of e-commerce systems which until recently had focused on the efficiency of shopping services [18]. Currently, almost all big online stores use recommendation systems. However, these systems are to a large extent based on a simple business analytics, limited computational intelligence, and reduced possibility of dynamic customer profiling.

3 Research Methodology and Experimental Platform

The Upsaily system, based on the B2C model, is geared towards current customers of the online internet shops. In the system database, not only are all customer transactions stored, but also basic data about their demographic and behavioral profile. The system is able to record customer reactions to offers directed at them through various contact channels. Functionally, the system can be considered as a Customer Intelligence solution, i.e. the one whose primary interest is current customers, and the aim is to increase customer satisfaction that translates into increasing turnover through the customers making follow-up purchases, increasing the value of individual orders by cross-selling or more valuable products (up-selling). The immediate goal of the system is not to help in acquiring new customers. The Customer Intelligence approach is related to conducting analytical activities leading to creation of a clear image of the customer so that one can find the most valuable customers and send them a personalized marketing message [19].

The results of research conducted as part of the RTOM project on Polish online stores operating in various industries that showed that in each of them over 75% of all customers are one-off customers, that is they never returned to the store after making a purchase, form the basis of such orientation of the system. Analysis of the average value of the order for a one-off customer shows that it is lower than for customers who make subsequent purchase. Interestingly, it is possible to see that there is a general trend consisting of an increase in the average value of the order with the increase in customer loyalty expressed in the number of purchases made by them. Usually, the average value of orders is hidden due to a company's confidentiality policy. From this observation, it was concluded that it is worth harnessing resources of the online store to build customer loyalty, for the simple fact that a loyal customer is ultimately more valuable than a one-off customer. It should also be pointed out that acquisition of a new customer is always related to the extra cost to be incurred to reach the customer with the marketing message in a selected medium. Without knowing a customer's previous transactions, we are unable to propose an effective offer tailored to the customer's preferences; therefore, in many cases the presentation of a marketing message will not cause projected customer reaction. In case of communication with current clients whose contact details are available and for whom all necessary marketing consents are established - at least at the assumptions level, it can be stated that reaching the customer should cost significantly less and the effectiveness of messages should be definitely higher.

Basing on literature [20–23], and drawing conclusions from the research carried out as part of the RTOM project [24] authors have proposed a schema of advanced data analysis in marketing [25]. Depending on the specific purpose, a group of customers to be covered by the campaign should be selected. In general, for the defined clients, the subject of the campaign is selected, e.g. product groups that they will potentially be interested in. The final stage is defining the conditions under which customers will be invited to participate in the campaign.

Functional architecture of the recommendation system Upsaily is presented in Fig. 1. The Upsaily system collects data from many sources, but the basis of its analysis is transactional data. Data from other sources such as marketing automation systems, social media, and systems analyzing activity on the store's website enrich the customer profile and thus expand the set of input data for analytical modules that, thanks to them, are able to provide better analyzes and better predictive models. The research platform on which the experiments are carried out has a significant place in the architecture of the system.

These experiments are evaluated in terms of business suitability, after their effects are positive; they are then transformed into regular modules operating in a production manner.

The system information outputs are integrated with the following:

- Marketing panel or application presenting the results of conducted analyzes, visualizing identified trends, found patterns, and segmentation effects. The recipient of this application are primarily managers and marketing analysts who, in using it, expand their own knowledge on the clients and their behaviors,
- A real-time recommender, an application whose aim is to offer an online store an offer that is as consistent as possible with its needs.
- Module "campaign for today" based on discovered trends and customer behavior patterns at the moment of launching, it is able to automatically indicate groups of customers and the product that they may be interested in at that moment.

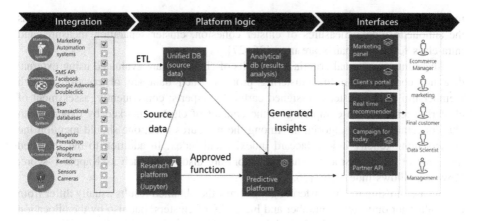

Fig. 1. Functional architecture of the Upsaily system

The results of the Upsaily system will be detailed in the next sections of the article.

4 Collective Clustering Assessment Methods

There are many algorithms that can be used in collective clustering approach [21, 22, 26]. In the project, the algorithmic composition was based on maximum variability and differentiation of clustering paradigms. Therefore the following algorithms were chosen:

- k-means based on the Euclidean distance between observations,
- Bisecting k-means acting on a basis similar to k-means, however, starting with all the observations in one cluster and then dividing the cluster into 2 sub-clusters, using the k-means algorithm,
- Gaussian Mixture Model (GMM), which is a probabilistic model based on the assumption that a particular feature has a finite number of normal distributions,
- DBSCAN identifying clusters by measuring density as the number of observations in a designated area. If the density is greater than the density of observations belonging to other clusters, then the defined area is identified as a cluster.

Usually the results of clustering algorithms are evaluated according to internal and external criteria. The internal criteria relate to the hierarchy of clusters, taking into account the similarity of observations within clusters and the similarity between clusters. The Davies-Bouldin[2] and Dunn[3] metrics are usually applied for assessment

---

[2] The Davies-Bouldin index is computed according to the formula: $DB = 0.5n \, \Sigma \, max \, ((si + sj)/d(ci, cj))$ where n is the number of clusters, the cluster centroids, si and sj mean d distances between the elements of a given cluster and the centroid. The algorithm that generates the smallest value of the DB indicator is considered the best according to the criterion of internal evaluation.

[3] The Dunn index is calculated according to the formula: $D = min(d(i, j)/max \, d'(k))$ where $d(i, j)$ means the distance between clusters i i j and $d'(k)$ the measure of distances within the cluster k. The Dunn index focuses on cluster density and distances between cluster. Preferred algorithms according to the Dunn index are those that achieve high index values.

measures. In addition to the mentioned measures, other functions of assessment such as the silhouette index, measures of cluster cohesion, cluster separation measure, and intra-class scattering matrix are used [26, 27].

According to external criteria, the results of clustering are evaluated using external data not considered in the clustering process. Such data are observations which membership in the cluster is assigned earlier by experts; consequently, assessment of clustering results from comparing of the content of clusters marked by experts with clusters created by the algorithm. Among the measures used, one should mention the clusters homogeneity index, Jaccard index, Rand index. In addition to the specified measures of the assessment, other indicators are also used, such as Kappa, F-score, Fowkes-Mallows index, etc. [26, 27].

In case of using many clustering algorithms, the obtained results usually differ from each other not only by the number and hierarchy of clusters, but also by the allocation of observations to clusters. In the article, we treat the set of algorithms as a collective of experts whose task is to make the grouping of the set of observations from the business point of view as best as possible. Discrepancies in grouping that appear in the results of the algorithms must be minimized. The solution to this problem is determined by the unification process.

In order to assess the results of clustering, it is often helpful to assign a category to collected observations. In the case of very large data sets, it is not possible to assign all observations by experts. Therefore, it has been proposed to enable the assignment of observation to the clusters through decision rules that define clusters selected by the expert in the form:

$$X_i \in C_j | if \, [(w_{11} \cap w_{12} \cap \ldots \cap w_{1k}) \cup (w_{21} \cap w_{22} \cap \ldots \cap w_{2m}) \ldots],$$

where X_i is a given observation, and C_j is a cluster in the conditional expression. Attributes used in conditional clauses indicate their importance and usefulness in the characteristics of clusters.

The decision rules are determined by the algorithm of inductive decision tree algorithm C4.5 [28]. These rules make in possible, on the one hand, to interpret the obtained clusters and, on the other hand, to symbolically determine the observations belonging to individual clusters. This solution makes it possible to find similar semantic clusters generated by different algorithms. The symbolic interpretation of clusters is enhanced by graphic display, which facilitates a quick identification of similar clusters. It should be noted that these works generally require significant involvement of marketing analysts.

In general, using the recommendation systems, the manager or marketing analyst is only interested in a few clusters describing similar clients, similar products, or similar transactions. Therefore, the first task concentrates on cluster identifying that can be a subject to unification. Although the task can be performed algorithmically, our experience has shown that much better results are obtained through selection of clusters by an analyst. If the visual selection is difficult, finding for a cluster C_i, a counterpart among clusters $C_j \in C_k$ obtained from another algorithm, then the formula of similarity between clusters $S(C_i, C_j)$ can be applied:

$$S(C_i, C_j) = max(|C_i \cap C_j|/|C_i|).$$

In cases where the cluster's observations C_i are distributed into several clusters from C_k, the assignment should take into account the distribution of S values and the weights of related cluster similarities.

After selecting the clusters obtained from different algorithms, one can start unifying the results. There are many methods of unification [29]. The most commonly used methods are the following:

- Consensus methods [30–33], which are used more in the first phase of unification to create initial clusterization than to unify the results,
- Multi-criterial grouping methods [30, 31, 34] are mainly used to harmonize criteria of different algorithms,
- Clustering methods supported by domain knowledge [35, 36].

The last group of unification methods was used in the Upsaily system. The domain knowledge of marketing has been used to direct the unification process of selected clusters. In the system, the earlier created decision rules are used to govern the process of unification, in particular, the conditional expressions of which are treated as grouping constraints. The idea of the proposed method consists in determining semantic relationships-constraints indicating observations that must be included in the cluster (called *must-link*), and those that should not be included in it (called *cannot-link*). In order to improve the quality of clusters, fuzzy logic has been proposed in some works [37–39] or characteristics of clusters such as values of inter-cluster distances, density [40, 41].

Let us now follow step by step the entire unification process, aiming at achieving consensus on the content of the final clusters without any significant loss of quality of the partitions. Let us assume that they were pre-designated as two similar clusters C_j i C_l, each generated by a different algorithm. As indicated, the interpretation of each cluster is given in the form of decision rules, namely:

$$C_j| \; if \; [(w'_{11} \cap w'_{12} \cap \ldots \cap w'_{1k}) \cup (w'_{21} \cap w'_{22} \cap \ldots \cap w'_{2m}) \ldots]$$
$$C_l| \; if \; [(w''_{11} \cap w''_{12} \cap \ldots \cap w''_{1k}) \cup (w''_{21} \cap w''_{22} \cap \ldots \cap w''_{2m}) \ldots]$$

The final cluster can be created by merging of conditions containing variables (attributes) indicated by the analyst based on domain knowledge. This operation can be called a subsumption according to which the more detailed condition is covered with a less detailed one. However, the resulting cluster may contain too many observations that are too far away from the class sought (as shown in Fig. 2). In narrowing the cluster's space, the observations given earlier by the expert might help, defined as a *must-link* or *cannot-link* marked in Fig. 2 in green and red respectively.

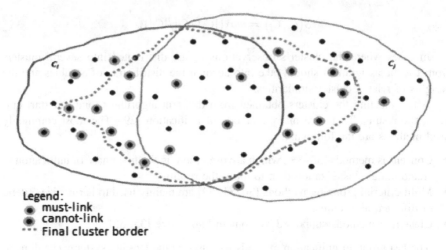

Fig. 2. Example of space of merged clusters. (Color figure online)

The boundary of the final cluster (green dotted line) is determined between the sum of observations belonging to two clusters minus the surroundings of ε observations belonging to the *cannot-link* relationship and the intersection of the observation plus the surroundings ε observations belonging to the *must-link* relationship. It can therefore be noted that the unified cluster includes observations lying in the space $|C_i \cup C_j| - \varepsilon$ *Xi/cannot-link* and $|C_i \cap C_j| + \varepsilon$ *Xi/must-link*. The radius of the surroundings ε can be determined based on ½ distance between the closest observations belonging to the *can not-link* and *must-link* relationships.

After the first unification of clusters, the process should be repeated for all similar clusters obtained from all algorithms. It should be noted that the order in which the clusters are selected influences the calculation time. We suggest choosing the most numerous clusters of interest in the first place. The next section will show examples of unification of the results of collective clustering.

Due to the thematic orientation of the Lecture Notes and the restricted volume of the article in the next chapter, we will concentrate on the business assessment of the results of clustering (domain knowledge) alone. The RFM analysis, which constitutes a traditional approach to analyze the customer behavior in the retail industry, will be used. Its acronym comes from the words "*recency*" (period from the last purchase), "*frequency*", and "*monetary value*". In this type of analysis, customers are divided into groups, based on information on the time which has elapsed since the last purchases, how often they make purchases, and how much money they spent [42].

The following observations explain why RFM is interesting for retail companies:

- Customers who have recently made purchases are more likely to make a new purchase soon.
- Customers who frequently make purchases are more likely to do even more shopping.
- Customers who spend a lot of money are more likely to spend even more money.

Each of these observations corresponds to one of the dimensions of RFM.

In the next section, the usefulness of this approach for assessing clustering algorithms is shown on the real marketing data.

5 Experiments and Research Findings

In order to show the practicality of the collective clustering method in specific business conditions, this section presents an experiment aimed at finding customer segments having similar behavior on the market. The clustering method should support a process of customer assignment to particular segment, assessment of proposed segments and interpretation of these segments. The segmentation example was inspired by the RFM method. The customer is defined by the following characteristics: frequency of their purchase (*frequency* dimension), the number of days which has passed since the last order (*recency* dimension), and the average order value (*monetary value*). We enrich the customer description by information about the number of orders. For an online store, such dimension is essential in order to determine the loyal customer. Customers were divided into 6 segments. For each segment, we calculated its value (the sum of all customers' orders from a given segment). The number 6 was chosen arbitrarily. Marketing employees were able to prepare 6 different marketing communication policies addressed to individual customers. With more segments, it would be very difficult for the marketing analyst to interpret segments and subsequently develop a tailored communication policy for selected customers. A larger number of segments will be justified only if the automatic recommendation mechanism uses this segmentation.

The experiment was carried out using three clustering algorithms: bisecting k-means, Gaussian Mixture Model, and DBSCAN[4]. After each experiment, an expert evaluated the results of the segmentation. The analysis covered 56 237 customers who had made at least 2 purchases in the online store.

When assessing segmentation, it is very helpful to visualize the data. With 4 dimensions, there has to be a possibility of presenting it on a surface (with only two dimensions). In order to prepare for visualization in the experiment, the four dimensions were reduced to two (X and Y), while the color means the segment number to which the given customer was assigned. Two methods to project the multidimensional space into a smaller number of dimensions have been applied. One of those methods is the Principal Component Analysis[5] (PCA). PCA is a popular technique for reducing multidimensional space [43].

---

[4] The HDBSCAN algorithm, which is an extension of the DBSCAN algorithm, was used. A library available on the GitHub platform was used for this purpose: https://hdbscan.readthedocs.io/en/latest/index.html

[5] In brief, the purpose of the PCA method is to find a linear subspace (in our case 2-dimensional) in which the variance after projection remains the largest. However, the PCA method should not easily reject the dimensions with the lowest variance. It builds a new coordinates system in which the remaining values are the most diverse.

An example of RFM segmentation using the k-means algorithm and visualization using the PCA method is presented in Fig. 3. One dot represents one real customer on the visualization (on left hand side of picture). Hovering over a selected dot will display values describing a selected customer. This solution will help the marketing analyst to understand the prepared segments.

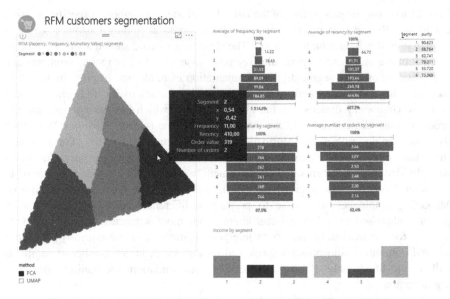

Fig. 3. Segmentation using the k-means algorithm and PCA visualization.

In the right part of the report are funnel charts presenting the average value of the given dimension attribute in individual segments; for example, average customer from segment 1 purchases with frequency of 14.22 days.

The column chart located in the bottom right corner of the report shows the sum of customers' orders in given segments. It can therefore be observed that the highest revenue was generated by customers from segment no. 6, the smallest in segment no. 5.

Another method of reducing dimensions that is useful for visualization is the Uniform Manifold Approximation and Projection (UMAP) [44]. It is a novel manifold learning technique for dimension reduction. UMAP seeks to provide results similar to t-SNE, a current state-of-the-art technique for dimension reduction well suited for visualization, with superior run time performance. The theoretical framework of UMAP is based on Riemannian (a non-Euclidian) geometry and algebraic topology. In overview, UMAP uses local manifold approximations and patches together their local fuzzy simplicial set representations. It is based on the approximation of the local manifold (local manifold approximations) and fuzzy simplicial sets. In contrast to a simple method such as PCA, where the projection is mainly based on two dimensions, the UMAP method takes all dimensions into account equally. An example of a visualization made using the UMAP method is presented in Fig. 4.

Visualization using two methods as well as presentation of the values of individual dimensions in clusters helps the analyst better understand individual customer segments and make an expert assessment of clustering.

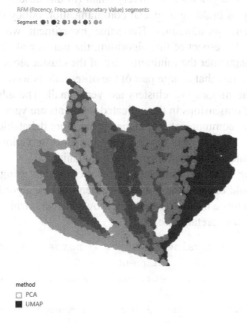

Fig. 4. Visualization of segmentation using the UMAP method.

Clustering using the k-means algorithm based on the Euclidean distance between observations has shown many shortcomings. These include the fact that the most varied dimensional values have the greatest impact (in our case, recency and frequency) when assigning customers to segments. The other dimensions influence to a lesser degree, and this can be observed in the low differentiation in the dimensions of average orders' values. In addition, it should be noticed that the boundaries between individual segments are not sharp. For example, segment 6, with the lowest average value, recency dimensions, includes both customers with a value of 0 and customers with a value of 147, these customers, from the perspective of the RFM method, made their purchases relatively long time ago. The fact that the segments are relatively well balanced (their size is relatively similar) constitutes the main advantage of this algorithm. It makes those segments valuable in creating a dedicated marketing policy.

The next algorithm of clustering used in the experiment was the bisecting k-means. Greater diversity was observed in individual dimensions while using algorithm than in the case of k-means. The clusters were again relatively balanced, however, the problem of the slight diversification of the 1 dimension remained, and in some segments there were customers located far away from the average value on a given scale.

Subsequent clustering was performed using the Gaussian Mixture Model algorithm. That method revealed significant differences in the value of individual dimensions, due to which we can observe interesting cases of outliers (e.g., segment 1 includes customers with a very large number of orders and very high value of orders). Unfortunately, the size of such segments is relatively small (in this case 34 customers), which makes the legitimacy of building a special communication policy targeting customers from such a segment questionable. The same experiment was repeated for the DBSCAN algorithm. In respect of this algorithm, the number of clusters was defined. Algorithm takes as parameter the minimum size of the cluster alone. The disadvantage of this approach is the fact that a large part of the observations were not assigned to any cluster; moreover, the majority of clusters are very small. The advantage is that the average values of the dimensions in the indicated segments are very diverse. The use of this algorithm to build communication policies is therefore debatable, but its advantage is the fact that clusters of relatively few but very similar observations are found, which can be used in the automatic recommendation mechanism.

For the marketing analyst, in order to perform clustering using all the mentioned algorithms, they should observe the boundaries identified by algorithms on individual dimensions, and then those borders to build their own clusters, which will be referred to as according to their interpretation, e.g.

```
If average order value> 1000 zł ∩ number of orders > 10
   ∩ recency < 300 ∩ frequency < 60
   then segment=„active frequent valuable buyers"

If average order value< 200 zł ∩ number of orders < 3
   ∩ recency > 250 ∩ frequency > 200
   then segment=„occasional past cheap buyers"
```

In the platform, customer filtering for clustering assignments can be done "manually" using the provided "sliders", presented in the upper right corner in Fig. 5.

In the last phase of the experiment, a collective segmentation was proposed, taking into account the results of the three selected clustering algorithms. Ultimately, because of the similar results of the k-means and bisecting k-means algorithms, the k-means was not used in the experiment. We created collective segments based on the results of 3 algorithms. The label of new clusters is constructed with the 3 numbers of clusters generated by the algorithms: bisecting k-means, GMM, and DBSCAN. For example, cluster 326 means that the customer had originally been assigned to clusters with numbers: 3 - bisecting k-means; 2 - GMM; 6 - DBSCAN. As a result, 52 segments were created (on 216 possible combinations), which is presented in Fig. 6.

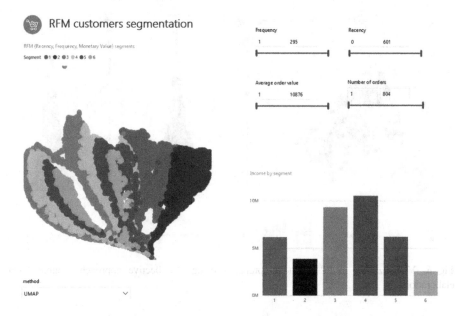

Fig. 5. Manual segmentation. Source: Own elaboration in the Upsaily.

Naturally, such a large number of segments do not allow for an in-depth analysis of each of them and for "manual" preparation of marketing policies. However, these segments can be successfully used in the automated recommendation mechanism.

In order to limit the number of clusters, similar segments may be merged if the marketing analyst wishes to analyze and interpret individual segments. After the analyst decides on the maximum number of clusters or the minimum cluster size, then segments below the thresholds are included in the larger segment meeting the criterion of cardinality. Clusters' merge can be made with the lowest distance between them. The distance of clusters is not determined by the Euclidian measure, as for each of the aforementioned methods, cluster number is just an identifier without any meaning. Such identifiers do not determine similarity of clusters (e.g., cluster 1 doesn't have to be closely related to cluster 2). Taking this fact into account, distance in this case should be understood as the number of algorithms indicating a different cluster number, e.g., between clusters 525 and 520 the distance is 1 - which means that the clusters differ by the result of 1 method. Between the clusters 320 and 525, the distance is 2. A number of conflicts appear after clusters that should be merged are identified - clusters of the same distance. In this experiment, we will resolve the conflict by selecting the highest cardinality cluster to which we attach a cluster that does not meet the criterion of cardinality.

The k-means, bisecting k-means or GMM algorithms require entering a pre-determined number of clusters that we would want to receive. The DBSCAN algorithm autonomously selects the number of clusters based on other parameters, but in its case a large part of the observations are excluded from resultant cluster. One can state that DBSCAN cannot be used in definition of marketing policies covering all customers; however, it is well suited for identifying smaller groups of observations that are very similar to each other.

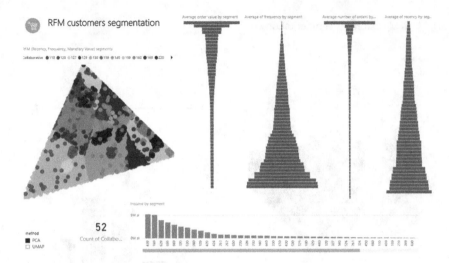

Fig. 6. Visualization of 52 segments prepared using a collective approach. Source: own elaboration.

In the next experiment, the objective was to unify two clusters using the previously described method, reinforced by domain knowledge. Having assumed that the focus was to concentrate campaign on customers purchasing most frequently, two clusters of customers with the lowest average days between purchases were generated by GMM and bisecting k-means algorithms. In case of bisecting k-means algorithm, it is cluster number 3 – further referred to as 3 BKM. Figure 7 presents the distribution of every dimension (highlighted values show selected cluster). The figure shows average values of every variable.

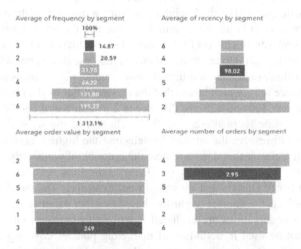

Fig. 7. Bisecting k-means cluster number 3-average values of dimensions among other clusters. Source: own elaboration.

GMM algorithm generated cluster number 6 with lowest average days between purchases, which is presented in Fig. 8. This cluster will be referred to as 6 GMM.

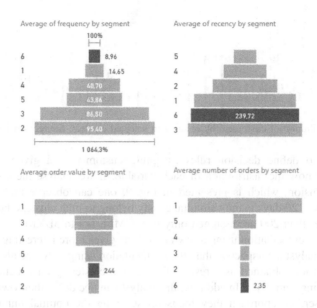

Fig. 8. GMM cluster number 6 - average values of dimensions among other clusters. Source: own elaboration.

Analysing the average values of each dimension, the clusters apparently differ a lot; however, the average does not show all the information on the real similarity of the clusters. If one analyses each dimension, the common parts can be identified. Table 1 presents not only the average value, but also the minimum and maximum value. For instance, analysing recency, one can see that the average value is 98,02 for bisecting k-means cluster 3 and 239,72 for GMM clusters 6 which seem to point to a significant difference. However, analysing the whole range of recency values of observations in both clusters, one can conclude that there are observations that belong to both clusters or that are very close.

Table 1. Avg, minimum and maximum value of each dimension.

	Bisecting k-means segment nr 3			GMM segment nr 6		
	Average	Min	Max	Average	Min	Max
Frequency	14.87	0	42	8.96	0	47
Recency	98.02	0	201	239.72	3	600
Order value	249	9	3384	244	9	753
Number of orders	2.95	2	804	2.35	2	13

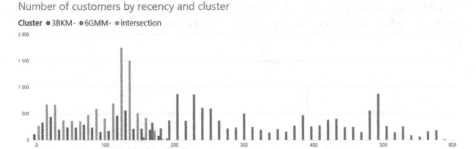

Fig. 9. Distribution of customers by recency in selected clusters. Source: own elaboration.

In order to define decision rules assigning customer to a given cluster, it is important to know the distribution of each variable. If we analyse the distribution of recency dimension, which is presented in Fig. 9, one can observe that clients with recency around 120 days mainly simultaneously belong to both clusters, but those with recency higher than 200 are assigned only to 6 GMM, not to 3BKM.

In general, segmentation using a few algorithms gives more interesting results from a marketing analyst's perspective than the segmentation using only one algorithm. First of all, the clusters obtained as a result of collective clustering have better and more useful marketing semantics. In addition, the analyst can decide on their own whether in using the described approach they focus on selecting the optimal number of large clusters, or analyse smaller clusters to identify hidden patterns of customer behaviour. The bar colour indicates the cluster. As can be seen, there are 3 clusters:

- intersection, which means that a customer belongs to both clusters,
- 3BKM, which consists of customers belonging to 3BKM and at the same time not belonging to 6GMM,
- 6GMM, which consists of customers belonging to 6GMM and at the same time not belonging to 3BKM.

In other words 3BKM consists of the sum of 3BKM and intersection. Figure 10 presents number of customers by average order value with similar logic of cluster presentation. In this case, one can observe that the most important difference could be summarized that customers with average order value higher than 650 are not assigned to 6GMM, only to 3BKM (but a number of such customers is limited).

If all dimensions are considered, the PCA visualisation can present observations being intersection of both selected clusters and observations that belong to one of the original clusters. However one can make a decision about the boundary of a final cluster following the algorithm presented in Sect. 4. Such border has been presented in an approximate form in a Fig. 11a. The following decision rule explaining the final cluster C_f stems from analysis of each dimension distribution by a domain expert

```
Cf | if [(0<=frequency<=47) ∩ (0<=recency <=200) ∩
        (50<=ave order value<=300) ∩ (2<= number of orders<=6)
```

Number of customers by average order value and cluster

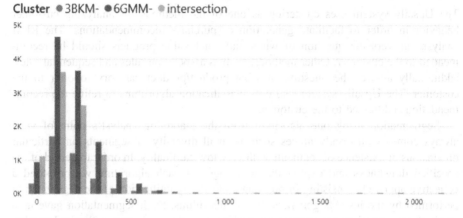

Fig. 10. Distribution of customers by average order value in selected clusters. Source: own elaboration.

Visualisation of final cluster and filter enabling domain expert to apply defined rule is presented in Fig. 11b.

The Davies-Bouldin indices for every cluster are as follows $DB_{3BKN} = 9489.7$ $DB_{6GMM} = 14445.7$ $DB_{Cf} = 4007.6$. The result of unification supported by domain knowledge is the cluster referred to as C_f that integrates customers belonging to cluster number 3 generated by bisecting k-means and a cluster number 6 generated by GMM. The results show that the final cluster is much more consistent (observations are more similar to each other) than in case of those two clusters were independently generated by these algorithms.

a)   b)

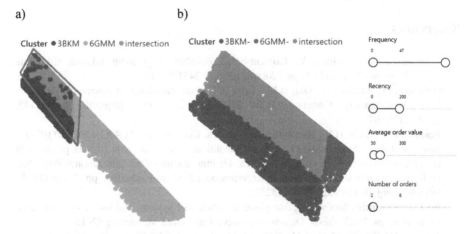

Fig. 11. Final cluster (a) borders (b) filters. Source: own elaboration.

6 Conclusions

The Upsaily system uses clustering as one of the methods for analyzing customer behavior in order to facilitate generation of purchase recommendations. The RFM analysis answers the question of when and what value products should be recommended to the customer. Other methods, such as association rules and sequential rules, additionally answer the question of what product/product category to offer to the customer. The Upsaily system also uses classification algorithms to refine the recommendations addressed to the customers.

Segmentation using one algorithm from the marketing analyst's point of view always comes with disadvantages such as small diversity of segments on particular dimensions or existence of segments with very low cardinality. In order to get rid of the specified drawbacks and exploit the advantages of each algorithm, we proposed a collective approach consisting in building a cluster by unification of the segmentation performed by the insights generated by all algorithms. Such segmentation gave us a result of more consistent segments with easier interpretation; however, the final number of segments is definitely higher than when using each algorithm individually. Small segments can be useful in situations where we build an automatic mechanism of generating recommendations based on the client's assignment to the segment, where the large number of segments constitute a problem. Segments consisting of a small number of customers are also useful in the task of identifying atypical clients as outliers. If one wishes to obtain a limited number of segments to define a tailored marketing policy to each segment separately, then the aggregation can be done on the criterion of cluster cardinalities.

In future studies, the authors intend to deal with the subject of collaborative clustering, automatic identification of the optimal number of segments and client clustering based on subsequent dimensions that also take their transactions and purchased products into account.

References

1. Balabanovic, M., Shoham, Y.: Content-based, collaborative recommendation. Commun. ACM **40**(3), 66–72 (1997). https://doi.org/10.1145/245108.245124
2. Goldberg, D., Nichols, D., Oki, B.M., Terry, D.: Using collaborative filtering to weave an information tapestry. Commun. ACM **35**(12), 61–70 (1992). https://doi.org/10.1145/138859.138867
3. Resnick, P., Varian, H.R.: Recommender systems. Commun. ACM **40**(3), 56–58 (1997)
4. Konstan, J.A., Adomavicius, G.: Toward identification and adoption of best practices in algorithmic recommender systems research. In: Proceedings of the International Workshop on Reproducibility and Replication in Recommender Systems Evaluation, pp. 23–28 (2013). https://doi.org/10.1145/2532508.2532513
5. Beel, J.: Towards effective research-paper recommender systems and user modeling based on mind maps. Ph.D. thesis. Otto-von-Guericke Universität Magdeburg (2015)
6. Jannach, D., Zanker, M., Ge, M., Gröning, M.: Recommender systems in computer science and information systems–a landscape of research. In: Proceedings of the 13th International Conference, EC-Web, pp. 76–87 (2012). https://doi.org/10.1007/978-3-642-32273-0_7

7. Ricci, F., Rokach, L., Shapira, B., Kantor, P.B. (eds.): Recommender Systems Handbook, pp. 1–35. Springer, Heidelberg (2011). https://doi.org/10.1007/978-0-387-85820-3
8. Jannach, D., Zanker, M., Felfernig, A., Friedrich, G.: Recommender Systems – An Introduction. Cambridge University Press, Cambridge (2010)
9. Lu, J., Wu, D., Mao, M., Wang, W., Zhang, W.G.: Recommender system application developments: a survey. Decis. Support Syst. **74**, 12–32 (2015). https://doi.org/10.1016/j.dss.2015.03.008
10. Said, A., Tikk, D., Shi, Y., Larson, M., Stumpf, K., Cremonesi, P.: Recommender systems evaluation: a 3D benchmark. In: ACM RecSys 2012 Workshop on Recommendation Utility Evaluation: Beyond RMSE, pp. 21–23 (2012)
11. Acilar, A.M., Arslan, A.: A collaborative filtering method based on artificial immune network. Expert Syst. Appl. **36**(4), 8324–8332 (2009). https://doi.org/10.1016/j.eswa.2008.10.029
12. Cornuejols, A., Wemmert, C., Gançarski, P., Bennani, Y.: Collaborative clustering: why, when, what and how. Inf. Fusion **39**, 81–95 (2017). https://doi.org/10.1016/j.inffus.2017.04.008
13. Kashef, R., Kamel, M.S.: Cooperative clustering. Pattern Recognit. **43**(6), 2315–2329 (2010)
14. Konstan, J.A., Riedl, J.: Recommender systems: from algorithms to user experience user modeling user-adaptation. User Interact. **22**, 101–123 (2012). https://doi.org/10.1007/s11257-011-9112-x
15. Carmagnola, F., Cena, F., Gena, C.: User model interoperability: a survey. User Model. User-Adapt. User Interact. **21**(3), 285–331 (2011). https://doi.org/10.1007/s11257-011-9097-5
16. Burke, R.: Hybrid recommender systems: survey and experiments. User Model. User-Adapt. Interact. **12**(4), 331–370 (2002). https://doi.org/10.1023/A:1021240730564
17. Kobiela, E.: Intelligent recommendation systems (pol. Inteligentne systemy rekomendacyjne). Network Magazyn (2011). http://www.networkmagazyn.pl/inteligentne-systemy-rekomendacji
18. Gemius 2017: The latest data on Polish e-commerce is now available (pol. Najnowsze dane o polskim e-commerce już dostępne). https://www.gemius.pl/wszystkie-artykuly-aktualnosci/najnowsze-dane-Polish-of-ecommerce-already-dostepne.html
19. Nazemoff, V.: Customer intelligence. In: The Four Intelligences of the Business Mind. Apress, Berkeley (2014). https://doi.org/10.1007/978-1-4302-6164-3_3
20. Chorianopoulos, A.: Effective CRM Using Predictive Analytics. Wiley, Hoboken (2016). https://doi.org/10.1002/9781119011583
21. Gordon, S., Linoff, M., Berry, J.A.: Data Mining Techniques for Marketing, Sales, and Customer Relationship. Wiley, Hoboken (2011)
22. Witten, I.H., et al.: Data Mining: Practical Machine Learning Tools and Techniques. Morgan Kaufmann, Burlington (2016)
23. Jordan, M.I., Mitchell, T.: Machine learning: trends, perspectives, and prospects. Science **349**(6245), 255–260 (2015). https://doi.org/10.1126/science.aaa8415
24. Pondel, M., Korczak, J., A view on the methodology of analysis and exploration of marketing data. In: Federated Conference on Computer Science and Information Systems (FedCSIS), pp. 1135–1143. IEEE (2017). https://doi.org/10.15439/2017F442
25. Pondel, M., Korczak, J.: Collective clustering of marketing data-recommendation system Upsaily. In: 2018 Federated Conference on Computer Science and Information Systems (FedCSIS), pp. 801–810. IEEE (2018). https://doi.org/10.15439/2018F217
26. Aggarval, C.C., Reddy, C.K.: Data Clustering: Algorithms and Applications. Chapman & Hall/CRC, London (2013)

27. Gan, G., Ma, C., Wu, J.: Data Clustering: Theory, Algorithms, and Applications. SIAM Series. SIAM, Philadelphia (2007). https://doi.org/10.1137/1.9780898718348
28. Quinlan, J.: Improved use of continuous attributes in C4.5. J. Artif. Intell. Res. **4**, 77–90 (1996). https://doi.org/10.1613/jair.279
29. Wemmert, C., Gancarski, P., Korczak, J.: A collaborative approach to combine multiple learning methods. Int. J. Artif. Intell. Tools, World Sci. **9**(1), 59–78 (2000). https://doi.org/10.1142/S0218213000000069
30. Strehl, A., Ghosh, J.: Cluster ensembles – a knowledge reuse framework for combining multiple partitions. J. Mach. Learn. Res. **3**, 583–617 (2002). https://doi.org/10.1162/153244303321897735
31. Ayad, H., Kamel, M.S.: Cumulative voting consensus method for partitions with variable number of clusters. IEEE Trans. Pattern Anal. Mach. Intell. **30**(1), 160–173 (2008). https://doi.org/10.1109/TPAMI.2007.1138
32. Nguyen, N., Caruana, R.: Consensus clusterings. In: International Conference on Data Mining, IEEE Computer Society, pp. 607–612 (2007). https://doi.org/10.1109/ICDM.2007.73
33. Pedrycz, W.: Collaborative and knowledge-based fuzzy clustering. Int. J. Innov. Comput. Inf. Control. **1**(3), 1–12 (2007)
34. Faceli, K., de Carvalho, A.C.P.L.F., de Souto, M.C.P.: Multi-objective clustering ensemble with prior knowledge. In: Sagot, M.-F., Walter, M.E.M.T. (eds.) BSB 2007. LNCS, vol. 4643, pp. 34–45. Springer, Heidelberg (2007). https://doi.org/10.1007/978-3-540-73731-5_4
35. Law, M.H., Topchy, A., Jain, A.K.: Multiobjective data clustering. In: IEEE Conference on Computer Vision and Pattern Recognition, vol. 2, pp. 424–430 (2004). https://doi.org/10.1109/CVPR.2004.1315194
36. Wagstaff, K., Cardie, C., Rogers, S., Schroedl, S.: Constrained k-means clustering with background knowledge. In: International Conference on Machine Learning, pp. 557–584 (2001)
37. Belarte, B., Wemmert, C., Forestier, G., Grizonnet, M., Weber, C.: Learning fuzzy rules to characterize objects of interest from remote sensing images. In: 2013 IEEE Geoscience and Remote Sensing Symposium (IGARSS), pp. 2986–2989 (2013). https://doi.org/10.1109/IGARSS.2013.6723453
38. Guo, H.X., Zhu, K.J., Gao, S.W., Liu, T.: An improved genetic k-means algorithm for optimal clustering. In: Conference on Data Mining Workshops, ICDM Workshops, pp. 793–797. IEEE (2006). https://doi.org/10.1109/ICDMW.2006.30
39. Grira, N., Crucianu, M., Boujemaa, N.: Active semi-supervised fuzzy clustering. Pattern Recognit. **41**(5), 1851–1861 (2008). https://doi.org/10.1016/j.patcog.2007.10.004
40. Bilenko, M., Basu, S., Mooney, R.J.: Integrating constraints and metric learning in semi-supervised clustering. In: Proceedings of the Twenty-First International Conference on Machine Learning, p. 11. ACM (2004). https://doi.org/10.1145/1015330.1015360
41. Gancarski, P., Cornueejols, A., Wemmert, C., Bennani, Y.: Clustering collaboratif: Principes et mise en oeuvre. In: Proceedings of BDA 2017, Nancy (2017)
42. Linoff, G.S.: Data Analysis Using SQL and Excel. Wiley, Hoboken (2015)
43. Ghodsi, A.: Dimensionality reduction a short tutorial, vol. 37, p. 38. University of Waterloo (2006)
44. McInnes, L., Healy, J.: UMAP: Uniform Manifold Approximation and Projection for Dimension Reduction. Preprint arXiv:1802.03426 (2018)

Specifying Security Requirements in Multi-agent Systems Using the Descartes-Agent Specification Language and AUML

Vinitha Hannah Subburaj[1]([⊠]) [iD] and Joseph E. Urban[2]

[1] School of Engineering, Computer Science and Mathematics,
West Texas A&M University, WTAMU Box 60767, Canyon, TX 79016, USA
vsubburaj@wtamu.edu
[2] Arizona State University, Tempe, AZ 85281, USA
urban@asu.edu

Abstract. Security has become an important concern with the development of large scale distributed and heterogeneous multi-agent systems (MAS). One of the main problems in addressing security during the development of MAS is that security is often an afterthought. The cost involved to patch existing systems against vulnerabilities and attacks after deployment is high. If developers and designers can spend some quality time investigating security aspects before beginning to code then this cost can be reduced significantly. Also, using formal methods to specify the complex behavior of large scale software systems has resulted in reliable software systems. This research effort was focused on using formal methods early in the development lifecycle to specify security requirements for MAS. New solutions are emerging to fix security related issues, but how much thought gets in during the early phases of development in terms of security needs to be answered. In this paper, analysis of security requirements for MAS, existing solutions to secure MAS, and the use of formal methods to specify security requirements has been studied. Descartes-Agent, a formal specification language for specifying agent systems has been taken into study to model the security requirements of MAS early on in the development process. Functional specifications of MAS are modelled along with the non-functional security requirements using the Descartes-Agent specification language. This paper also describes the extensions made to the Agent Unified Modeling Language (AUML) to represent the security requirements of MAS. The extensions proposed to AUML are in accordance with the extensions made to the Descartes-Agent specification language. A case study example is used to illustrate the specification of security requirements in MAS using the Descartes-Agent.

Keywords: Multi-agent systems · Security requirements · Formal methods · Descartes-agent

© Springer Nature Switzerland AG 2019
E. Ziemba (Ed.): AITM 2018/ISM 2018, LNBIP 346, pp. 93–111, 2019.
https://doi.org/10.1007/978-3-030-15154-6_6

1 Introduction

MAS are a set of software agents that work together to solve problems that are beyond the individual capacity of a single software agent. MAS are a comparably new software paradigm, which has been accepted widely in several application sectors that involve large and complex tasks. The autonomous, pro-active and dynamic problem solving characteristics of MAS have recently caught the attention of several application areas, such as: banking, transportation, e-business, and healthcare. In all these mentioned services, it is imperative that security must be assured. These services will face serious deployment issues if the security requirements are not being enforced. This approach is possible by considering the agent properties and the security aspects that relate with those specific properties.

The use of MAS in open, distributed, and heterogeneous applications, however may cause problems with security issues which in turn may affect the success of the various applications. Security in MAS is an advancing field in a well-established field of study, such as security in networks, P2P, and web services communication. Hence, this paper analyzes the basic security concepts required to be applied to security of MAS.

This paper includes a review of the past and present work related to the security issues of MAS. Also, the research effort has studied the existing security technologies used as solutions to address the security issues of MAS. Mobile agents, host security, agent communication, and delegation are some of the current security technologies that are used to address security issues [1, 2].

The need for systematic and secure system development has increased the use of formal methods. The following are some of the specific characteristics of using formal methods to specify secure software systems [3]:

- enable reasoning from logical/mathematical specifications of the behaviors of computing devices,
- offer accurate proofs, so that all system behaviors meet desirable properties,
- crucial for security goals,
- rule out a range of attacks,
- provide guidance for gapless construction, and
- always use models.

Implementing formal methods in various areas such as verification of hardware systems, embedded systems, analysis and testing of software has improved the quality of computer systems. There is a forecast that formal methods can bring similar improvement in the security of software systems. Formal methods have been associated with security applications for a while [4], thereby offering new techniques for security goals across a wider range of components. Without the implementation of formal methods, security will always remain weak. In this paper, one such formal method has been used to specify the security requirements of MAS.

Wing, in her paper, has stated that security always had played a vital role in the development of formal methods in the 70 s and early 80 s [5]. There are a few questions that might arise regarding formal methods. Has the scenario changed? Are the formal methods now ready to have a significant role in the production of more secure systems? The answer is yes, formal methods now have an important role in security systems. In this paper, limitations of formal methods and a summary of the results on how model checking and theorem proving tools were discussed. Also, the challenges and opportunities for formal methods in analyzing the security of systems, beyond the protocol level are also elaborated. Formal methods need integration with (1) other methods that address issues on formalization (analysis must include several factors such as risk, hazard, fault, and intrusion detection) and (2) into the entire software development lifecycle (such as during requirements analysis, testing, and simulation). Finally, there is a necessity to introduce human factors (cannot be ignored), which in principle is part of the system's environment. Research conducted on modeling of human behavior, human-computer interaction, and management of processes and organizations can all aggregate the formal nature of research on formal methods.

MAS design is a developing field with its roots still not established in industry due to the lack of a de facto standard. The Foundation of Intelligent Physical Agents (FIPA) and Object Management Group (OMG) work together to relate agent technology in industry with the de facto standards. AGENT UML [6, 8], an extension of the Unified Modeling Language (UML) was proposed to facilitate developers with an agent development process. AUML is a graphical modeling language standardized by FIPA [7] that uses agent-specific features to support agent development. In this paper, the security aspects associated with a multi-agent system has been specified using extensions made to AUML. Security requirements of agents along with their interactions have been captured effectively using AUML.

The remainder of this paper is structured as follows:

Section 2 discusses the existing work related to security issues in MAS, security solutions for MAS, and the use of formal specification to specify security requirements in MAS. Section 3 discusses the earlier extensions done to the Descartes specification language to specify agent systems. Section 4 discusses the security framework developed in this research effort to specify the security requirements of MAS using Descartes-Agent. Section 5 discusses the extensions made to the AUML interaction diagram to specify security requirements of MAS. Section 6 provides a case study example that illustrates the application of the developed security framework with an e-commerce application. Section 7 summarizes the paper with a brief discussion of future work.

2   Related Work

Jung et al. [9] surveyed existing research efforts that related to security in MAS, with a special focus on access control and trust/reputation. The paper concluded that security of agent based environments is critical. In spite of several efforts, many problems still remain and appear to be challenging with the continuous development of new technologies that are developed.

The research described in the research paper [10] identified the various security issues encountered by MAS. In order to assure MAS security, the paper examined the following: (1) basic concepts of security in computing, (2) characteristics of agents and MAS that introduce new threats, and (3) different strategies to prevent attacks. However, despite the similarities, security in MAS has specific requirements which need the autonomy, mobility, and other agent features that are not usually found in most conventional systems.

A model (based on the concepts and models regarding agent's role and communications) is presented [11] for securing MAS. The model provides an adequate way to ensure the security requirements and design are combined with system functionalities during the development process. The proposed model also incorporates the general security requirements at the agent and system levels. The paper has considered and addressed several system level threats, such as (1) corrupted mobile agents attack the main system host, (2) fake agent, (3) insecure communication among the platforms, and (4) agent level threats. The research work has attempted to extend the Gaia methodology with the security model. Further research work is needed in order to provide developers with security solutions for MAS based on the Gaia methodology.

A secure-critical system is difficult to develop and there are several known research issues regarding the security weaknesses in many sectors. Hence, a good methodology to support secure systems development is immediately needed. The research paper [12] presents the aim to assist the difficult task of developing security-critical systems using an approach of the Unified Modeling Language. The extension UMLsec of UML [12] (that allows expressing security relevant information within the diagrams) in a system specification is described in this paper. The UMLsec is defined in the form of a UML profile using the standard UML extension mechanisms. In particular, the related constraints provide criteria to classify the security aspects of a system design, by attributing to the formal semantics of a simplified fragment of UML. Formal evaluation is possible since the behavioral parts of UMLsec are considered with formal semantics. Hence, even the security experts who undertake a formal evaluation for certification purposes also may benefit from the possibility of using a specification language that may be more adaptable than some conventional formal methods.

Even though security has a major role in the development of MAS, security requirements are usually considered after the design of a system. The main reason is because of the fact that agent oriented software engineering methodologies have not unified security concerns throughout their developing stages. Mouratidis and Giorgini [13, 14] in their paper, introduce extensions to the Tropos methodology to enable them to model security concerns throughout the entire development process. This paper also describes the new concepts and modeling activities getting integrated to the current stages of Tropos. Tropos is characterized by the following three key aspects:

- deals with all the phases of system development, adopting a uniform and homogeneous way,
- attends to early requirements (emphasizing the need to understand organizational goals), and
- builds a model of a system that is refined and extended from a conceptual level to executable level, by a sequence of transformational steps.

The Tropos methodology includes five main software development stages, such as early and late requirements analysis, architectural design, detailed design, and Implementation. In order to extend Tropos with security related concepts, factors such as security concepts and security modeling activities are detailed in the paper. A real life case study from the health and social care sector is used to illustrate the approach using Single Assessment Process (eSAP) system.

MAS have become a promising architectural approach for constructing Internet-based applications. Recent research work in software architecture have resulted in the necessity to define languages for designing and formalizing agent architectures and more specifically secure ones. This paper describes the basic fundamentals for an architectural description language (ADL) to specify secure MAS. Mouratidis et al. [13, 14] in their paper introduce a set of system design primitives that is conceptualized with the Z specification language to build secure MAS architectures. The main concepts of SKwyRLADL, including the security aspects, are described in this paper. The Z specification language is used to describe SKwyRLADL concepts. Z is widely used as a formal specification language as it is clear, concise and easy to learn. The three sub-models of SKwyRLADL: agent model, security model, and architectural model are detailed in this paper. The concept is applied on an e-commerce example to illustrate the research effort. The illustration involves the description of formally specified architectural aspects, such as interfaces, knowledge bases, security objectives, security mechanisms, and plans of the e-Media system. Hussain et. al. [15] in their paper describe the formal specification of security properties using Z notation.

Oheimb and Mödersheim [16] in their paper introduces ASLan++, a specification language designed to specify web services, service-oriented architectures, and their security protocols. The paper also provided an example on how web services along with their securtity features can be specified using ASLan++. Hagalisletto and Haugsand [17] in their paper discuss a formal specification language called LS, for specifying security properties. Modal logic operators were used to specify the security properties. The framework developed was applied to a variety of agents and security properties such as trust, confidentiality, trustworthiness, non-repudiation and authenticity were specified.

3 Background

The Descartes specification language, developed by Urban [18] was designed to be used throughout the software life cycle. The relationship between the input and the output of a system is functionally specified when using this specification language. Descartes defines the input data and output data and then relates them in such a way that output data becomes a function of input data. The data structuring methods used with this language are known as Hoare trees. These Hoare trees use three structuring methods namely direct product, discriminated union, and sequence.

Direct product provides for the concatenation of sets of elements. Discriminated union provides for the selection of one element out of a set of elements. A plus sign (+) is used to denote discriminated union. Sequence represents zero or more repetitions of a set of elements. Sequence is indicated by an asterisk (*) suffixed to the node name.

By definition of Hoare trees, a sequence node is followed by a sub node. A single node can accommodate a sequence of direct product or a sequence of discriminated union. In the Descartes specification language, a literal is any string that is enclosed within single quotes. Consider the following example,

agent 'autonomous_agent' wherein autonomous_agent is a literal.

The Descartes specification language was extended in 2013 by Subburaj [19] for specifying complex agent systems. The extensions made to the Descartes specification language follows a top-down modular development allowing for the decomposition and incremental development of large agent systems. Six new concepts were added to Descartes for specifying and validating agent software systems. The added concepts were: (1) agent construct; (2) agent goal; (3) agent attributes; (4) agent roles; (5) agent plans; and (6) communication protocol.

Agent systems consist of multiple autonomous agents. Each of the agents has a specific goal to achieve and a set of actions to perform in order to achieve a goal. The agent construct in an agent system is used to define the behavior of an agent, including the goal, different roles, type of events, the plans, and the knowledge base. Each agent in an agent system has a structure. The notion of declaring an agent can be compared to the identification of objects in an object oriented methodology. The declaration of an agent module is pre-pended with a unary "agent" reserved word. Consider the following example,

agent AGENT_MODLUE_NAME_(INPUT)

Every agent has a goal of achieving a certain state or task. For example, imagine an agent that would start running with a goal of cleaning a house. The initial goal of such an agent is to clean the house and perform actions accordingly to achieve the goal statement. In Descartes-Agent, the agent goal is specified by using a new primitive, "goal", added to the Descartes syntax. An agent goal is an important attribute to be specified in an agent system. The plans that are executed by an agent solely depend upon the goal defined for a specific agent.

The agent roles are used to identify the key roles in an agent system. The notion and description of role models has been adopted from the Gaia methodology [20].

One of the most important aspects of agents is that they act autonomously to achieve their goals. This characteristic of agents to act autonomously in an environment is realized through the plans part in an agent system. The plans consist of a sequence of actions that an agent will take when a corresponding event occurs. The first part of the plan specified the list of events that trigger the execution of a specific plan by the agent.

The second part context describes the contexts when the plan is applicable. The context part is used to specify the current beliefs of the agent system. This part consists of a set of rules that can be specified with respect to specific agents. The context part also communicates with the knowledge/belief component in the agent framework to update and read agent specific rules. The next extension is the reserved keyword "plans" used to specify the agent plans. The keyword triggered_events is used to list the triggered events. The keyword context is used to specify the agent specific rules and belief. The keyword method is used to specify the list of actions to be taken. In order to specify the context of the plan, new logical primitives were added to Descartes-Agent.

The knowledge/belief base in an agent system contains the knowledge that the agent has about itself and its environment. An agent's plan reads and modifies the knowledge/belief base. The knowledge/belief base consists of logical rules that are known initially before the agent starts to execute the plans. Also, based upon the execution of plans by the agents in the agent systems, the knowledge/belief base gets updated according to a current belief. In the Descartes-Agent processor, the knowledge/belief base was implemented as a separate component. The processor before executing the agent plans and also after executing the agent plans will access the knowledge/belief component to take appropriate decisions.

The last extension to Descartes-Agent for specifying agent systems is the communication protocol. Agents interact with other agents in the agent system and also with the environment to realize agent goals. The communication protocol in the extended Descartes is set up by the name tag (in upper case letters) of the calling agent module within parentheses followed by a period and the name of the relevant message within parentheses followed by the "^" symbol and then the name tag (in upper case letters) of the called agent module within parentheses.

4 Specifying Security Requirements Using the Descartes-Agent

4.1 MAS Properties

Wooldridge and Jennings [4] software agents come with the following properties:

- "Autonomy: An agent has its own goal and the ability to operate without any human intervention; more importantly, agent has control over its own state and can regulate its own functioning without outside assistance.
- Sociability: An agent is capable of interacting with other agents and humans using an agent communication language. This approach allows an agent to seek and provide services.
- Reactivity: An agent is capable of perceiving and acting on its close environment. The agent can respond to changes that occur in its surroundings.
- Pro-activeness: Agents are not only capable of responding to the stimulus from their surroundings, but are also capable of exhibiting a goal-oriented behavior by taking initiatives."

In addition, there are some other characteristics, such as situadeness, mobility, rationality, veracity, and benevolence. Situadeness means agents are capable of sensing a special condition based on the inputs received from the environment.

The term software agents covers a wide range of more specific agent types [21]. Etzioni and Weld [22] and Franklin and Graesser [23] provide a list of attributes that each agent must possess to a lesser or greater degree. The software agent attributes are as follows:

- "Reactivity: the ability to selectively sense and act.
- Autonomy: goal-directedness, proactive and self-starting behavior.
- Collaborative behavior: can work in concert with other agents to achieve a common goal.
- Communication ability: the ability to communicate with persons and other agents with language more resembling humanlike "speech acts" than typical symbol-level program-to-program protocols.
- Inferential capability: can act on abstract task specification using prior knowledge of general goals and preferred methods to achieve flexibility.
- Temporal continuity: persistence of identity and state over long periods of time.
- Personality: the capability of manifesting the attributes of a "believable" character such as emotion.
- Adaptivity: being able to learn and improve with experience.
- Mobility: being able to migrate in a self-directed way from one host platform to another."

4.2 Security Requirements in MAS

The autonomous, pro-active, and dynamic nature of software agents thought proven to solve challenging problems, also comes with security concerns. Often, these security aspects get unnoticed until the deployment of the end-deliverables. Patching the security flaws after deployment has always resulted in high costs.

From the above properties, it is evident that software agents operate in an open environment and are free to interact with their surroundings to achieve their goal. This openness gives rise to a number of security and trust issues. Some of the commonly occurring security problems with agent based systems [9] are: confidentiality, integrity, availability, accountability, and non-repudiation.

Based on agent characteristics, there [9, 14] have been presented a list of security requirements of the MAS. Table 1 associates agent characteristics with their associated security problems.

Table 1. Agent properties and associated security concerns

Agent property	Description	Security concerns
Situatedness	If the agent gets to sense the input from its local host, then problems are less. But, instead if the information is coming from the Internet then there comes the problem of trust	Trust, authentication, and integrity
Autonomy	Malicious agents can intrude without any request from humans or other agents	Authorization
Social ability	Enabling secure communications among agents and between humans and agents	Confidentiality, integrity, availability, accountability, and non-repudiation
Mobility	By being able to self-migrate from one platform to other platforms, agents are prone to a number of security attacks	Authentication, confidentiality, integrity, privacy, and faulty tolerance Damage, DoS, breach of privacy or theft, harassment, social engineering, event-triggered attack, compound attacks, masquerading, unauthorized access, copy-and-reply, and repudiation
Cooperation	Many agents cooperatively working together to access resources and internal status of other agents. This leads to security concerns	Authentication and authorization

4.3   Descartes-Agent Security Specifications

Among the list of security concerns listed above, in this paper we focus on two concerns namely: access control and confidentiality.

To provide access control there are two steps involved: first is to provide authentication to a group of agents enabling them to establish their true identity and then authorization that allows us to define the type of access privileges each agent obtains.

Every agent has a goal of achieving a certain state or task. In the secure agent framework specified by using the primitive, "goal" being prepended by a "!" symbol. With the specification of the secure agents, the goal is enclosed within a * symbol denoting the goal of secure agents.

Figures 1 and 3 illustrate the Descartes-Agent framework for specifying MAS and the Descartes-Agent secure framework for specifying MAS.

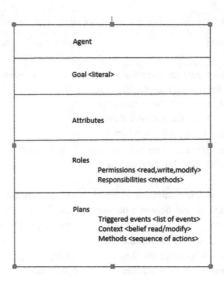

Fig. 1. The Descartes-Agent framework for MAS

A. Formally specifying authentication requirements for software agents

The authentication block in the security framework specified in Fig. 3, is decomposed as user authentication and resource authentication. Within the user

```
agent TRANSACTION_AGENT
    goal
            *! To successfully complete a secure transaction *
    user1
            public+
                true
                false
            users
                files
                    'list of files that can accessed'
                servers
                    'list of servers that user1 can talk to'
            protected
                password
                alphanumericstring
    resource1
            public+
                true
                false
            resources
                users
                    'list of users that can this resource'
            protected
                password
                alphanumericstring
```

Fig. 2. Authentication example using secure Descartes-Agent

authentication, the node named public is a discriminated union meaning the public attribute can either be true or false. Resources in a secure agent system define the different types of resources that the secure agent can access. The protected attribute defines the method of authentication used by that user. There can be unique credentials such as passwords, encrypted passwords, and public-key-infrastructure schemes. The resource block is the same as the user except that there is a list of users that are given permission to access particular resources. Figure 2 illustrates the authentication requirement using Descartes-Agent specifications.

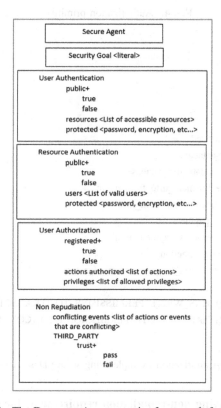

Fig. 3. The Descartes-Agent security framework for MAS

B. Formally specifying authorization requirements for software agents

The user authorization block specified in the secure agent framework consists of three parts: registered, actions authorized, and privileges. The first part of the user authorization block specifies whether the user is a registered user or not. The second part of the authorization block allows one to specify all the actions that an authorized user can perform. The third part allows for the specification of all the privileges or access rights to specific resources. In order to specify the access privileges of users, new logical primitives were added to Descartes-Agent. The example given in Fig. 5 illustrates the specification of an authorization requirement using Descartes-Agent specifications. Figure 4 lists the newly added authorization primitives.

(<userx>)_HAS_READ_PERMISSIONS_TO_(<resourcex>) – user X has read permission to access a specific resource

(<userx>)_HAS_WRITE_PERMISSIONS_TO_(<resourcex>) – user X has write permission with a specific resource

(<userx>)_HAS_APPEND_PERMISSIONS_TO_(<resourcex>) – user X has append permission with a specific resource

(<userx>)_HAS_EXECUTE_PERMISSIONS_TO_(<resourcex>) – user X has execute permission with a specific resource

Fig. 4. Authorization primitives

```
user2
        registered+
            true
            false
        actions_authorized
            update_database
                    'update_the_database'
            receive_payment_info_from_agent
                    'receive_payment_info'
            process_payment
                    'process_payment_info'
            confirm_transaction
                    'confirm_the_completion_of_a_transaction'
    privileges
            (USER2)_HAS_WRITE_PERMISSIONS_TO_(TRASACTION_RECORD)
            (USER2)_HAS_EXECUTE_PERMISSIONS_TO_(COMMIT_QUERY)
```

Fig. 5. Authorization example using secure Descartes-Agent

C. Formally specifying non-repudiation requirements for software agents

In multi-agent systems, non-repudiation service generates evidence that proves the action that took place between two agents are valid and irrefutable. The non-repudiation can be implemented using two approaches. The first approach uses a trusted third party t to resolve conflicts and to prove the origin and destination of messages. The second approach enforces non-repudiation without the involvements of a thirst party trusted agent and denoted as weak-repudiation [17]. The non-repudiation block in the security framework specified in the Fig. 6, consists of two parts: conflicting action or conflicting event and trusted third party. The conflicting action or evidence that needs to be resolved gets specified under the first part and the third part being used to justify and provide irrefutable evidence regarding the claim gets specified in the second part. In the following example, the conflicting event is the message transfer between the agents SENDER and RECEIVER. The conflicting action is specified in the first part and then the trust node is used to justify if the message was actually sent by the SENDER and then RECEIVER received the message that was sent. Descartes specification Hoare tree consists of two types of nodes namely the reference nodes and the match nodes. A match node acquires a value through matching and must appear in lower-case letters. A reference node acquires a value from a previously matched node or from a parameter or a module call and must appear in upper-case letters. In the following example, trust is a match node that appears in the analysis tree that will either take a value of pass or fail. Depending on the repudiation of the event or action specified, the trust node can be used to prove or dispute the claimed event.

This basic communication protocol gets used most often in networking and the extensions made to Descartes-Agent can be used to specify such security protocols.

```
agent SENDER
   goal
         *! To successfully transmit message to receiver*
   conflicting_events
            send_message_to_receiver
                  'send_message_to_receiver'
   third_party
            trust+
                  pass
                  fail


agent RECIEVER
   goal
         *! To successfully receive message from sender*
   conflicting_events
            receive_message_from_sender
                  'recieve_message_from_sender'
   third_party
            trust+
                  pass
                  fail
```

Fig. 6. Non-repudiation example using secure Descartes-Agent

5 AUML Security Specifications

Agent UML (AUML) a framework proposed by Bauer [6] is used to model agent and agent interactions in multi-agent system design. AUML is a graphical modeling language standardized by FIPA that uses agent-specific features to support agent development. In our previous research effort, the extensions made to the Descartes specification language to specify multi-agent systems has been specified using AUML [24]. To accommodate the requirements of an agent system, AUML standard evolved as a cooperative effort between the Foundation of Intelligent Physical Agents (FIPA) and the Object Management Group (OMG). This section describe the extensions made to AUML to support the specifications of security requirements in MAS. Previous work that was done in the area of AUML [6–8, 25] has been taken into study to propose the extensions.

In this paper, AUML interaction protocols have been taken into study and have been extended to specify security requirements.

 is a symbol used in the interaction diagram that specifies user/agent/object with security constraints.

With AUML interaction diagrams, an interation constraint is used to denote constaints used in the interactions. There are different kinds of intration operator used with UML 2.4, such as alt, opt, loop, and break. In this research effort, a new security constraint is proposed with a secure keyword. The interation operator secure defines the security policies asscoiated amongst the multi-agents taking part in that interation. The notion used to denote this secure fragment is given above.

The list of secure actions, privileges granted, accessible resources, authenticated users, protection algorithms, etc... can be specified within this secure fragment. When agent interaction gets specified using the AUML interaction diagrams, these secure constraints will prevail as long as the agents' interaction exists. This approach ensures that security is enforced all the time when agents are communicating with each other and with the external environment.

Figure 7 gives a simple example incorporating the security extentions proposed with AUML in this research effort. The key symbol next to actors and objects denote that these have security constraints attached to them. The security fragment attached with these actors/agents/objects list all the security constraints that they have to abide by to take part in the interation. The admin is a user who is authorized to peroform read/write operations on DB1 and also has rights to interact with the transaction agent. The list of accessible resoucres by this user is also specified in the interation diagram.

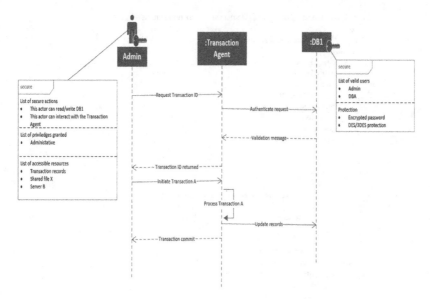

Fig. 7. AUML interation diagram with security extensions

DB1 also has a secure fragment listing the authenticated users who can have access along with the protection scehmes enforced. The proposed model can be extended to add more security policies and protocols in the future.

6 Case Study Example

MAS are used to provide efficient e-commerce solutions, but different security related issues are associated with the agent solutions of e-commerce applications. A case study example of a real time MAS for e-commerce applications [26] is described for illustrating the security framework introduced in this research effort. The real time multi-agent architecture for an e-commerce application consists of four agents namely: UserAgent, QuotingAgent, TrendWatchingAgent, and BuySellAgent.

The main goal of the USER_AGENT is to determine the user requirements, such as the risk level, amount of money to spend, and the market sector preferences. The USER_AGENT specifies the quality threshold to ensure if the actual stock price lies within the threshold value [27]. Security requirements associated with this user agent requires authentication, authorization, and confidentiality.

The following Descartes-Agent specification adds the security requirements to the USER_AGENT. Figure 8 illustrates the specification of the USER_AGENT that includes authentication, confidentially, and non-repudiation security requirements.

```
agent   USER_AGENT_(RISK_LEVEL)_AND_(AMT)_AND_(PREFERENCE)
    goal
            "!to_determine_user_requirements_securly"
    attributes
            RISK_LEVEL
                INTEGER
            AMT
                FLOATING_POINT
            PREFERENCE
                STRING
    user_authentication
            public+
                true
                false
            resources
                files
                    'list_of_files_that_can_be_accessed_by_user_agent'
                servers
                    'list_of_servers_that_can_be_accessed_by_user_agent'
                protected
                    password
                        alphanumericstring
    user_confidentiality
            registered+
                true
                false
            actions_authorized
                check_stock_price
                    'check_stock_price'
                check_risk_level
                    'check_risk_level'
                decide_on_stock
                    'make_decision_based_on_price_value'
                confirm_transaction
                    'confirm_the_completion_of_a_transaction'
            privileges
                (USER_AGENT)_HAS_READ_PERMISSIONS_TO_(USER_PROFILE)
                (USER_AGENT)_HAS_WRITE_PERMISSIONS_TO_(RISK_RECORD)
                (USER_AGENT)_HAS_EXECUTE_PERMISSIONS_TO_(THRESHOLD_QUERY)
    conflicting_events
            message_from_quoting_agent
                'recieve_message_from_quoting_agent'
    third_party
            trust+
                pass
                fail
return
        GOAL
        USER_AUTHENTICATION
        'with'
        RESOURCES
            FILES
            SERVERS
            PROTECTED
            'with'
            PASSWORD
        USER_CONFIDENTIALITY
            REGISTERED
            ACTIONS_AUTHORIZED
        CONFLICTING_EVENTS
        THIRD_PARTY
```

Fig. 8. Case study example using secure Descartes-Agent

7 Discussion of Research Findings, Conclusion, and Future Work

A security framework that allows developers to formally specify the security requirements of MAS has been discussed in this paper. The security framework has been built as a part of the Descartes-Agent formal specification language. The key point on the developed security framework is that it can be applied early on in the development process of MAS. The identification of these security requirements early during the development of agent systems reduces the security patching cost involved with MAS development. One of the main benefits of using Descartes-Agent is that it allows partial specifications to be developed and executed. This feature allows for specifying security requirements with a high-level of abstraction.

Three important security issues with MAS, namely authentication, authorization, and confidentiality, and non-repudiation were taken into study. The security framework built in this research effort allows for the specifications of security requirements that would implement these security solutions in MAS. The challenging aspect of incorporating a formal executable specification language to specify security requirements for MAS has been accomplished in this research effort. From the extended Descartes-Agent specifications, the security requirements were also represented using AUML interaction diagrams. The simplistic nature of AUML interaction diagram constructs were used and extended to specify the security constraints of the MAS. The extensions proposed to an AUML interaction diagram can be used as a model to specify security aspects of MAS in other design diagrams, such as class diagram, activity diagram, state chart diagram, and communication diagram. A case study example has also been discussed to illustrate the use of the security framework built in this research effort. The case study discussed in this paper serves as a basis for formally specifying security requirements for MAS and can be applied to different applications in similar fields.

As future work, the security framework developed will be extended to provide solutions to other security issues, such as integrity, availability, and accountability. Extending the security framework to enforce security with distributed MAS will be a future challenging effort.

References

1. Borselius, N.: Mobile agent security. Electron. Commun. Eng. J. **14**(5), 211–218 (2002). https://doi.org/10.1049/ecej:20020504
2. Borselius, N. Security in multi-agent systems. In: Proceedings of the 2002 International Conference on Security and Management (SAM'02), pp. 31–36 (2002)
3. Chong, S., et al.: Report on the NSF Workshop on Formal Methods for Security. arXiv preprint arXiv:1608.00678 (2016)
4. Wooldridge, M., Jennings, N.R. (eds.) Intelligent agents: Theories, Architectures and Languages, Lecture Notes in Artificial Intelligence, vol. 890 (1995), ISBN 3-540-58855-8. https://doi.org/10.1007/bfb0013568

5. Wing, J.M.: A symbiotic relationship between formal methods and security. In: Proceedings of Computer Security, Dependability and Assurance: From Needs to Solutions, pp. 26–38 (1998). https://doi.org/10.1109/csda.1998.798355
6. Bauer, B., Müller, J.P., Odell, J.: Agent UML: a formalism for specifying multiagent software systems. Int. J. Softw. Eng. Knowl. Eng. **11**(03), 207–230 (2001). https://doi.org/10.1007/3-540-44564-1_6
7. FIPA Agent UML Web Site. http://www.fipa.org/activities/modeling.html
8. Huget, M.-P., Odell, J.: Representing agent interaction protocols with agent UML. In: Odell, J., Giorgini, P., Müller, Jörg P. (eds.) AOSE 2004. LNCS, vol. 3382, pp. 16–30. Springer, Heidelberg (2005). https://doi.org/10.1007/978-3-540-30578-1_2
9. Jung, Y., Kim, M., Masoumzadeh, A., Joshi, J.B.: A survey of security issue in multi-agent systems. Artif. Intell. Rev. **37**(3), 239–260 (2012). https://doi.org/10.1007/s10462-011-9228-8
10. Cavalcante, R.C., Bittencourt, I.I., da Silva, A.P., Silva, M., Costa, E., Santos, R.: A survey of security in multi-agent systems. Expert Syst. Appl. **39**(5), 4835–4846 (2012). https://doi.org/10.1016/j.eswa.2011.09.130
11. Hedin, Y., Moradian, E.: Security in multi-agent systems. Procedia Comput. Sci. **60**, 1604–1612 (2015). https://doi.org/10.1016/j.procs.2015.08.270
12. Jürjens, J.: UMLsec: extending UML for secure systems development. In: Jézéquel, J.-M., Hussmann, H., Cook, S. (eds.) UML 2002. LNCS, vol. 2460, pp. 412–425. Springer, Heidelberg (2002). https://doi.org/10.1007/3-540-45800-X_32
13. Mouratidis, H., Giorgini, P., Manson, G.: Modelling secure multiagent systems. In: Proceedings of the Second International Joint Conference on Autonomous Agents and Multiagent Systems, pp. 859–866 (2003). https://doi.org/10.1145/860710.860713
14. Mouratidis, H., Giorgini, P.: Secure Tropos: a security-oriented extension of the tropos methodology. Int. J. Softw. Eng. Knowl. Eng. **17**(02), 285–309 (2007). https://doi.org/10.1142/s0218194007003240
15. Hussain, S., Dunne, P., Rasool, G.: Formal specification of security properties using Z notation. Res. J. Appl. Sci. Eng. Technol. **5**(19), 4664–4670 (2013)
16. von Oheimb, D., Mödersheim, S.: ASLan++—a formal security specification language for distributed systems. In: Aichernig, Bernhard K., de Boer, Frank S., Bonsangue, Marcello M. (eds.) FMCO 2010. LNCS, vol. 6957, pp. 1–22. Springer, Heidelberg (2011). https://doi.org/10.1007/978-3-642-25271-6_1
17. Hagalisletto, A.M., Haugsand, J.: A formal language for specifying security properties. In: Proceedings for the Workshop on Specification and Automated Processing of Security Requirements – SAPS 2004. Austrian Computer Society (2004)
18. Urban, J.E.: A specification language and its processor. Ph.D. dissertation. Computer Science Department. University of Southwestern Louisiana (1977)
19. Subburaj, V.H., Urban, J.E.: A formal specification language for modeling agent systems. In: 2013 Second International Conference on Informatics and Applications (ICIA), pp. 300–305. IEEE (2013). https://doi.org/10.1109/icoia.2013.6650273
20. Cernuzzi, L., Juan, T., Sterling, L., Zambonelli, F.: The Gaia methodology: basic concepts and extensions. Multiagent Syst. Artif. Soc. Simulated Organ. **11**(2), 69–88 (2004). https://doi.org/10.1007/1-4020-8058-1_6
21. Żytniewski, M., Sołtysik, A., Sołtysik-Piorunkiewicz, A., Kopka, B.: Modelling of software agents in knowledge-based organisations. Analysis of proposed research tools. In: Ziemba, E. (ed.) Information Technology for Management. LNBIP, vol. 243, pp. 91–108. Springer, Cham (2016). https://doi.org/10.1007/978-3-319-30528-8_6
22. Etzioni, O., Weld, D.S.: Intelligent agents on the internet: fact, fiction, and forecast. IEEE Intell. Syst. **4**, 44–49 (1995). https://doi.org/10.1109/64.403956

23. Franklin, S., Graesser, A.: Is it an agent, or just a program?: A taxonomy for autonomous agents. In: Müller, J.P., Wooldridge, M.J., Jennings, N.R. (eds.) ATAL 1996. LNCS, vol. 1193, pp. 21–35. Springer, Heidelberg (1997). https://doi.org/10.1007/BFb0013570

24. Subburaj, V.H., Urban, J.: Intelligent agent software development using AUML and the Descartes specification language. In 2011 14th IEEE International Symposium on Object/Component/Service-Oriented Real-Time Distributed Computing Workshops, pp. 297–305 (2011). https://doi.org/10.1109/isorcw.2011.43

25. Kahloul, L., Barkaoui, K., Sahnoun, Z.: Using AUML to derive formal modeling agents interactions. In: The 3rd ACS/IEEE International Conference on Computer Systems and Applications, p. 109. IEEE (2005). https://doi.org/10.1109/aiccsa.2005.1387098

26. DiPippo, L.C., Fay-Wolfe, V., Nair, L., Hodys, E., Uvarov, O.: A real-time multi-agent system architecture for e-commerce applications. In: Proceedings of the 5th International Symposium Autonomous Decentralized Systems, pp. 357–364. IEEE (2001). https://doi.org/10.21236/ada477877

27. Subburaj, V.H., Urban, J.E.: Formal specification language and agent applications. In: Kołodziej, J., Correia, L., Molina, J.M. (eds.) Intelligent Agents in Data-intensive Computing. SBD, vol. 14, pp. 99–122. Springer, Cham (2016). https://doi.org/10.1007/978-3-319-23742-8_5

Information Technology and Systems for Business Transformation

An Adaptive Algorithm for Geofencing

Vincenza Carchiolo[1]([✉])(iD), Mark Phillip Loria[2], Michele Malgeri[3](iD),
Paolo Walter Modica[2], and Marco Toja[2]

[1] Dip. Matematica e Informatica, Universitá di Catania, Catania, Italy
`vincenza.carchiolo@unict.it`
[2] See Your Box, 2 Cormont Road, London SE5 9RA, England, UK
`{mloria,pmodica,mtoja}@seeyourbox.com`
[3] Dip. Ingegneria Elettrica Elettronica e Informatica, Universitá di Catania,
Catania, Italy
`michele.malgeri@unict.it`

Abstract. Location based services play a key role in creating fully automated and adaptive systems that support Supply Chain Management and complex inter-modal logistics. IoT technology allows companies to part from statistical analysis in favour of proactive management by leveraging data collected in real time from the goods and processes that sustain their business. This paper describes a real world implementation of proactive location-based services suitable for application scenarios with strong time constraints, such as real-time systems, called Proactive Fast and Low Resource Geofencing Algorithm within a centralized, thin-client IoT system.

Keywords: IIoT · Geofencing · Algorithm · Supply chain

1 Introduction

Nowadays, Location Based Services (*LBS*) are *crucial for many businesses* [1], as well as for government organizations, as they play an important role in decision-making processes, company activities and in any control and policy system in modern computer organizations.

Most applications exploiting LBSs are based on the idea of presenting location-specific information when the user asks for it. A relatively small amount of new applications act *proactively*, delivering information directly to the end user without he/she asks for it explicitly.

The most discussed and requested proactive LBS nowadays is *Geofencing*, which allows to determine the topological relation between a moving object and a set of delimited geographical areas, enabling to detect and monitor when a mobile device *enters*, *leaves*, *crosses* or *bypasses* a precise geographical area delimited by a virtual perimeter, called geofence [2,3], then alerting the user via geo-notifications. A geofence can be dynamically generated, like a circular area surrounding the current position of a mobile device or can be made of

© Springer Nature Switzerland AG 2019
E. Ziemba (Ed.): AITM 2018/ISM 2018, LNBIP 346, pp. 115–135, 2019.
https://doi.org/10.1007/978-3-030-15154-6_7

a predefined set of boundaries, which may be arbitrarily drawn by the user or specific for a place or a building. Geofencing services can be classified, depending on the geographical references used to check device's position, in [4] static that check the geographical position of a mobile device in respect to a fixed area, dynamic that operates according to the position of a mobile device in respect to a changing area and peer-to-peer that use the geographical position of a mobile device with respect to other mobile devices.

This paper introduces a framework for geofencing-based services, which exploits a novel geofencing algorithm well suited for proactive applications using a smart approach to manage performance. The algorithm, called Proactive Fast and Low Resource Geofencing Algorithm (PFLGA), represents an innovative solution for implementing proactive LBSs suitable for application scenarios with limited resources and strong time constraints, such as IIoT-based real-time monitoring systems for Supply Chain Management. This paper highlights the main features of PFLGA and of the framework, which have both been utilized to implement a geofencing service used by See Your Box, an IT company offering Business-to-Business services which allow early detection of logistic issues happening in Supply Chain Management across several industry verticals.

PFLGA proposes a centralized, thin-client solution to the geofencing problem, exploiting a compact, self-explanatory data format and tree-based index structures for the representation, collection and indexing of geospatial geometric shapes. These features allow the proposed solution to face two classic challenges of Geofencing: reducing the energy consumption of the mobile device and allowing the matching process within the centralized solution to scale [5].

Several algorithms have been proposed in technical literature for the implementation of geofencing functionality. The paper compares PFLGA [6] with *Parallel Spatio-temporal TOpological joiN*(PISTON) [7], *Scan-Line Algorithm and Grid Compression (SLGC-1)* [8] and *Geofencing via Hybrid Hashing* [9].

PFLGA is designed to detect the occurrence of both complex topological events, such as the entering, leaving, or crossing of a geofence, or simply the presence of a device inside an area, depending on the available geographical information about the device in exam, which varies both in quantity and accuracy of the measurements and on the detail level requested for the analysis. The algorithm returns the result of this test in a few hundred milliseconds.

Section 2 presents some Geofencing algorithms and a comparison with PFLGA. Section 3 introduces the application scenario and deeply discusses the requirement of a geofencing solution for a Supply Chain Management (SCM) system. Section 4 deeply discusses PFLGA and one of its possible implementations and provides a comparison between the algorithm mentioned above and those existing geofencing designs which better fit with the service requirements of the considered application scenario. Section 5 provides an overview of the results that have been obtained in two different real world applications. Finally, conclusions and ideas for future developments are discussed in Sect. 6.

2   Related Work

The application scenario of the geofencing service proposed in this paper is that of IoT-based industrial services supporting SCM and logistics for remote monitoring of goods and assets using mobile devices, smart cards, tags or similar technologies. This kind of services are placed in the context of Industry 4.0. In particular, the application scenario presented in this paper is a system using uniquely identifiable mobile objects, henceforth called *trackers*, which transmit real-time location data with a configurable frequency, which may change over time. The system is centralized and thin-client, meaning that the trackers have limited resources and processing capabilities, in order to save battery power to provide a long-lasting monitoring service.

The geofencing-based services that run within the system are powered by a custom developed algorithm. Its functionality and performance are compared with other geospatial analysis algorithms which resolve similar geofencing problems. These algorithms are compared based on the set of features requested by the application scenario the proposed solution has been developed for.

The Hybrid Hashing adopts a very efficient filtering strategy, based on the use of two in-memory hash tables, to reduce the time spent for the point-in-polygon test. Moreover, it builds or updates the in-memory hash tables for the geofences during system spare time, shifting some computation from the "point-in-polygon test" stage (which is often time critical) to non-time-critical processing stage. This algorithm shows a low response time. The main drawbacks are the high storage requirements, the time required for the construction and update of index and data structures for the geofences. Finally, Hybrid Hashing is not able to return trajectory-based spatio-temporal topological join predicates.

SLGC-1 algorithm uses QuadTree compression algorithm to store data regarding geofences, which reduces the amount of memory requested for the index structure, the complexity of the storage is less than $O(n)$ and the approach to geofencing is a simple and straightforward point-in-polygon based solution. Lastly the point-in-polygon test time does not increase with the number of edges of the analyzed geofence. As the previous algorithm, SLGC-1 is not able to return spatio-temporal topological join predicates, so the geospatial analysis is not deep.

PISTON adopts a parallel in-memory indexing for trajectories and spatial geofences, which is a very scalable approach. Moreover, it evaluates the spatio-temporal topological join predicates with a sequence of topological relations that may hold between the trajectory of the moving object and the geofences at different time units. The trajectory index IR is optimized for high rate of location updates and can handle both coordinate-based and trajectory-based queries. PISTON adopts an efficient trajectory-filtering strategy and it is scalable due to its native multi-threaded setup. Main problems deal with the time required for the construction and update of the R-Tree index for the geofences, which is high, and the high memory requirements.

PFLGA adopts an in-memory, tree-based indexing for the spatial polygons representing the geofences of interest. The time required for the construction and update of the in-memory index for the geofences is low. Moreover, it adopts an efficient trajectory-filtering strategy which checks for intersections between the MBR of the analyzed trajectory and the MBRs inside the in-memory index and can return the trajectory-based spatio-temporal topological join predicates describing the relation between the moving object and each area in the set of geofences. Lastly, the algorithm can also evaluate the simple point-in-polygon test for the current position of the moving object if a simple geospatial analysis is required. The main drawback is the response time of the trajectory-based topological join query, which is not the shortest among all.

Table 1 shows the comparison among the following features: In-Memory Spatial Index (IMSP), Spatio-Temporal Topological Join Predicates (STTJP), Use of Trajectory-Filtering/Filtering Strategy (TFFS), Geofencing via evaluation of Point-In-Polygon (PIP), Geofencing via evaluation of spatial intersection with trajectory SEGmentS (SEGS), Geofencing via evaluation of spatial intersection with complex TRAJectories (TRAJ).

Table 1. Comparison of features

	IMSP	STTJP	TFFS	PIP	SEGS	TRAJ
Hybrid Hashing	Yes	Yes	Yes	Yes	-	-
SLGC-1	Yes	-	Yes	Yes	-	-
PISTON	Yes	Yes	Yes	-	Yes	Yes
PFLGA	Yes	Yes	Yes	Yes	Yes	Yes

3   Application Scenario

3.1   Geofencing and Supply Chain

This section focuses on the application of geofencing algorithms in services related to SCM, which involve the movement and storage of raw materials and unfinished products from the point of origin to the point of destination and/or consumption. SCM was traditionally driven by Enterprise Resource Planning systems, which provided plans and estimation regarding the different aspects of the business activity. In recent times, a quiet revolution has been taking place thanks to the use of Location-based technologies and innovative solutions to track and trace transportation equipment, materials and drivers across all the steps of the supply chain [10]. LBSs allow the enterprise to dynamically tender and dispatch shipments in real time, divert a route because of weather conditions or a severe accident that is causing major delays in the transportation route, or transmit notification messages to the stakeholders whenever a shipment arrives at a warehouse [10] making the whole process more efficient and less expensive.

For all these reasons, LBS can be considered a disruptive technology for the supply chain that will bring great opportunity for logistics innovation. The evolution in mobile telecommunication technology, together with the advances in electronics and the introduction of the IoT paradigm, has enabled the networking of portable wireless devices and wearable computers that can provide new types of usable knowledge to all the members and stakeholders of a globally dispersed supply chain [11].

These devices, equipped with sensors and actuators, exploit their connection capability to transmit to the Service Provider's servers, in a Machine-to-Machine communication, all the data regarding the status of the shipment which are important for the service to function. The installation of M2M nodes in pallets, containers, vehicles and warehouses, along with new types of inference algorithms and techniques, will enable seamless, efficient, and transparent movement of raw materials and products through the global supply chain [11], allowing the business's customers to look at all the critical points of the chain. Therefore, M2M communication, together with geofencing, map-matching and localization services, represent the enabling technologies for developing and deploying a location-based service.

3.2   Geofencing Challenges

Developing a Location-Based Service, founded on M2M Communication, to support the SCM raises several technical challenges, the most important of which are: geographical diversity and telecommunication coverage, location awareness, response time, accuracy of the result, power conservation, security and privacy.

Geographical Diversity and Telecommunication Coverage: along their trip, from the moment goods are packaged for shipping to the moment they arrive at destination, containers and cargo go to many places where mobile network coverage is poor to non-existent. Thus, the use of dual mode GSM-satellite M2M devices, for instance, is crucial to provide uninterrupted service to customers. Satellite communication therefore is always available as a back-up technology to transmit the device's position. Furthermore, mathematical statistical interpolation may be used to fill the missing data.

Location Awareness: in some application scenarios, such as air transport, the ability of the LBS to switch operative mode depending on devices' position could be an important feature both to meet customer needs and legislative restrictions (e.g. IATA restrictions on network-enabled electronic devices [12]).

Response Time: the algorithm behind the LBSs services should return the result of the computation within a specific deadline from the moment the packet, transmitted by the device, is received. This is important in order to guarantee the responsiveness of the application which uses the service and is crucial for time-critical applications.

Accuracy of the Result: the precision of devices' location depends on the hardware and software used in the mobile communication system, as well as on the positioning service [13]. The accuracy level requested to the Location-Based Service, both for position tracking or route-matching, influence the service's response time and varies depending on the application scenario in which the service will be used.

Power Management: energy efficiency and power consumption are critical aspects when developing an LBS using battery-powered M2M devices. Containers and cargo trips from source to destination may last over 75 days, so the device attached to them should work properly for long periods of time, often without the possibility of recharging the battery.

Security and Privacy: customer concerns about security and privacy are another challenge for location-based technologies applied to SCM. With regards to shipment security, it is desirable that the LBS integrates a priority function which immediately alerts the customer in case of illicit manipulation of the container holding the goods. On the other hand, the M2M devices should transmit the shipment status and location data using data security instruments, such as cryptography, to keep them confidential and avoid interception of sensible information.

Among all available tools which contribute to the establishment of applications and systems for SCM, geofencing plays an important role in the context detection of proactive applications, which can automatically adapt business and industrial operations to the geospatial context a user, or a mobile device, is currently in.

3.3 Geofencing Service Features for SCM Systems

Geofencing allows to detect and monitor changes in the topological relation between a mobile device and a bound geographical area (the *geofence*). The topological relation can be expressed in terms of the spatio-temporal predicates *enter, leave, cross* and *bypass*, which are obtained as the result of *trajectory-based topological join queries*. These queries test the intersection between the whole or part of the trajectory of a moving object and a geofence, returning the spatio-temporal predicate describing their relationship based on the intersections found. These queries are powerful instruments for geospatial analysis, but they are also computationally intensive.

This represents a challenge, as it requires to identify or construct the most efficient algorithm or method which, under the operating conditions of the specific system and application scenario, resolves geofencing problems, returning the result of trajectory-based topological join queries in a period that is acceptable for interactive, ad-hoc geospatial analysis services.

The requirements of a good geofencing for SCM are:

- static, meaning that the spatio-temporal predicates are verified by checking the trajectory of the moving object with respect to fixed, bound areas;

- geometric and symbolic addressed, so that the geofences could be defined with both geometric shapes or symbols, such as words and alphanumeric codes, which identify precise locations;
- centralized, so that the matching between the trajectory of the moving object with the set of associated geofences is executed by the servers, which are the main part of the system;
- capable of operating effectively with different and variable location accuracy, tracking rate and device speed.

3.4   Real Time Monitoring Ecosystem

A real time monitoring ecosystem uses industrial IoT technology to gather, process and analyze smart data collected directly on goods stored and moved across the world. IoT technology allows companies to shift the attention from low information data collection, such as fleet management or warehouse management, to a high value data collection and real time monitoring. This creates the need for a system capable to record and transmit data globally without the need of a dedicated telecommunication infrastructure. The system must be battery powered, wireless and its dimensions must be such to allow a pervasive monitoring of goods. These points lead to a real time monitoring system that must be adaptive from its core by changing how business intelligence is applied to incoming data in real time. In this paper we discuss See Your Box system focusing on PFLGA, which represents the core component of its *geofencing service.*

When we shift the attention from a simple logistics process in terms of fleet management to a solution that monitors a complex logistics process following goods during their transformation from raw material all the way to the end user, the inter-modal logistics process requires a new approach in terms of how we process data. Inter-modal risk monitoring requires therefore an embedded AI system capable of adapting both to a variety of goods and a variety of logistics scenarios. If not, such lack would force to create so many different technologies that would result in an unsustainable business model.

The system is composed of two main elements that are the smart sensing devices and a centralized cloud-based infrastructure with a high performance rules engine that processes incoming data. A web-based management dashboard offers immediate access to the risk monitoring platform while REST APIs enable full M2M integration with the system. The architecture of the cloud platform and smart sensing device have been described in detail in previous work.

The whole cloud architecture is based on a fully scalable infrastructure based on virtual machines that are responsible of fulfilling specific tasks. A lot of research and effort was invested in creating an efficient self-load balancing system that could use the full potential of the available hardware. This allows the system to take advantage of instant and dynamic vertical scaling driven by the actual load of the system [14]. The cloud platform is subdivided in three main components:

- Gateway, accepts incoming requests from devices, authenticates and decrypts data, forwards data within the system and delivers messages to devices.

- Rules Engine, applies business logic to the incoming data according to the risk sub model.
- Databases, the system uses a multiple DBMS approach to leverage the strengths of relational and no-sql engines [14].

The gateway can process incoming data both asynchronously and synchronously. The former is the standard approach for most applications where smart sensing devices act mainly as a telemetry system offering a real time overview of the logistics process. The latter is used in all those applications where the smart sensing device must change configuration parameters upon a result of the processing of the transmitted data. An example where this approach is used with location-based services is anti-theft monitoring where a device will record location in a low-power mode for power efficiency and swap to a high precision mode when a geofence is trespassed raising the alert of a possible theft. Each delay that occurs while processing a response for the device puts the possibility to deliver a response to the device at risk since the transmission channel is characterized by a very short time out. For this reason, each component that processes incoming data must be carefully optimized for processing speed. The complexity of location-based services can easily become a bottleneck.

Information content of incoming data is limited if the system is not able to correlate a context to it. It's fundamental that incoming data must be processed with business rules that are relevant to the specific phase of the logistics process. For this reason, the system was designed with a fully adaptive rules engine where small business rules can be continuously not only activated and deactivate, but also adapted with parameters or data processed by offline processes, such as data mining systems. A typical example is a time bound geofencing rule used for detecting theft that can adapt its time constraints by correlating traffic and weather information. A truck failing to reach a checkpoint in time could represent a hint for an anomalous behaviour during a clear day with no traffic, or perfectly acceptable behaviour if an accident has happened along the way or bad weather is slowing down the transport. These needs lead us to develop a way to describe and model a complex location-based service with a data structure that could be easily understood by customer domain experts and customized by external services. The result is a dictionary-based structure that can be easily ported across systems in JSON format and is compatible with the GeoJSON format for the description of the geofencing areas involved.

4   An Efficient Solution to Geofencing Problem

4.1   Geofencing Use Case Modeling

PFLGA was designed as an innovative solution for implementing proactive LBSs suitable for time-critical industrial applications in the context of Supply Chain Management, whose specific requirements have been extensively discussed in the previous work. However, the performance of an algorithm for the resolution of trajectory-based topological join queries represents just one concern for designing a geofencing service for real-world applications in inter-modal transport and SCM. The main challenges regarding the design of such a geofencing service concern:

- *data collection* and *telecommunication coverage:* the environment set up for testing the algorithms used to solve geofencing problems exploits ready-to-use collections of geographical data which do not consider the problems concerning the supply of this data by the sensing devices. These devices transmit the data collected from their sensors through an existing telecommunication infrastructure. Transmissions may occur *synchronously,* with a predefined frequency, or *asynchronously* depending on telecommunication coverage, system policies or provided services. However, the geofencing service to be implemented should be capable of returning a proper response for the considered geofencing problem independently from the moment device updates are received;

- *customers' requirements:* geofencing services could be applied to a broad array of customers' businesses, each featuring a set of peculiarities and specific requirements which contribute in defining an even broader array of possible use cases, which are often very distant from the academic scenarios considered for geofencing algorithms testing. These requirements make the resolution of geofencing business problems dependent from other aspects different from the *topological predicate* alone;

- *time reference:* time represents a critical variable in the industrial context as it allows to define processes deadlines, schedule events and specify time boundaries to define the beginning and the end of business cases. The supply chain management activity of a company develops geofencing scenarios where the interest on precise topological events is bound to their occurrence in a specific sequence and/or within predefined time intervals. Therefore, an efficient time constraints representation is needed to depict geofencing use cases within the service to be implemented;

These challenges raise the need to describe complex geofencing business cases using a model that:

- allows the service to adapt to the different updating frequencies of the data transmitted by the trackers;
- allows the correct representation of customers' geofencing business cases and their peculiar requirements;
- is easily intelligible for customer domain experts and customizable by external services;
- is compliant with See Your Box adaptive rules engine system.

These prescriptions lead us to develop the *geofencing rule* model. The geofencing rule model depicts geofencing business cases as a set of *stories* describing sequentially the events the customer is expecting the tracker to go through during the shipment. Using this schema, a geofencing use case is translated into a customizable business intelligence rule which is continuously evaluated by See

Your Box's rules engine. The geofencing rule model shares most of its structure with See Your Box generic rule model but is characterized by the set of stories introduced just above. Each story of the set is defined using the *geofencing sub-rule* schema, a model representing a precise spatio-temporal behaviour of the tracker, relative to a delimited geographical area, whose occurrence is important for the client's business on that shipment. A geofencing rule is executed when a position update is received from the device assigned to the shipment to which the geofencing service is provided. Each sub-rule of the set is evaluated, and the occurrence of a scenario described by a geofencing sub-rule is said to *trigger* that sub-rule.

4.2   Geofencing Sub-rules Schema Specifications

The geofencing sub-model is one of the most important part of the geofencing service implemented within See Your Box system. The elements which make up this model are presented below.

Geofence. Geofences are represented using geometric and polygonal shapes drawn on the *WGS 84* (EPSG 4326) geodetic system, which is the standard U.S. Department of Defense definition of a global reference system for geospatial information and is the reference system for the Global Positioning System (GPS) [15]. WGS 84 is based on a consistent set of constants and model parameters that describe the Earth's size, shape, gravity and geomagnetic fields, which make it consistent within ±1 m. The geofences, drawn on WGS 84 as mentioned above, are then represented using GeoJSON data format [16]. GeoJSON is used and supported by a large plethora of both front end and back end software tools and libraries, providing a compact, self-explanatory representation of bounded areas of any possible shape, from regular polygons (triangles, squares, etc.) to the complex perimeter of a building, such as airports, stadiums, etc.

Topological Predicate. The predicate describes the action performed by the tracker towards a specified bounded area, the geofence discussed above, in terms of the topological relation between the trajectory travelled by the tracker and the geometric shape defining the geofence. The behaviour of a moving device relative to a bounded area can be defined using the spatial predicates *enter*, *leave* and *cross*, proposed for the first time by Erwig and Schneider in 1999 [17]. Whether a moving object enters, leaves, or crosses a given geofence is determined by resolving a *trajectory-based topological join query*, consisting in examining one or more segments of the trajectory travelled by the device, checking if they intersect with the geofence and evaluating the intersections found. The aforementioned predicates provide a complete description of any case study considered for academic purposes to which geofencing could be applied to. However, the application of a geofencing service to real world use cases must take into consideration that device position update is discrete, and it is strongly bound to the telecommunication coverage of the area the device is currently in. Even so, the geofencing functionality must still be able to determine device behaviour, providing the customer with the expected service. Considering the challenges delineated above and **PFLGA** algorithm features, we decided to exploit the following topological predicates for geofencing sub-rule creation, to support what we found to be the most plausible use cases geofencing could be applied to:

- *inside:* the sub-rule triggers when the device is inside the geofence;
- *outside:* the sub-rule triggers when the device is outside the geofence;
- *arrival:* the sub-rule triggers when the device enters the geofence;
- *departure:* the sub-rule triggers when the device leaves the geofence;
- *cross:* the sub-rule triggers when the device crosses the specified bounded area in just one position update.

Inside and *Outside* have been included in the domain of the topological predicates for the geofence sub-rules to support the simplest geofencing use cases and those ones where the customer wants to know whether its shipment reached a precise location along its journey to the final destination.

Time Reference. The geofence and the topological predicate described above define the spatial aspect of geofencing sub-rules. These components alone are not enough to classify the behaviour of a monitored tracker. The time component is essential to define completely the scope of each sub-rule and to help design complex use cases. The *time reference* defines the temporal window within which the occurrence of the topological predicate of a precise sub-rule must be checked. From the analysis of real application scenarios of geofencing it has been possible to define the following types of time reference:

- *any:* the occurrence of the topological predicate specified in the sub-rule is not expected within a precise time interval. Geofencing sub-rules whose time reference is set to *any* are checked at every position update sent by the tracker;
- *absolute:* the occurrence of the topological predicate specified in the sub-rule is expected within a precise time interval defined by a start date and an end date. Geofencing sub-rules whose time reference is set to *absolute* are checked at every position update sent by the tracker within the absolute time interval defined by the start date and end date;
- *relative:* the occurrence of the topological predicate specified in the sub-rule is expected within a precise time interval from the moment another sub-rule of the same set, referred to as *reference sub-rule*, is triggered and for a defined time interval, expressed in minutes. Geofencing sub-rules whose time reference is set to *relative* respect to another sub-rule of the set are checked at every position update sent by the tracker from the moment the reference sub-rule is triggered to the end of the specified time interval.

The temporal references described above allow to depict complex customers' use cases, featuring long spatio-temporal sequences and event dependency, into manageable geofencing rules.

Processing and Notification Options. The geofence, the topological predicate and the time reference described above define the *geofencing event* the system is listening to. In order to represent the largest possible number of real-world use cases, the geofencing sub-rule model has been provided with a set of options which define the actions the system must perform during the geofencing rule check or after the occurrence of the event depicted in the three points mentioned above. The geofencing sub-rule model features:

- an option which tells whether the occurrence of the event described by the geofencing sub-rule should be used to trigger the execution of another consecutive action within the system, called *raise trigger*. This option helps to design system rules to solve precise geofencing-dependent customers' requests, such as context-dependent trackers' configuration swapping;
- an option which tells whether to continue or stop performing the check once the sub-rule has been triggered for the first time, referred to as *execute while not triggered*. This option helps to design geofencing rules for all those use cases where it is important for the customer that an event occurs *just once*, such as a sequence of checkpoint placed along a predefined route the shipment has to travel along;
- an option, present if the sub-rule time reference is set relative to another sub-rule, which tells whether the sub-rule should be checked or not if its reference has not been triggered yet, also called *evaluate even if reference is not set*. This option helps to design all those use cases where it is important to notify the customer of both the occurrence or the absence of a geofencing-dependent event;
- an option which tells whether the occurrence of a precise tracker behaviour should trigger or not the transmission of a notification to the customer, referred to as *alert if triggered*;
- an option which tells whether the missed occurrence of a precise tracker behaviour should trigger or not the transmission of a notification to the customer, referred to as *alert if missed*.

4.3   The Algorithm in Details

Proactive Fast and Low Resource Geofencing Algorithm (PFLGA) is proposed as an innovative solution to the geofencing matter, inspired by the *ray-casting* algorithm and designed for implementing proactive location-based services suitable for time-critical, IoT-enabled industrial applications in the context of Supply Chain Management.

The proposed design provides every tracker for which geofencing service is enabled with a set of one or more geofences, i.e. geospatial objects, such as polygons and circles, whose boundaries are drawn over a specific geodetic coordinate system.

The data periodically transmitted by the tracker carries its geographical position, expressed in terms of latitude and longitude coordinates, enabling the location update for each tracker. These geographical points are used to determine the most plausible *path travelled* by the device between location updates, exploiting route-matching services with different levels of detail. The *travelled path* is then used to determine the topological relation between the moving object and the set of geofences assigned to the shipment the device is attached to.

Although the algorithm is designed to determine the topological relation between a moving object and a set of geofences using its trajectory, it can also perform the geofence inclusion test using other geospatial objects, from a geographical location point to a single segment of the whole complex trajectory travelled by the tracker, depending on the available geospatial information regarding the moving object and the complexity required for the geofencing analysis. This allows the algorithm to be potentially applied to different use cases, from those which require an examination with low level of detail, in favour of a low query response time, to those that require a detailed geospatial analysis regardless of the query response time.

Since the application scenario in which the geofencing service will be used allows each tracker to be assigned a set of one or more geofences, and the trajectory-based topological join queries are rather compute-intensive, it is important that data structures containing geospatial data support the retrieval of elements of an arbitrarily large size in an efficient way, therefore the proposed geofencing algorithm uses an *in-memory tree-based index structure* for indexing the set of geofences assigned to each tracker for which the geofencing service is required.

The insertion strategy for these structures has a computational complexity of $O(n)$, while the search operation has a computational complexity of $O(\log n)$, which permits a fast object retrieval in time critical applications.

The use of this kind of spatial index enables the application of an efficient filtering strategy on the set of geofences on which the intersection test with the trajectory will be performed.

PFLGA searches for any intersection between the route travelled by the tracker and progressively smaller bounding areas, called *Minimum Bounding Rectangles* (MBRs), which contain one or more geofences within them. In case the trajectory doesn't have any intersection with those bounding areas, the test ends without checking the set of geofences, otherwise the test continues with smaller bounding areas, until a precise geofence is found and tested.

PFLGA is based on the theory behind trajectory-based topological join queries. Given a set of geofences, represented as polygons or circular shapes, and the whole or a part of a trajectory defining the path travelled by the moving object, represented as a polyline geometric object, the algorithm verifies the existence of intersections between this polyline and the set of MBRs containing the geofences to be analyzed. If the polyline defining the trajectory intersects one or more MBRs, the algorithm performs the following steps on each geofence contained within the MBRs of interest:

- gets the previous position of the device and checks whether it was inside or outside the current geofence;

- calculates the intersections between the geofence and the trajectory travelled by the device, if there is any;
- analyzes the result obtained above and returns a composite topological predicate [18], which tells whether the object entered, crossed or left that area.

---

input : $\mathcal{F}$: set of geospatial objs making geo-fences
$\quad\quad\quad idx$: index of the set of geofences
$\quad\quad\quad route$: trajectory travelled by the object
output: $predicate$, position with respect to the fence

```
1  // list of idxs of the MBRs in the index intersecting the route
2  I = getIntersection(idx, route)
3  foreach pos ∈ I do
4  │    prev_pos = getPrevPosition(route);
5  │    // checks if the prev_pos was inside the current MBR
6  │    Intersections = getIntersections(pos, route)
7  │    if getIntersection(pos, prev_pos) is not null then
8  │    │    if Intersections number is odd then
9  │    │    │    the object left the fence
10 │    │    else
11 │    │    │    the object is still inside
12 │    │    end
13 │    else
14 │    │    if Intersections is empty then
15 │    │    │    the object is still outside
16 │    │    else
17 │    │    │    if Intersections number is odd then
18 │    │    │    │    the object entered the fence
19 │    │    │    else
20 │    │    │    │    the object crossed the fence and it is outside
21 │    │    │    end
22 │    │    end
23 │    end
24 end
```

Algorithm 1. PFLGA description

The algorithm (Algorithm 1) implies the a-priori construction of the in-memory, tree-based index, which will use a time interval proportional to the dimension of the set of geofences in exam (since the insertion algorithm for this tree-based index structure has a computational complexity of $O(n)$). Since the set of geofences is quite static and it is updated rarely, compared to the location of the moving object and its trajectory, the additional processing required for the index is bearable, especially if it is compared to the query processing speed up offered using this index structure. The algorithm, whose possible implementation in pseudo-code is shown below, has a computational complexity of $O(\log n)$.

4.4 Performance Comparison

The performance of PFLGA is compared against the above discussed algorithms. Test results are normalized according to the outcome of PFLGA on each test and reported in Fig. 1 below. The test has been executed on a laptop computer loaded with Intel Core i7 4720HQ CPU (Quad Core, 2.60 GHz up to 3.60 GHz) and 8 GB DDR3 RAM, running Linux Ubuntu 14.04 LTS using Apache Bench (also indicated as ab), a tool designed for benchmarking Apache installations and any HTTP server in general [19].

In order to allow a fair comparison and avoid data dependencies, every test uses the same dataset used by the algorithm's author to determine the performance.

To compare PISTON vs PFLGA we used the following datasets:

1. Geofences Dataset: US TIGER® Texas, a real-world spatial-objects dataset which contains 6694 geofences drawn in the Texas area [20];
2. Trajectories Dataset: 10000 trajectories between couples of random location point inside the Texas area, generated according to the specifications in the PISTON paper [7].

The test requires the execution of a geospatial query for each of the trajectories contained in the dataset.

For the comparison of Hybrid Hashing against PFLGA we used two different datasets, according to the paper [9]. The first dataset is provided by the ACM Open GIS Cup 2013 [9], which includes two location point files and two polygons files. For this comparison we selected two of these files, one for each category:

1. Geofences Dataset: Poly10 file, which contains 32 instances of 10 different polygons;
2. Locations Dataset: Point500, which contains 39289 instances of 500 different points.

The test requires the execution of 10000 geospatial queries for each of the trajectories contained in the dataset, according to the experiment specification in the paper.

The second dataset, according with Hybrid Hashing's Authors, is synthesized as follows:

1. Geofences Dataset: Poly-OSM1, which contains 200 instances of 20 different polygons, selected from the Land Polygon dataset.
2. Locations Dataset: Point-OSM1, which contains 80000 instances of location points randomly selected from the MBR area of each polygon.

The test requires the execution of 10000 geospatial queries for each of the trajectories contained in the dataset.

Finally, to compare SLGC-1 against PFLGA the datasets are constructed according to the SLGC-1 paper [8]. This geofences dataset contains 5 different polygons, respectively having 5, 10, 50, 100 and 223 vertexes, and a circular area. Each of these geospatial objects covers a geographical area almost equal to $4000\,\mathrm{km}^2$, and Locations Dataset, 125000 different GPS location points limited in the geofences' areas. For each couple of GPS points a trajectory connecting them is calculated. The test requires the execution of a geospatial query for each of the trajectories contained in the dataset.

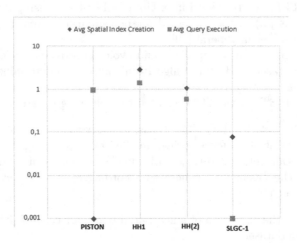

Fig. 1. Time performances of others algorithms vs PFLGA (PFLGA/other)

Figure 1 summarizes the results of the performance comparison discussed above. PFLGA performances are comparable to, and in some case better than, those of the other designs, both in terms of average spatial index creation time, in the pre-processing stage, and average query execution time, while offering some features which makes it more adaptive than its competitors to different application scenarios (Table 1).

5   Results and Business Cases

In this section we will present two real world business cases where PFLGA was used to support SCM in two different fields: *grocery home delivery* and *anti-theft solution for HVA* (high value assets) in the industrial spare part vertical.

5.1   Food Home Delivery

The client is in need for a tech solution to monitor an average of 3000 daily deliveries within a fast-paced inter-modal logistics process where a mistake in handling the goods or managing the cold chain could cost the stakeholders the loss of market share or run out of business. Real time availability of data is fundamental since within the matter of hours groceries are delivered to the end customer directly at his home with no further possibility to verify the status of the goods. The typical logistics process consists of three different logistics operators that lasts between 24 and 72 h (Fig. 2). The short duration of the average shipment translates quickly into a high turnover of used devices. This means that if the system itself can't automate procedures it becomes impossible to handle or manage. In this application the client's requirements were to be able to have real time visibility of the goods location and if these were handled according to its service level agreements.

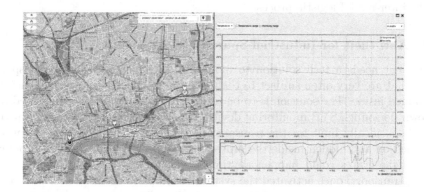

Fig. 2. Grocery delivery real time monitoring

The first way that the geofencing system supported the client's needs was by ensuring that the goods reached the end customer within the maximum time and in full compliance of the cold chain specifications. Up to this moment the client relied on the delivery tracking system, but internal auditing required an autonomous detection of delivery. This use case was handled with a time relative geofencing rule that would notify the client if the package reached the end customer within the maximum allowed number of hours and a full report on temperatures registered during transport.

The system is capable of autonomously detecting the different phases of the logistics process and automatically switch off the devices once they return to the main warehouse. In this case the geofencing algorithm was instructed to detect only a return within the warehouse premises. The predicate return is different from entering since the application must support two use cases:

- A device is switched on inside the warehouse, placed inside a delivery box and returns after delivery is complete.
- A device is switched on inside the R&D department located in a different area, transported to the main warehouse before starting the standard cycle.

Lastly the client desired a continuous performance evaluation and auditing of the logistics operators to make sure they would respect the agreed upon delivery times. The geofencing solution allowed again a fully independent solution to track the location of the goods without intervention of the logistics operator and without inserting new infrastructure such as RFID portals, bar-code scanners and so on.

In this case the performance of the single operator was to be considered independently from the others. The algorithm was setup to ensure a relative arrival to the next checkpoint using as a time reference the arrival time at the current warehouse.

Currently the provided system has proven to be able to handle all requirements providing a pervasive and automated monitoring of the different phases of the inter-modal logistic process.

5.2   Anti-theft for Industrial Spare Parts Transport

The client needs a tech solution to monitor the transport of industrial spare parts that are very often subject to theft due to the quantity of precious metals contained inside. The solution is to be totally autonomous and not operated by its own personnel. SYB monitoring devices were placed inside the custom-made crates specifically built for the transport by one of the suppliers. Devices were switched on and hidden inside the protective foam structure. Since the production of the crates could happen anytime between days or months before the actual transport, once activated the system would place them into an ultra-low power mode for energy consumption optimization. Thanks to a first geofencing rule the system would detect the arrival at the client's warehouse and change configuration to acquire location more frequently and monitor the movement of the spare parts.

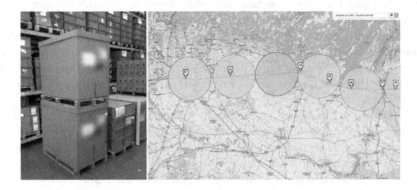

Fig. 3. Spare parts monitoring (Color figure online)

Transport was performed over a predefined route with a tight departure schedule. Therefore, the system was configured with a series of relative geofence checkpoints placed along the route that would be set relative to a precise moment in time. The arrival at destination was registered with an entry geofence over an area and the automatic switch-off was performed upon 48 h of a stationary location registered inside the destination geofence.

Any given time a geofence checkpoint was not respected the system would swap configuration into a high precision location acquisition mode to ensure the best possible tracking at the cost of battery life. A missed check point would trigger a notification in real time allowing the client to monitor the position of the crates during transport. Figure 3 represents a typical scenario that could occur. The arrival geofence at the client's warehouse (blue circle) is used by the system to start monitoring the handling and transport of the spare parts. Green circles represent checkpoints that have been respected while a red geofence indicates a checkpoint that wasn't crossed.

6   Conclusions

This work describes the evolution process of a geofencing algorithm in becoming a full-fledged location-based service for real time monitoring of inter-modal logistics processes.

The paper presents PFLGA, a geofencing algorithm specifically designed to build proactive location-based services for Supply Chain Management systems with strong time constraints and describes its implementation within See Your Box's system. The results are derived from the use of the algorithm in production stage of development within real life application.

A geofencing algorithm powering a Location-Based Service for Supply Chain Management needs to provide solutions to both point-in-polygon inclusion tests and complex trajectory-based geofencing problems, depending on the available geospatial information regarding the moving object and on the requests of the specific case. Both are separately available in existing algorithms such as SLGC-1 [8] and PISTON [7] respectively. PFLGA shows better performances and a broader set of features than other existing algorithms presented in technical literature, making it more adaptive to different application scenarios.

PFLGA specifications emphasize the role of ray-casting algorithm, in-memory indexing structures and trajectory-based topological joint queries as founding concepts of a solid design to solve the geofencing problem.

The paper highlights how business intelligence rules modelling is as a fundamental step for the establishment of a SCM system. Traditional elements of LBS, such as point-in-polygon tests and trajectory-based topological joint queries are only the first step for creating effective LBS whereas the inclusion of context awareness, temporal relations between events and multi-sensor analysis prove to be necessary in translating domain knowledge into business intelligence.

The study, based on real world data and usage in B2B scenarios, is limited by the number of verticals that have been taken into consideration and the amount of collected data points.

Despite these limitations, the use of PFLGA and geofence based business rules for different clients operating in food and industrial fields show clearly that the scenarios sometimes present similar characteristics which could be traced back to a pattern. It's easy to imagine as for future developments the possibility of identifying patterns that will allow for a standardization of geofence powered location based services on one side and machine elaborated geofencing rules on the other.

References

1. Feng, F., Pang, Y., Lodewijks, G.: Towards context-aware supervision for logistics asset management: concept design and system implementation. In: Ziemba, E. (ed.) AITM/ISM -2016. LNBIP, vol. 277, pp. 3–19. Springer, Cham (2017). https://doi.org/10.1007/978-3-319-53076-5_1
2. Sachin, W., Rahate, D.M.S.: Geo-fencing infrastructure: location based service. Int. Res. J. Eng. Technol. **3**, 1095–1098 (2016)
3. Rouse, M.: Geo-fencing. http://whatis.techtarget.com/definition/geofencing. Accessed 2016
4. Allen, G.: Internet of things, industrial internet of things, industry 4.0 - it's all connected! (no pun intended). https://redshift.autodesk.com/industrial-internet-of-things-iot-terms/. Accessed 2015
5. Garzon, S.R., Deva, B.: Infrastructure-assisted geofencing: proactive location-based services with thin mobile clients and smart servers. In: 2015 3rd IEEE International Conference on Mobile Cloud Computing, Services, and Engineering, pp. 61–70, March 2015. https://doi.org/10.1109/MobileCloud.2015.31
6. Carchiolo, V., Modica, P.W., Loria, M.P., Toja, M., Malgeri, M.: A geofencing algorithm fit for supply chain management. In: Ganzha, M., Maciaszek, L.A., Paprzycki, M. (eds.) Proceedings of the 2018 Federated Conference on Computer Science and Information Systems, FedCSIS 2018, Poznań, Poland, 9–12 September 2018, pp. 737–746 (2018). https://doi.org/10.15439/2018F238
7. Ray, S., Brown, A.D., Koudas, N., Blanco, R., Goel, A.K.: Parallel in-memory trajectory-based spatiotemporal topological join. In: 2015 IEEE International Conference on Big Data (Big Data), pp. 361–370, October 2015. https://doi.org/10.1109/BigData.2015.7363777
8. Lin, K., Chen, Y., Qiu, M., Zeng, M., Huang, W.: SLGC: a fast point-in-area algorithm based on scan-line algorithm and grid compression. In: 2016 11th International Conference on Computer Science Education (ICCSE), pp. 352–356, August 2016. https://doi.org/10.1109/ICCSE.2016.7581606
9. Tang, S., Yu, Y., Zimmermann, R., Obana, S.: Efficient geo-fencing via hybrid hashing: a combination of bucket selection and in-bucket binary search. ACM Trans. Spat. Algorithms Syst. **1**(2), 5:1–5:22 (2015). https://doi.org/10.1145/2774219
10. Allen, G.: Harnessing the power of location based services. http://blogs.dcvelocity.com/supply_chain_innovation/2016/03/harnessing-the-power-of-location-based-services.html. Accessed 2016
11. Rao, B., Minakakis, L.: Evolution of mobile location-based services. Commun. ACM **46**(12), 61–65 (2003). https://doi.org/10.1145/953460.953490
12. IATA: Guidance on the expanded use of passenger portable electronic devices (PEDs) (2014)
13. Rein, A., Ülar, M.: Location based services-new challenges for planning and public administration? Futures **37**(6), 547–561 (2005). https://doi.org/10.1016/j.futures.2004.10.012
14. Carchiolo, V., Loria, M.P., Malgeri, M., Toja, M.: An efficient real-time architecture for collecting IoT data. In: 2017 Federated Conference on Computer Science and Information Systems (FedCSIS), pp. 1157–1166, September 2017. https://doi.org/10.15439/2017F381
15. ICAO: DOC 9674/AN 946 - WGS84 Manual (2002)
16. Butler, H., Daly, M., Doyle, A., Gillies, S., Hagen, S., Schaub, T.: The GeoJSON format. RFC 7946, RFC Editor, August 2016. https://tools.ietf.org/html/rfc7946

17. Erwig, M., Schneider, M.: Developments in spatio-temporal query languages. In: Proceedings of Tenth International Workshop on Database and Expert Systems Applications. DEXA 1999, pp. 441–449 (1999). https://doi.org/10.1109/DEXA.1999.795206
18. Pfoser, D., Jensen, C.S.: Capturing the uncertainty of moving-object representations. In: Güting, R.H., Papadias, D., Lochovsky, F. (eds.) SSD 1999. LNCS, vol. 1651, pp. 111–131. Springer, Heidelberg (1999). https://doi.org/10.1007/3-540-48482-5_9
19. TAS Foundation: ab - Apache HTTP server benchmarking tool. https://httpd.apache.org/docs/2.4/programs/ab.html. Accessed 2018
20. U.S. Census Bureau: Tiger/line shapefiles and tiger/line files (2006)

Digital Distribution of Video Games - An Empirical Study of Game Distribution Platforms from the Perspective of Polish Students (Future Managers)

Witold Chmielarz[✉] and Oskar Szumski

Faculty of Management, University of Warsaw, Warsaw, Poland
{witold.chmielarz,oskar.szumski}@uw.edu.pl

Abstract. The aim of this article is to execute a comparative analysis of services and distribution platforms used to purchase computer games. The article is a continuation of the research focused on the popularity, use and impact of games on the behavior of a prominent population and analysis of the typical e-shops with games. Authors has chosen four the most common amongst students computer game services and platforms simultaneously found in the first hundreds of searches in Google to carry on analysis. To support this research authors decided to use CAWI methodology to assess nine groups of features: transparency, site navigation, quality of information, product search quality, advertising, the quality of the order processing, way of visualization and product promotion from the customer's perspective. Platform analysis was carried out according to: installation package support, application design, search engine quality, transparency, product presentation and security. A qualitative study was conducted to select a sample of selected students using the point method and the point method with preferences to evaluate the distinctive features of the services. A group of over seven hundred randomly selected people from the university was examined. This approach was based on the structure of the article consisting of the presentation of the research hypothesis, the description of the methodology and the research sample, and the analysis of the results and their discussion together with the resulting conclusions. The results of the work may be used by the owners of computer distribution services or platforms and website designers.

Keywords: Computer games · Digital distribution platforms ·
User's assessment

1 Introduction

Increasing popularity of computer games lead to dynamic development of game distribution platforms. Challenge to offer the successful game might take a few layers including: game itself, direct and indirect marketing as well as channels of distribution namely distribution platforms where prospects can purchase or achieve in other way the game. In addition to that prior studies in the area of e-gaming indicate that gamers are difficult to satisfy, making the quality of games and attractiveness of accompanied

© Springer Nature Switzerland AG 2019
E. Ziemba (Ed.): AITM 2018/ISM 2018, LNBIP 346, pp. 136–154, 2019.
https://doi.org/10.1007/978-3-030-15154-6_8

channels of distribution an important issue. This article is the fifth of the series of studies carried out among the representatives of academic, young society concerning the possibility of using computer games in education, entertainment, sport, etc. Following study focuses on the identified as leading in Poland distribution platforms that provide access to various types of games. The main objective of this study is to analyse the quality of selected game distribution platforms used by distributors of computer games and making possible recommendations to address the concerns of gamers to meet their needs. The digital distribution of computer games is considered by the authors to be a method of products' dissemination that consists of making installation files or a source code required to run the application via the Internet, that publisher provides to a player. In general the process of distribution of installation files is carried out via the dedicated service available through the platform that is designed especially to provide the sale and post-sale support to the customers. For the purpose of this research authors used working definitions of distribution platform understood as the whole solution that consist of different components and interfacing methods as website (further referenced as website) or supporting application (further referenced as application) that games and other game related services are enabled for the use of the users.

This study was inspired and crafted as an answer to the needs of one of the computer companies operating in the digital games market and was aimed to carry on the study into the popularity of games among students who are of the most active within the groups of electronic players on the market. Initially, the research had only the preliminary nature and was focused mostly on the number of players, devices that are used for playing games, the frequency of playing games as well as types of games and the most frequently used titles. Subsequently, the aspects related to perceiving computer games as sport and entertainment were considered. The next step was a possibility to use the games for didactic purposes. The penultimate stage of the research analysed the most popular shops offering computer games. The logical consequence of the conducted studies was the research that focused on the selected distribution platforms.

The study considers the data provided by GamesIndustry.biz and a report on the global gaming market in 2017 [1]. Currently e-gaming business is the most dynamic and dominant entertainment market. According to the published data, the value of the entire gaming market in 2017 amounted to 116 billion dollars, which represents an increase of 10.7% in relation to 2016. It is noticed that mobile device gaming becomes the leader within the market with the share in the total value amounted to 42% (an increase by 23% in relation to 2016). The income from games running on personal computers and consoles presented a very similar tendency, and it amounted to 27% and 31%, respectively [1, 2]. Considering the scope of this market within the entertainment area rapid growth of interest both from the user and vendors' perspective, it truly appears to be the research field which deserves further analyses. It is worth to mention that the share of the digital platforms used for distribution of computer games in the entire market amounts to around 92% [3]. In the literature, one may point to the sources which evaluate the influence of the digital gaming platforms on the players [4] or on the natural environment [5], however, there is no comparative assessment of particular platforms from the point of view of users.

The conducted analysis is designed to determine the most important characteristics and features of platforms distributing computer games as well as motivations of individuals visiting those touchpoints and making game purchases.

2 The Assumptions of the Research Methodology

Preliminary to the research authors decided to identify the most representative platforms that offer digital games. Four platforms were selected for the above-described comparative analysis: GOG (CD Projekt – Poland, (https://www.gog.com)), Origin - (Electronic Arts Inc.- USA, (https://www.origin.com)), Steam (Valve Corporation – USA, (https://store.steampowered.com)) and Uplay (Ubisoft Entertainment – France, (https://store.ubi.com)). The rationale for choosing these platforms was their greatest recognition in Poland and popularity of use (segment leaders) and the diversity of platforms' ownership location. The probing of platforms used in this research has been supplemented and verified by an additional analysis of the frequency of the responses given to searches of individual platforms in the first hundred Google search results accompanied by the results of the initial part of the survey distributed among students.

The analysis has been divided into four parts. Part one covered the frequency of the use of games, platforms and devices (e.g. PC, Playstation), payment options; second part included comparative analysis of websites of distributors; third one analysed installed applications and the last one included comments of end users that are also important from the perspective of future development paths and recommendations with regards to this market segment.

Authors decided to apply a set of thirty-seven indicators, divided into nine groups to analyse selected distribution platforms. Following indicators were verified in previously carried out research studies [6, 7]: website clarity (first impression, assessment of visual aspects, accumulation of elements, graphic elements, the arrangement of elements, colour scheme, lettering); website support (registration, intuitiveness, the location of navigational tools, the functionality of navigational tools, terms of use, restrictions for unregistered users); information quality (the amount of information presented on the website, simplicity of access to information, the possibility to ask questions, the manner in which questions may be asked); the quality of the product search engine (the number of modifications, the number of filters (criteria), the accuracy of the response, the clarity of the results scheme); advertising on the site (location of windows, excessive and intrusive advertising, the accuracy of recommendations); quality of the ordering process (payments options, clarity of the ordering process, information on the expected delivery time); the method of product distribution (supported Digital Right Management (DRM) platforms), supported operating systems, a method of getting access rights, reactivation of access rights); presentation of the product (product information, hardware requirements, information transparency, relevant information); promotions (discounts on one-off purchases, promotions for occasional customers, loyalty programs for regular customers).

Authors fulfilled the need for extended analysis through the research of digital distribution applications (applications) for PCs with Windows systems. The applications of the same distributors which were analysed in the first part of the research, namely Valve Corporation (Steam), Electronic Arts Inc. (Origin), Ubisoft Entertainment (Uplay) and CD Projekt (GOG Galaxy). The installation of Windows 10 on a virtual machine using VirtualBox 5.0 was used for the assessment. Six groups of parameters were analysed consisting of such criteria as: installation package (size and form of access accompanied with provided ways of its distribution), the appearance of the application (ergonomics of component, scalability to the screen size), search engine (search efficiency), transparency (presentation of notifications and messages, menu information that is easy to notice), product presentation (information about products and equipment), security (applied security methods e.g. payment security, access to purchased products).

Under the circumstances of a dynamic and complex market environment as well as high innovation and competitiveness of solutions, the following questions were queried:

- what characteristics and form should the design of websites and applications adopt to increase their attractiveness to the client as the digital distribution platform?
- what set of attributes and functionalities seem the most important for digital platform users?

Answers to stated questions can be provided by means of an extended analysis of the requirements defined by users of online platforms. The quantitative and qualitative research into users' opinions is needed for this purpose, and the study should examine, on the one hand, the use of applications and, on the other, the websites that provide the gaming source. Taking into account the fact that there are few and random studies regarding this area, both in national literature [8–10] as well as foreign sources [5, 11–13], the research was based on the authors' own approach consisting of the following steps:

1. selection of the test group,
2. designing an online survey characterizing websites and distribution platforms from the client's point of view,
3. verification of the survey based on the test group and selection of the most important assessment criteria from the users' point of view,
4. identification of the most important factors influencing the behaviour of the users of websites and game distribution platforms and making the revised survey available again on the Internet, along with the distribution of information about the possibility of its completion,
5. analysis and discussion of the findings,
6. defining conclusions from research and design recommendations for game distribution platforms to achieve the advantage over others within the market.

The simplified, standardized scoring method of Likert was used for the assessment of each specified criterion. On this scale, each criterion was evaluated as follows: 0.00 - the criterion is not implemented, 0.25 - the criterion is implemented on a minimal, sufficient level, 0.50 - the criterion is implemented on the medium level, 0.75 - the criterion implementation level is good, 1.00 - full implementation of the criterion with the most effective (lowest) economic impact.

The selection of online gaming stores was made based on the frequency of the first hundred of Google search results, after entering the keywords "witryny dystrybutorów gier" (computer games distribution websites) and "platformy dystrybutorów gier" (platforms of computer game distributors). This list has been cross verified by taking into account the opinions of so called game experts - students who frequently and intensely play computer games via digital platforms.

The research was carried out in the second half of November 2017, on a sample of 713 randomly selected members of the academic community. 549 people completed the survey (over 77% of respondents), where - after a thorough analysis - 368 survey participants provided complete answers regarding the selected four platforms, which constitutes 67% of the respondents. 33% of the sample used other platforms than the four websites selected for the present analysis. Over 20% of students declare that they do not play games at all.

The online survey was deployed on the servers of the Faculty of Management at the University of Warsaw. The sample included the representatives of the academic community, students of all types of studies at two universities: the University of Warsaw and the Vistula Academy of Finance and Business, who indicated interest in completing the online survey. The study was carried out in two stages. The first stage concerned the evaluation of the game distribution platforms that are the most popular among students and what assessment criteria are the most suitable to evaluate distributors' websites and separately criteria that should be applied to evaluate the applications of the selected game platforms. In the second stage, the services and selected applications were analysed according to user-defined criteria for the four identified online game distribution platforms.

The survey was completed correctly by 368 respondents, evaluating only those that referred to the defined four websites analysed in the study. The results are: 55 people evaluated two websites and 26 respondent assessed three websites. This resulted in a total of 446 observations. Origin was rated by 121 respondents, GOG by 116 people, Uplay by 108 and Steam by 103 individuals. The gender distribution among the survey participants was divided into 72.5% of women and 27.45% of men. The average age of respondents was 20.6 years (from 20–23 years), which was typical for BA and BSc students, mainly with secondary education (over 94%). Bachelor's education was indicated by 4.08% of the sample, and higher education by 1.36% of the share. Over 42% of respondents were non-working students, and almost 58% were working students. Almost 30% of respondents declared coming from the city of over 100,000 residents, over 26% from cities with 11-100 thousand inhabitants, and over 43% from villages or towns up to 10,000 residents.

3   Analysis and Discussion of Survey Results Concerning Computer Game Distributors

The questionnaire was divided into three parts: an introductory part comprising eight questions, an analytical part (37 questions about websites and 6 questions regarding the application), a field of opinions, comments and recommendations of users, evaluation of installation process. As comprehensive element of the questionnaire survey also included a data sheet describing the test sample (demographical data).

3.1 Introductory Information

In order to analyse the collected data, the scoring method was applied. Each of the respondents assessed individual criteria in a subjective way. The assessments were added together, structured and averaged, followed by a reference to the maximum possible assessment of each indicator, both in the cross-section of websites/applications and the criteria applied on top of the respondents evaluating them.

Authors assume that the mass scale of the research allows for averaging of scores and minimizes the subjectivism of the assessments despite the scoring method is criticized for the subjectivism of the evaluations. The simplicity and standardization of the evaluations result in the fact that respondents make relatively few mistakes and participate in such surveys more willingly than in the case of surveys conducted by means of other methods. From the authors' experience, the findings obtained with the application of comparative analyses of websites are just as valuable as those received in the case of more sophisticated methods (AHP/ANP, Electre, Promethee and others) [14].

The first question concerned the moment when people who use distribution platforms started playing computer games. Nearly 53% of respondents said that they started playing computer games in primary school, more than 12% in pre-school age, almost 11% have been playing games from middle school, high school and college, and 24% did not play computer games at all.

The gamers declared the frequency of e-game playing and thus it allowed authors to emphasize presented experience within the area. The results are a s follow: almost 47% play games occasionally (once or twice a month), nearly 21% several times a week, 15% of the share - several times a month, more than 10% very rarely - several times a year, and more than 7% play computer games daily. After specifying this question, it turned out that 59% of the sample spend less than an hour a week playing computer games, and 16% play only 1–2 h a week. Over 21% play from 3 to 12 h per week. Those who play over 13 h – that is almost 2 h daily constitute the share of almost 4% of respondents.

Division of devices used looks like follow: thirty percent of gamers use only a smartphone for their games, over 23% a PC or a desktop computer, 19% use a PC and a notebook, over 20% use a console or a portable console, and 8% - a tablet.

The next question concerned PC and console platforms where students have their accounts. Over 25% have an account on the Origin platform, over 21% on Steam, almost 10% on GOG and Uplay, and the remaining 33% of the share on the Windows Store, Xbox Games Store, Battle.net, PlayStation Store and Nintendo eShop.

Over 53% describe themselves as experienced players (many years of experience and a wide range of games they played), 9% believe that they are advanced players (they play almost every day, different games on different equipment at least from elementary school, 15% claim that they are casual players (novices or people playing only occasionally, e.g. once a month or every three months), and 23% do not play at all.

The students play mainly games that are free of charge - 74%, they do not spend any money on it. Considering the remaining 26% - 13% of this share spend up to PLN 20, and only a little over 1% of the respondents spend over PLN 100.

3.2   Analysis of Survey Results Related to Websites

Analyses of the findings related to the evaluation of websites of the selected computer game distributors have been made in two cross-sections: service oriented and the evaluation criteria focused. The first cross-section was created by averaging the scores obtained by particular service for all specified criteria. The assessment for the detailed criterion was calculated as its percentage share in the potential maximum score that could be obtained during the implementation of a given criterion (it was equal to the number of criteria multiplied by the highest rating, i.e. 1). All websites included in the ranking have achieved ratings exceeding 50% of the maximum possible score, so it indicates that the clients are generally satisfied with the services they offer (Fig. 1).

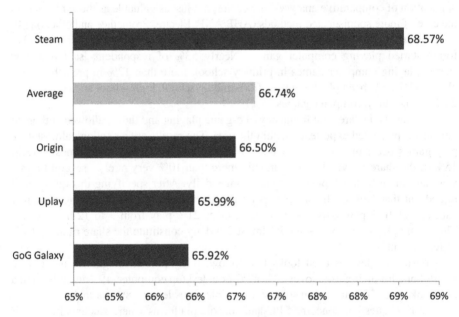

Fig. 1. Cross-section 1: Ranking of websites of selected game distributors

The average assessment in the respondents' opinions is close to 67%. Among the analysed websites, Steam received the highest rating with over 68%, the lowest rating was indicated in the case of GOG Galaxy - almost 66%. Thus the spread of results is in the range of 2.65%, which is very low value with regard to services. The leading position in the case of Steam was resulted by the highest score obtained for such groups of criteria as: product distribution, website clarity, the quality of product search and ordering process quality - where the average rating of these four criteria was 72%. The lowest rating of the GOG Galaxy website resulted from the highest rating in three categories: on-page ads, information quality and website navigation, with an average of these three criteria equal to 63%. Origin, where product presentation received the highest scores and Uplay (the best promotions) have taken the middle positions (it should be noted that Uplay platform uses website that is not equal to the Ubisoft domain but is recognized by the users as equivalent and compound within the whole platform). The Steam service was the only website which ranked above the average; however, the difference amounted to less than 2 percentage points, the rating of the remaining services was slightly below average.

The second cross-section considered all the parameters specified by all nine groups of criteria, the highest scores were assigned to the product presentation (76.63%), the quality of the ordering process (72.05%) and the quality of the product search engine (69.67%). This demonstrates the pragmatism of website designers, who first of all pay attention to the most important factors from the point of view of sales that may encourage the clients to visit the website again. The lowest scores were recorded in the case of quality of advertising presented on the website (55.02%), information quality (61.51%) and promotion (64.08%). This is an interesting finding, which shows that there is a growing dissatisfaction (compared to previous surveys of websites) with the excessive and redundant advertising on the website. The discrepancy between ratings is very large in this case, reaching 23 percentage points. The scores which are above average (which amounts to 66.74%) were recorded in the case of four groups of criteria – i.e. the above-mentioned factors listed in the three positions, as well as the criterion described as website navigation (67.15%).

Analysis of the detailed criteria within the groups of assessment criteria enables the authors to look more closely at the problem of the factors determining success or failure of the websites of selected platforms of computer game distributors. Among the analysed platforms, the criteria on the Steam website were rated highest - as many as 15 of them took the first position among the ones selected for analysis and as few as 7 took the last position. The second website was Origin, in the case of which 9 items were rated as the highest, and 7 as the lowest as compared to others. The other two places are more difficult to assess because the GOG Galaxy platform website had the 8 best-rated criteria, but as many as 16 were rated the worst, and the Uplay platform site - although only 5 rated best; there were 5 fewer aspects which rated worse than in the case of GOG Galaxy. The best ratings were: product information - 84.67%; hardware requirements and information clarity on the Origin platform (all scores were over 80% of the maximum rating which was seen as satisfactory from the user's point of view); clarity of the layout of results, accuracy of answers and ease of access on the Steam platform (all scores exceeding 74%). On the GOG Galaxy website, they were: registration, intuitiveness and functionality of navigational tools (over 71% for all aspects). On the Uplay website, it was an accumulation of graphic elements (77.56%) and well below the average: discounts on one-off purchases and colour scheme (above 68%). On average, the worst in the respondents' opinion were the following: intrusive advertising (43%), the way of asking questions via search engine (51%) and restrictions for unregistered users (53%). The advertisements received the best scores in the case of the Origin platform website - 42%, and the worst on the Uplay website - 44%. The discrepancy between the average ratings of the maximum and minimum criteria was 38%.

3.3   Opinions, Comments and User Recommendations

A careful analysis of players' comments and opinions leads to the following main conclusions:

- the research showed that the leading position within the game distribution platforms has been granted based on the level of quality of service offered by the providers, fulfilling expectations of demanding users such as e-players,
- all analysed websites consist of some common features, e.g. they do not allow advertisements of other stores, websites and platforms distributing games, each platform presents clearly visible logo, in the main section of the page there is a large banner with the game currently being promoted,
- the overall layout and structure of websites (except Origin) is very similar, almost resembling a template, as compared to other online stores.

Conclusions for Steam website are as follows:

- has a very clear page layout in dark colours. The layout and structure is clear and readable, and the elements that are important to the seller are easy to find due to the use of green colour,
- there are many language versions, including Polish,
- user-friendly – the website interactively reacts to navigating by displaying additional information,
- well-designed product presentation – a short product description, popular tags, when visiting the website, a movie with scenes from the game starts and a few screens with game images are displayed as an incentive to make a purchase. The rating system, presented under the description of the game, containing: a summary of the latest assessments and the overall aggregate rating, may be seen as important from the client's point of view,
- well-functioning shopping basket - each purchase added is presented in the form of: photos, description, list of systems in which it operates, as well as price and additional information for the customer,
- promotions are a very strong point of the Steam website, e.g. weekend promotion (a discount on the prices of all products of a given publisher), promotion related to a particular title or a collection, the possibility of using the full version from Friday to Sunday, etc.,
- products that were combined into subject related sets or different versions of the game e.g. a basic version, special edition with gadgets, the version with a selected set of additions e.g. the extended versions which are associated with extra costs for the user.

Conclusions for Origin website are following:

- the main page has a minimalistic design and layout, different from a typical website of an online store. Nevertheless, it is very clear and easy to navigate, but it leaves the impression of not targeting the novice but rather a player who has already dealt with it,
- easy to notice, large search engine box, login and registration button,
- large advertising banners with game scenes and short product information,

- a large selection of options for changing the language on the displayed page, including Polish,
- navigating the menu is easy, it provides readable, understandable and logical information,
- there is a problem with fast navigation on the page, e.g. in the Origin Access section, information about available titles is available when purchasing a sub-scription, but - even after clicking – the user is not informed about their content. The same applies to the information which platforms these titles can use,
- according to the information provided on the website, games are available on a PC and Mac. But unfortunately, the availability on the Mac is limited (Origin Access only in the PC version),
- product presentation is seen as modern: a short description of the content, infor-mation about the possibility of making a purchase, the possibility of downloading the trial version. However, movies or scenes from the game can be found on different (next) page, along with game modes, a full product description, infor-mation about the producer and hardware requirements,
- no product ratings by users,
- the purchasing process is therefore accessible and clear, but there is no shopping cart option. The only solution is the option to buy immediately after selecting the product and approving the payment method,
- promotions available to the client in the case of the Origin website include: the possibility of buying individual titles, at slightly reduced prices and a beneficial promotional program Origin Access, for example: providing specific games without restrictions, subscription holders can try new games before the premiere and pay 10% less, they receive information about new products, they can use the one-time payment option (greater cost) or pay for a subscription, etc.

Conclusions for Uplay (Ubisoft) platform website:

- a clearly visible search box, a minimalistic menu, a login box and a shopping cart. In the main part there is an advertisement of the promoted product, in the next section there are promoted games with figures from these games and packages of games of one product already released,
- website in light and aesthetic colours, messages are clearly visible and readable,
- only English language version available,
- the website is clear and easy to navigate, however, you need 3 clicks and two reloads to make a purchase, which is not very convenient,
- despite the fact that the information is easily accessible and navigating through the website does not cause any problems, it does not encourage the client to access more information,
- there is a choice (though sometimes limited) of accessibility between end devices (PC, Playstation 4, Xbox One, Nintendo Switch or VR),
- person can order sets (boxes) with additional figures, maps and accessories that are not available anywhere else comparing to other distributors,
- the product presentation is created in a tabular manner (after clicking on a given element), which is inconvenient for the client. The information is sufficient, but there are no buyers' opinions or assessments,

- user-friendly shopping cart, after adding a new item, a buyer may see the entire basket with the selected items and it is possible to quickly remove the product. Unfortunately, the process of adding products is already time-consuming, which is a considerable disadvantage of this website; also, moving to payment section requires several full page reloads,
- three types of promotion are used, i.e. presale, weekend discounts, and club loyalty points that can be exchanged for a percentage promotion.

Conclusions for GOG website are below:

- this is a traditional online shop layout with a pleasant colour scheme,
- has a transparent menu with a shopping basket and search options. In the main section, there is a clear presentation of all the products sold along with prices, including news and promoted products,
- there is no Polish language version, even though we deal with a Polish distributor/provider,
- a transparent page description with sufficient information which is easily and smoothly navigated, has an interactive menu with a modern layout that works well with the user,
- shopping - if an item has been added to the cart, it will be marked with a cart icon on the list. Each product is marked with an operating system icon that game is compatible with,
- the functionality related to adding a product to the basket is running quickly, it is easy to remove the item from the basket,
- GOG client information specifies all available hardware platforms such as Windows, OS X, Linux,
- the most interesting option offered by GOG is DRM-Free content. Customer buys a game that has no protection against copying or verification of purchased rights through a license server (no restrictions),
- product presentation on a website is very similar to Steam. We get a lot of useful information in the foreground: movies, scenes from the game, possible language versions, supported operating systems, standard information about recommended and minimum requirements with regard to the player's hardware and opinions of other customers about the items,
- a wide promotion program - for specific titles, publisher's products and weekend promotions [15].

Conclusions for all four web site comparison:

- Steam and Ubisoft present only a few products from the list, the full list is available after the Search button. Steam, on the other hand, offers full information with a photo and price in the proposed content, Ubisoft - only suggests product names,
- on the Steam and GOG websites, you can move quickly and get rich information about products. In addition, the product description includes information about the hardware platforms for which they are intended (PC, Linux, with some VR - virtual reality glasses),

- each site offers user-friendly search engine, the user is given hints after typing in a few letters. However, should be indicated that in the case of GOG and Origin websites, all search results are immediately displayed on the webpage (if they exceed the page, the number of results is displayed).

3.4 Comparative Analysis of Installed Digital Applications (Platform Client)

Analyses of the evaluation results of the installed applications of the selected computer game distributors were also made in two cross-sections: according to hardware plat-forms (devices) and according to the evaluation criteria. The first of them was based on the average, calculated for each distribution platform based on detailed assessments. The calculation indicates the absolute domination of the Steam application, expressed by the five highest average ratings in five categories of criteria, out of all six possible. In the opinion of respondents, only in the group of the product presentation (i.e. information about products and tools), the GOG Galaxy application gained the advantage of 3 percentage points. At the same time, it is a group of criteria with the highest average assessment (74.02%). The lowest score (67.98%) on all platforms was assigned to the installation package (size and simplicity of access and ways of its distribution). The difference between the maximum and minimum scores amounts to 6 percentage points. Only the Steam application with its results is above the average of all results. The lowest score was obtained in the case of the GOG Galaxy application with the result of 69.93% by 4 percentage points less than Steam. The scores of Origin and Uplay applications were only about one percent higher. The ranking of the final digital distribution applications for PCs is shown in Fig. 2.

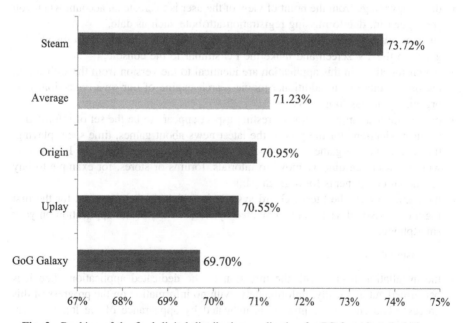

Fig. 2. Ranking of the final digital distribution application for PC for selected platforms

The order of the groups of detailed criteria determined the ranking order. The average for Steam was 73.72%. This was mainly due to the high search engine rating (in terms of usability and mode of operation), the appearance of the application, the layout of the elements, scalability to the screen size, clarity and readability (presentation of notifications and messages and the ease of finding information on the menu). The evaluations of Origin (70.95%) and Uplay (70.55%) are only slightly lower. The presentation method and the quality of the search engine received high scores, the worst scores were assigned to the installation package in each of the selected applications. Apart from this feature, the scores below the average (amounting to 71.23%) were indicated in the case of security – i.e. securing payments and access to purchased products.

For this study, the installation files of applications were downloaded directly from the distributors' websites in the second half of November 2017, bypassing intermediaries. The application designed for the Windows platform was evaluated because all platforms offer and operate on this operating system. Uplay has no alternative to other devices, while other platforms also provide Mac installations, and Steam also distributes installations on Linux. All installation files were easily accessible from the distributor's website.

Steam installation:

- installation process is in Polish, using standard Windows install engine. A license agreement for acceptance is presented in English, for people who are over 13 years old, with the option of choosing the interface language and installation location. The installation process is completed with starting the application which downloads additional data, which can be seen as the proper installation, and finishes with a welcome screen where user can log in or set up a user account,
- the application in the look and feel is an identical copy of the website,
- the disadvantage from the point of view of the user is to create an account when you are logged in, due to missing registration attribute such as date,
- an interesting solution is the Big Picture mode, which allows you to display the game on the TV screen and make the PC similar to the console,
- search functions in this application are identical to the version from the website. In the library there is an additional movie search engine of our own collection, thus organizing access to games,
- on this application, the most interesting aspect appears to be the set of information about productions for the player: the latest news about games, time spent playing, the date of the last game, a set of achievements in the game. From the Information window, user can quickly move to tutorials, forums or stores, for example to buy additional components for a given game,
- the platform uses the Steam Guard system, in which the key required for the first login on a given device can be obtained by email or the Steam application on your smartphone.

Origin installation:

- the installation begins with the initiation of the dedicated application, then it is performed automatically, unfortunately, with no information on the progress of this process. The end of the process is indicated by appearance of the login screen, which also allows to set up an user account,

- it is a modern platform but requires high-level hardware and memory resources, which can negatively affect the functioning and stability of the game,
- application in addition to basic services: purchase, download and the ability to use the purchased content allows communication with other players,
- it also ensures constant updating of the titles owned and the possibility of accessing the demo versions,
- the operation of the application is similar to that of the website. Speed and quality of use are also similar,
- transparency of graphics and the logic of the structure and the layout of information on the application do not raise any objections,
- two additional security measures are applied to ensure the user's security in the game. The first of them is the verification question (defined by the user, or chosen from the given list) and the answer to it, that user should remembered for the future use. The question is a mandatory step in setting up an account. The second security option (optional) is the ability to obtain a verification code (by e-mail, an authentication application or in the form of an SMS).

Uplay installation:

- the installation process starts with selecting the installation language, viewing the license agreement, and selecting the installation location. Then the automatic installation process begins. Afterwards, you can activate the game, where the login panel appears at the beginning with the option to create own account,
- it is a very simple application, starting from the news - current promotions and the possibility sign on to the beta testing program of finalised products,
- minimalistic approach to content: news, games (that user owns) and free games,
- the store operates using the same layout as the previously assessed Ubisoft website. In addition, we have the opportunity to directly enter the product activation code, communicate with other players and modify your profile,
- on this platform, user cannot find a visible search engine, which makes it difficult to navigate through resources,
- there is only basic information about owned product,
- application requires one or two-step verification by the application, as with the Origin platform.

GOG Galaxy installation:

- first step includes the language version pick up, the license agreement is accepted and the place of installation is chosen. Then the actual installation process begins. After its completion, user can launch the application and a login screen appears (where one can create a new account or reset current password),
- the application has a similar design as the website. The additional menu contains information about the currently owned products and the possibilities to run them. There is a compliance of the website and application. When purchasing an item, after adding a product in the application, a shopping basket is also visible on the website,
- the platform has a search engine to search the library of purchased games, operating similarly to the one on the website,

- the application is to serve as a device to use the purchased licenses and store them,
- at the product description level, user has a possibility to buy additional items related to the title,
- security – application requires two-step verification, the code is sent to the e-mail address provided on logging in. The only option is to log out of all logged applications with one button.

All platform applications require an active account. Each of them offers the opportunity to work offline, and the ability to add games from outside the platform. The installation process on all platforms proceeded in a similar manner and was quite intuitive. The most consistent and simplified installation process occurs on the Origin application. Installation on other applications of comped platforms is similar, with minor differences resulting from the order of the approved activities, which does not significantly affect the user's perception. It should also be noted that the installation is usually required to be performed once.

4   Analysis of the Findings with the Application of a Scoring Method with Preferences and the Discussion of the Findings

Customers have different expectations towards platforms depending on their level of experience and use of communication technologies for sharing knowledge [16]. One of the methods limiting the subjectivity of the experts' evaluations of users in the case of a scoring method (apart from the prior averaging of scores) is the application of unitary preferences, to particular criteria or selected criteria sets. In this study, the authors divided the criteria into three groups which are important or particular categories of users:

- novice – this category of a user is characterised by the interest in what person may evaluate at first sight, as well as the ease of obtaining a product and making a payment (mainly the technical aspects – the clarity of the website (first impression, the evaluation of the visual aspects, the number and distribution of graphic elements, colour scheme, lettering), promotions (promotions, loyalty schemes), the quality of the ordering process (simplicity of placing the order, information on delivery time, payment options),
- gamer – a person who perceives a game as entertainment, frequently plays games at the beginning that are available free of charge on their smartphone, then switches to PC or console games (mainly takes into account the service-related aspects: navigation of a website (location and intuitiveness of navigation, way of registering, terms of use, restrictions for unregistered users), distribution of products (channels and methods of obtaining games and reactivating access rights, DRM platforms supported, operating systems), advertising on the website (validity or recommendations, location of pop-up windows, excessive and intrusive advertising),
- professional – a person who plays very frequently (on a daily basis), passionate about playing games, plays all the newest games and is ready to pay for using them, plays professionally and can even earn money on the activity, etc. (mainly

interested in the functional aspects: the presentation of the product, the quality of information (the amount of information on a website, the possibility and manner in which one may ask questions, ease of access to information), the quality of the product search engine (the number of modifications, the number of filters, accuracy of answers, clarity of the scores).

For each group, the authors adopted one variant with a group of dominating criteria:

- novice (70% for technological aspects, 15% for the remaining ones),
- gamer (70% for service-related criteria, 15% for the remaining ones),
- professional (70% for functional criteria, 15% for the remaining ones).

Assigning preferences to particular groups of criteria resulted in changes in the rankings. The greatest changes could be observed in the case of the novice category in the case of games where Uplay platform moved from the last place to the second position in the ranking. In the remaining cases, the authors only recorded the reduction of the distance in relation to the previous approach. Small differences confirm that despite the significant differences with regard to the strategy of the development of the examined platforms, there emerges a specific standardization of the product/services ranges offered to clients. The summary of the positive features of the ranking points to the dominating position of the Steam platform. Only in the variant of an e-gamer, the scores obtained for the Steam and Origin platforms were above the average, and in the case of a gamer only Steam platform reaches the scores beyond average, in the case of the novice, such scores were obtained for Steam and Uplay platforms. The results of the ranking carried out by means of a scoring method with preferences are presented in Fig. 3.

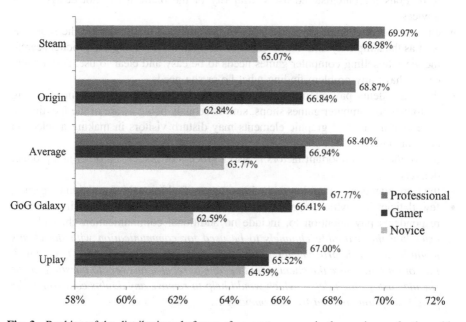

Fig. 3. Ranking of the distribution platforms of computer games in the scoring evaluation with preferences for different kinds of players

5 Conclusions and Recommendations

The conducted survey, supplemented with the opinions and comments of customers of computer games shops (the original wording of the respondents' opinions was retained), lead to the following conclusions:

- the majority of users are satisfied with the appearance and functionality of the platforms (websites and applications) distributing computer games, which is evidenced (mostly) by high scores (above 50%) of the specified criteria and their average values, both in the case of the selection of the examined companies as well as the evaluation criteria sets,
- the respondents emphasise the fact that in the case of the analysed platforms they pay particular attention to the features which allow them to easily obtain information on the content of the game (product information – 83% on average, and the information clarity – over 78%), as well as to find out whether they will be able to use all the functionalities of the game (hardware requirements - over 78%), ease of registration and payment (registration method and payment options – over 72% of approval),
- the lowest scores were obtained in the case of the excessive and intrusive advertising on the platforms (over 43%), despite the fact that these are mainly advertisements aimed at self-promotion,
- due to the fact that most of the individuals using the platforms consider themselves to be gamers, or even advanced gamers (65% in total), they are not interested in the manner and possibility to ask questions (51% and 56% respectively), as well as restrictions for unregistered users. Majority of the platforms is not designed for novices,
- clients value the simplicity and clarity of the analysed platforms and the scores as well as the simplicity and intuitiveness of navigation, including the product search, the website selling computer games needs to be easy and clear to use, and a client cannot have any problem finding what he or she needs,
- the respondents pay attention to an important role of visualisation in attracting customers to computer games shops, simultaneously being aware of the fact that an excessive number of graphic elements may disturb visitors in making a selection and purchase,
- one of the most important factors is also a process of placing an order and product delivery,
- the respondents pay attention to the importance of additional information on games,
- few deficiencies which, apart from an excessive amount of advertising that the respondents pay attention to, include no additional communication channels: … *extending the available channels to be used for communication with the clients might be seen as improvement (…) an interesting option is a possibility to chat with the consultant, where the client would be able to receive answers to questions he or she may ask without delay, which would help to remove any doubts concerning the products/options offered by the company….*

At present, Steam is a world leader in the category of computer games distribution, and its high score in this study confirms its position and the awareness of the market where it operates. The lower scores indicated in the case of other platforms may be explained with the fact that it is targeting a focused (narrow) group of recipients, who do not mind certain shortcomings with regard to the website since they are satisfied with the high quality of the final product they purchase. Origin and GOG have a modern look and very good interfacing tools to communicate with the user. The design of the Ubisoft website appears to be obsolete, and thus it may be seen as unattractive. Moreover, another disadvantage of Ubisoft is the lack of consistency with regard to the naming of the website and the application which is installed on a PC to use the purchased games.

Also companies analyzed in paper should remember about newcomers, which are attracting consumers with new approach to digital distribution. One of this companies is Robot Cache that gives opportunity to users to resell their games and mine cryptocurrency IRON [17]. Depending on fast changes in consumers' needs this kind of competition can rapidly become popular and threaten the actual leaders.

Another significant phenomenon in gaming industry is mobile platform which rapidly increases popularity. In author's survey 30% of gamers use only a smartphone for their games. It proves the statement defined in the other studies that the mobile gaming is taking the lead over other platforms – changing also the characteristics of played games.

One of the limitations of the study was undoubtedly focusing on only four distribution platforms. These are the leading platforms on the market, and in total they constitute – according to statistics - approximately 70–80% of the market share. Authors research also mimicked similar output, where 33% of the sample used other platforms than the selected four. In future research authors will extend survey to identify which of other platforms are most popular and what are their main advantages.

The diversity of the opinions concerning the computer games platforms causes some difficulties with regard to generalizing the evaluations. In the case of platforms offering games from independent designers there emerge various phenomena (such as "fake games") [18], which may negatively affect the rating of a particular platform. Despite the high popularity of this type of platforms, the similarity of their evaluations to the evaluations of internet shops in other areas of business [19]. Thus, it may be stated that there occurs a specific standardisation of views on how the website should look like. On the other hand, it gives also the idea on the discrepancy between the users' expectations and the projects of their creators. Moreover, one may conclude that the traditional principles of designing websites and applications are still up-to-date and applicable.

References

1. GamesIndustry.biz: GamesIndustry.biz presents … the year in numbers 2017 (2017). https://www.gamesindustry.biz/articles/2017-12-20-gamesindustry-biz-presents-the-year-in-numbers-2017. Accessed June 2018
2. SuperData Research: Worldwide digital games market: April 2018 (2018). https://www.superdataresearch.com/us-digital-games-market. Accessed June 2018

3. Lifewire: Top PC game digital download services (2018). https://www.lifewire.com/top-pc-game-digital-download-services-813065. Accessed Sept 2018
4. Polygon: In the long run, do Steam sales harm gamers? (2014). https://www.polygon.com/2014/1/15/5313142/in-the-long-run-do-steam-sales-harm-gamers. Accessed June 2018
5. Buonocore, C.E.: Comparative life cycle impact assessment of digital and physical distribution of video games in the United States. Master's thesis, Harvard Extension School (2016). https://dash.harvard.edu/handle/1/33797406?show=full. Accessed June 2018
6. Chmielarz, W., Szumski, O.: Analysis of users of computer games. In: Ganzha, M., Maciaszek, L., Paprzycki, M. (eds.) Volume 8, Proceedings of the 2016 Federated Conference on Computer Science and Information Systems, 11–14 September 2016, Gdańsk, Poland, pp. 1139–1146. PTI, Warsaw and IEEE, New York City (2016). ISSN 2300-5963
7. Chmielarz, W., Szumski, O.: Analysis of predispositions of e-gamers and its relevance in the use of computer games didactic process. In: Ziemba, E. (ed.) Information Technology in Management, New Ideas and Real Solutions, 11-th Conference of ISM and 14-th Conference of AITM part of FedCSIS 2016 Book. Lecture Notes in Business Information Processing, Gdańsk, Poland, vol. 277, pp. 77–102 (2017). ISBN 978-3-319-53075-8. https://doi.org/10.1007/978-3-319-53076-5_5
8. Ziemba, E. (ed.): Technologie i systemy informatyczne w organizacjach gospodarki opartej na wiedzy. Wydawnictwo Wyższej Szkoły Bankowej w Poznaniu, Poznań (2008)
9. Wielki, J.: Modele wpływu przestrzeni elektronicznej na organizacje gospodarcze. Wydawnictwo Uniwersytetu Ekonomicznego we Wrocławiu, Wrocław (2012)
10. Ziemba, E. (ed.): Towards a Sustainable Information Society. People, Business and Public Administration Perspectives. Cambridge Scholars Publishing, Newcastle upon Tyne (2016)
11. Nielsen, J.: Projektowanie funkcjonalnych serwisów internetowych. Helion, Gliwice (2003)
12. Nielsen, J.: Mobile Website and Application Usability. Nielsen Norman Group Press (2013)
13. Nielsen, J.: Tablet Website and Application UX. Nielsen Norman Group Press (2014)
14. Chmielarz, W., Szumski, O., Zborowski, M.: Kompleksowe metody ewaluacji witryn internetowych. Wydawnictwo Wydziału Zarządzania UW, Warszawa (2011)
15. GOG: GOG weekly sale (26.11) - Syberia, Phoning Home and more up to-80% (2018). https://www.gog.com/promo/20181126_weekly_sale. Accessed Nov 2018
16. Ziemba, E., Eisenbardt, M., Mullins, R.: Use of information and communication technologies for knowledge sharing by polish and UK-based prosumers. In: Ziemba E. (eds.) Information Technology for Management: New Ideas and Real Solutions, ISM 2016, AITM 2016. Lecture Notes in Business Information Processing, vol 277, pp. 49–73. Springer, Cham (2017). https://doi.org/10.1007/978-3-319-53076-5_4
17. Forbes: This Steam competitor lets you resell digital games, mine crypto for new ones (2018). https://www.forbes.com/sites/jasonevangelho/2018/01/16/new-steam-competitor-resell-your-digital-copies-mine-crypto-for-games. Accessed June 2018
18. USgamer: Valve removes nearly 200 "Fake" games from Steam (2018). https://www.usgamer.net/articles/valve-removes-nearly-200-fake-games-from-steam. Accessed Sept 2018
19. Chmielarz, W.: Determinanty rozwoju serwisów dystrybucji treści komercyjnych w Polsce. In: Problemy Zarządzania, Wydawnictwo Naukowe Wydziału Zarządzania UW, Problemy wykorzystania systemów informatycznych zarządzania w gospodarce, vol. 13, nr 2 (52), t.1, pp. 51–65 (2015). ISSN 1644-9584. https://doi.org/10.7172/1644-9584.52.4

Exploring BPM Adoption Factors: Insights into Literature and Experts Knowledge

Renata Gabryelczyk[(✉)] [iD]

Faculty of Economic Sciences, University of Warsaw, Warsaw, Poland
r.gabryelczyk@wne.uw.edu.pl

Abstract. The main aim of the proposed research is to identify factors that create an environment conducive to successful Business Process Management (BPM) adoption. The research methodology includes two triangulated approaches: the first - the process of theorization based on a literature review and procedure for analysis of qualitative data; and the second - the process of acquiring knowledge from experts based on assumptions of the Delphi technique and coding of acquired qualitative data. Factors predicting successful BPM adoption have been identified within the TOE (Technology-Organization-Environment) framework. The following factors are proposed: complexity of BPM system and notation, satisfaction with existing systems, technology readiness, top management commitment, leadership, perceived strategic benefits, extent of coordination, organizational readiness, performance measurement, culture and communication, employee competency and commitment, market pressure, and, regulatory and legal pressure. Study results have the potential to fill the research gap by contributing to the development of a theoretical model of BPM adoption that has not been proposed in studies thus far. In practical aspects, the proposed study can influence the understanding of the factors predicting successful BPM adoption and is the first step towards the development of a measuring instrument allowing the assessing of an organization's readiness to adopt BPM.

Keywords: Business Process Management · BPM adoption · TOE framework

1 Introduction

The main aim of the proposed research is to identify factors that are favorable or restrictive to Business Process Management (BPM) adoption. The identification of such factors can be helpful in the prediction of successful BPM adoption and use of this management concept. Achieving this goal may also contribute to the development of the BPM adoption model, including an instrument for measuring the readiness of an organization in its adoption of BPM.

BPM has been developing for over 25 years in Information Systems (IS) research [1, 2], and also in management practice [3]. BPM combines the identification, modeling, automation, implementation, control, measurement and improvement of business processes to support organizational goals and increase its effectiveness and efficiency [4]. In each of these BPM areas there are a number of studies, which, however, lack a

© Springer Nature Switzerland AG 2019
E. Ziemba (Ed.): AITM 2018/ISM 2018, LNBIP 346, pp. 155–175, 2019.
https://doi.org/10.1007/978-3-030-15154-6_9

coherent, theoretical adoption model [5, 6]. This evident gap in BPM research and expected contribution for theory and practice are the main motivations for this proposed study.

The term "*adoption*", in the context of this research, is defined as the use and acceptance of BPM assumptions in an organization relating to: process-based organizational structures, employee communication, process documentation, process execution, use of IT tools to support implementation and control of processes, performance measurement, process ownership, and taking into account customer requirements [7]. The level of organization involvement in BPM initiatives and programs determines process maturity, i.e., the higher the process maturity of an organization, the higher the level of BPM adoption. However, we can examine closer process maturity only when the organization decides to adopt BPM and starts the first associated initiatives and programs. In the proposed study, we identify technological, organizational and environmental conditions that are conducive to the successful adoption of BPM before the decision on this adoption is taken. Therefore, the BPM adoption model refers to factors that are predictors of the successful use and acceptance of BPM and are conducive to the development of BPM maturity.

BPM adoption factors, to the best of our knowledge, have not been identified thus far. Therefore, they need initially to be understood and they merit in the first step systematic literature review and qualitative approach [8, 9]. Thus, this research aims at the identification of the initial list of BPM adoption factors based on the triangulation of two research approaches: the theoretical and empirical. The theorization process is based on the methodology of qualitative research on literature sources. A literature review is the obvious basic workshop of every researcher in summarizing previous studies and developing new knowledge [9]. The methodology of qualitative research proposed by Jabareen [8] will be used in reasoning the initial set of factors based on literature studies. In the empirical approach, the knowledge of experts was acquired in the first round of the Delphi survey. The results of the literature studies will be compiled and compared with the results of an empirical analysis of experts' opinions [10].

To group BPM adoption factors the TOE (Technology-Organization-Environment) framework was used as one of the most recognized concepts for innovative solutions adoption on the organizational level [11, 12]. The proposed study is an indispensable basis for the initial formulation of research hypotheses for the BPM adoption model.

The BPM adoption model should elucidate what factors predict successful BPM use in an organization, and, as a model to develop a theory, it should provide predictability based on clearly defined assumptions and be precise and falsifiable [13]. These reasons led to the proposed use of the TOE. The TOE framework was introduced by Tornatzky and Fleischer [12] to indicate widespread theoretical perspective on factors influencing business innovation in organizations. This framework explains how a technological, organizational, and environmental context influences the adoption and implementation of innovations [11, 12].

BPM as a driver of organizational innovation [14, pp. 3–15] enables the development and implementation of process innovations [15, 16]. Previous research on BPM indicates that not only are resources within an organization important for BPM adoption, but also in the broadly understood context and external environment [3].

There is also strong evidence-based research showing a relationship between Information Systems (and general Information Technology) and BPM in organizations [17–20].

These relationships are also confirmed by theories widely adopted in the field of Information Systems [21] and used to explain BPM [22]. Based on inference conducted by Trkman [22]: *task-technology fit theory* explains the relationship between processes and IT, *dynamic capabilities theory* refers to the purposefully adaptation of resources in the continuous improvement process, and, *contingency theory* points to the fit between the environment and processes. BPM critical success factors should be considered based on the combination of all of these three theories. Indicated theories refer respectively to the technological, organizational and organizational context. These arguments led to the use of the TOE framework as the theoretical lens of BPM adoption's determinants. Thus, to realize the main aim of the proposed research three research questions are formulated in this study:

RQ1: Which technological factors are conducive to successful BPM adoption?
RQ2: Which organizational factors are conducive to successful BPM adoption?
RQ3: Which environmental factors are conducive to successful BPM adoption?

This paper will be organized as follows: firstly, the literature underlying the BPM adoption will be presented, followed by a literature review on BPM Critical Success Factors (CSFs) and the factors identified in the research using the TOE framework. Next, the research process and methodology will be presented. Subsequently, the obtain results obtained will be exposed and discussed in both based on the analysis of the literature and on the empirical study of the BPM experts. Finally, a discussion, contribution, and direction of future research will be also proposed.

2 Background

2.1 Adoption of BPM

The topic of BPM is widely explored in empirical research [2] and used in organizations primarily to increase organizational effectiveness, prepare organizations to implement IT systems and increase customer satisfaction [22, 23]. One common definition of BPM is proposed in [4, pp. 87–88]: "*Business Process Management (BPM) is a discipline involving any combination of modeling, automation, execution, control, measurement, and optimization of business activity flows in applicable combination to support enterprise goals, spanning organizational and system boundaries, and involving employees, customers, and partners within and beyond the enterprise boundaries*". This definition was created as a result of a broad discussion of the researchers of the phenomenon and practitioners of BPM implementation, and because it covers both, the BPM technological context (BPM as a technology) and the business context (BPM as a management discipline), it is considered the most comprehensive.

Despite the great popularity of process-based management concepts and the benefits they bring, BPM is still not adopted as a practice in many organizations, particularly in those of the public sector. It is unclear what causes this lack of acceptance

[22]. Moreover, the term "*adoption*" in the context of BPM is seldom used in literature, although it seems to be analogous to the area of Enterprise Resource Planning (ERP) systems research [18]. This is particularly notable if we wish to explore factors that can explain the use and acceptance of BPM assumptions in an organization [5, 24].

Previous BPM adoption studies that have used the "*adoption*" term have focused on success factors or single, selected aspects of BPM implementations and applications. Hribar and Mendling [5] in quantitative research analyzed the role of organizational culture for the successful adoption of BPM. According to this study organizational culture influences the success of BPM adoption. Moreover, this research includes an analysis of the types of organizational culture and indicates which culture types to a greater extent contribute to the success of BPM adoption and the resulting increased performance.

Malinova and Mendling [6] in their qualitative research proposed a conceptual framework for the adoption of BPM indicating possible causes of adoption, action and implementation strategies, and the anticipated effects of this adoption. However, there is no measuring instrument in the study, so it cannot serve as a model for adoption in accordance with the principles of modeling in organizational science [13]. Eikebrokk, Iden, Olsen and Opdahl [24] applied a similar approach to the analysis of factors that influence the acceptance and use of process modeling in organizations: a process modeling acceptance model was developed and tested empirically using survey data from companies.

In general, research on BPM devotes much more attention to BPM after the adoption decision. Studies on the entire BPM life cycle and studies examining different aspects of BPM maturity are definitely dominant. In addition to the afore mentioned studies of the type of culture as a predictor of successful BPM adoption [5] and research on the acceptance of BPM tools [24], literature sources on BPM prediction are virtually non-existent.

2.2   BPM Critical Success Factors

In the context of the successful adoption of BPM there have been several studies on critical success factors (CSFs) [22, 25–30]. Researchers used different terms for identical factors frequently critical to the success of BPM. These terms include: matching processes to organizational strategies, selecting appropriate project management and management methods, supporting top management, using the right information technology, and building a BPM-driven organizational culture.

All these factors are important for understanding the factors behind a successful BPM adoption. However, the adoption model should provide predictability based on clearly defined assumptions and be precise and falsifiable [13]. A BPM adoption model should explain which factors are positive or negative predictors of BPM adoption. For this reason, a review of critical success factors diagnosed after BPM (ex-post) adoption may be a starting point to consider which of these factors can be predicted earlier. For example, if top management support is a BPM critical success factor, then this factor probably also occurred in other organizational change projects implemented in the organization. If top management did not support other projects, it can be assumed that it will not support BPM initiatives and programs. Thus, the review of BPM CSFs studies is the first step to diagnosing prediction factors and for the development of a BPM adoption model, which is missing in BPM research. Table 1 presents a summary of a literature review on BPM CSFs.

Table 1. BPM critical success factors

BPM CSFs	Literature sources
Top management support, Management involvement, Leadership	[25] Bai and Sarkis; [26] Bandara, Alibabaei and Aghdasi; [27] Buh, Kovacic and Stemberger
Information technology, Development of service-oriented business applications and adapting the IT infrastructure, IS support	[25] Bai and Sarkis; [26] Bandara, Alibabaei and Aghdasi; [27] Buh, Kovacic and Stemberger; [29] Ravesteyn and Batenburg; [28] De Bruin and Rosemann; [30] Skrinjar and Trkman; [22] Trkman
Strategic alignment, Alignment of processes to organizational goals	[25] Bai and Sarkis; [26] Bandara et al.; [27] Buh, Kovacic and Stemberger; [28] De Bruin and Rosemann; [30] Skrinjar and Trkman; [22] Trkman
Governance, Clearly defined process owners, Appointment of process owners	[27] Buh, Kovacic and Stemberger; [28] De Bruin and Rosemann; [22] Trkman
Methods, Methodology	[26] Bandara, Alibabaei and Aghdasi; [27] Buh, Kovacic and Stemberger; [29] Ravesteyn and Batenburg; [28] De Bruin and Rosemann
Project management, Change Management, Ability to implement the proposed changes	[25] Bai and Sarkis; [26] Bandara, Alibabaei and Aghdasi; [27] Buh, Kovacic and Stemberger; [29] Ravesteyn and Batenburg; [30] Skrinjar and Trkman; [22] Trkman
Performance measurement, Measurement and control	[25] Bai and Sarkis; [26] Bandara, Alibabaei and Aghdasi; [27] Buh, Kovacic and Stemberger; [29] Ravesteyn and Batenburg; [30] Skrinjar and Trkman; [22] Trkman
People, Level of employee's specialization, Training and empowerment of employees, Motivated employees	[26] Bandara, Alibabaei and Aghdasi; [27] Buh, Kovacic and Stemberger; [28] De Bruin and Rosemann; [30] Skrinjar and Trkman; [22] Trkman
Culture, Communication, Teamwork, Social Networks	[25] Bai and Sarkis; [26] Bandara, Alibabaei and Aghdasi; [27] Buh et al.; [28] De Bruin and Rosemann

2.3   TOE as a Conceptual Framework for BPM Adoption

To identify and group BPM adoption factors in an organization the TOE framework is applied. The technological context of the TOE concerns the availability of internal and external technologies and new technologies relevant to the organization; the organizational context describes the characteristics of the organization such as communication processes and internal resources; the environmental context refers to the environmental conditions in which the organization operates, e.g. nature and/or strength of competitors and government regulations [11, 31].

The TOE framework takes into account the three aforementioned perspectives important for the adoption of new solutions, and have therefore been chosen as the theoretical basis in various areas of IS research such as cloud computing adoption [32, 33], e-business adoption [31], enterprise resource planning systems (ERP) adoption [34] and e-government assimilation [35]. In BPM research, the TOE framework was used to study BPM software adoption [36]. In order to identify contextual factors a literature review on TOE framework applications and on success factors of BPM implementations was conducted. Table 2 provides an overview of the factors using in the research with TOE framework. The factors are grouped according to the technological, organizational and environmental context. Factors are listed according to the name under which they occur in the research. However, some names have the same meaning.

Table 2. Factors affecting innovation adoption based on TOE framework

	Factors in research using the TOE framework	Literature sources
Technological Context	Complexity, Compatibility, Satisfaction with existing systems, Technology Competence, Technology readiness, Technology integration	[32] Alshamaila, Papagiannidis and Li; [33] Borgman, Bahli, Heier and Schewski; [37] Chau and Tam; [36] He and Wang; [38] Ismail and Ali; [39] Ramdani, Kawalek and Lorenzo; [40] Zhu, Kraemer and Dedrick; [41] Zhu and Kraemer
Organizational Context	Perceived benefits, Perceived costs, Perceived barriers, Top management support, Organizational readiness, Extent of coordination, Employees knowledge, Financial commitment	[32] Alshamaila, Papagiannidis and Li; [33] Borgman, Bahli, Heier and Schewski; [37] Chau and Tam; [38] Ismail and Ali; [42] Kuan and Chau; [31] Oliveira and Martins; [35] Pudjianto, Zo, Ciganek and Rho; [39] Ramdani, Kawalek and Lorenzo; [41] Zhu and Kraemer
Environmental Context	Perceived environmental pressure, Market uncertainty, Regulatory policy and support	[37] Chau and Tam; [42] Kuan and Chau; [31] Oliveira and Martins; [34] Pan and Jang; [39] Ramdani, Kawalek and Lorenzo; [43] Zhu, Dong, Xu and Kraemer

3 Methodology

The methodology in this study results from the triangulation of the theoretical and empirical approach that allowed us to obtain the quality of qualitative analysis and "*to check out the consistency of findings generated by different data collection methods*" [44]. First, in the process of theorization, we used the literature review and the procedure for constructing the conceptual framework by Jabareen [8] to analyze the qualitative data obtained in the literature sources. Second, in the process of eliciting experts' knowledge, we used assumptions of the Delphi technique to collect qualitative comments and coding methods to analyze this inquiry. The research model is presented in Fig. 1.

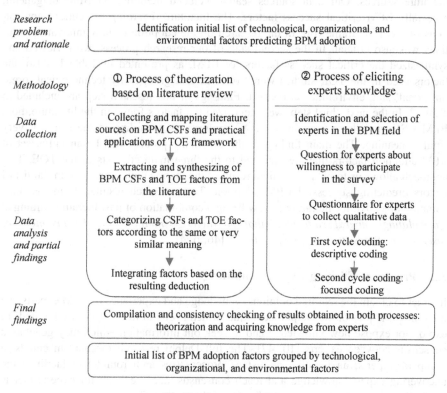

Fig. 1. Research model.

There are three main reasons why we have combined different types of qualitative methods. Firstly, as previously mentioned, is to achieve triangulation within qualitative investigation and to check the consistency of results [44]. Secondly, the procedure of Jabareen [8] defines framework as an integrated set of factors that enable the theoretical explanation of the studied phenomenon. Thus, according to this definition, the chosen procedure can be used for the preliminary identification of factors. Moreover, it is a methodology of qualitative research that can be based on literature review research, this being the initial step of every researcher as the necessary basis for developing new knowledge and systematizing the existing one [8, 9]. The literature review creates a foundation for the development of new models and theories [9], and this is the main aim of proposed research: to create a foundation for the BPM adoption model. Thirdly, experts opinion, based on their practical experience, exerts an influence on the development of BPM with full conviction [45].

3.1   Process of Theorization

Jabareen's procedure for building conceptual frameworks from existent multidisciplinary literature is a process of theorization [8]. According to the chosen research approach, we have used in this study the following research steps presented on Fig. 1 (①). In the first step of our research process we collected, mapped, and read the literature sources. Our data sources search included literature on BPM in general, especially BPM critical success factors. The literature regarding the current applications of the TOE framework in the research on the adoption of new innovative solutions was also crucial. In the second step of our research process, we reviewed and synthesized the critical success factors for BPM, as presented in Table 1. Also, the factors used in the TOE studies were collected and grouped by technological, organizational, and, environmental context. Findings of this research step are included in Table 2. In the next, third step, we categorized the factors found in the literature, both BPM CSFs and those used in the TOE applications according to the same or very similar meaning. The main finding of the theorizing process will be an initial set of BPM adoption factors that are assigned to the three main contexts of the TOE. This approach allows us to identify as final result of the theorization process an initial list of factors predicting successful BPM adoption. This approach resulted from the most common objective for literature review being a combination of past literature aiming at "*formulating general statements that characterize multiple specific instances of research, methods, theories, or practices*" [46, p. 4].

3.2   Process of Eliciting Experts Knowledge

In order to obtain the required opinions, knowledge and experience of BPM experts, we used the principles of the Delphi technique, which is one of the best-known methods to explore or expose new knowledge and to seek out information which may generate a consensus between experts [10, 47]. The full Delphi research mechanism entails: a group of experts, an iterative multistage process (research rounds) to facilitate the uncovering expert knowledge and reach consensus, and feedback for experts that is gradually systematized by the coordinator of the study [47].

As the research suggests, even an initial questionnaire allows the eliciting of expert knowledge, and the qualitative data gathered from it can be used as valuable research material [10, 48]. In accordance with this approach, we carefully identified and selected BPM experts with the prerequisite professional knowledge and/or practical experience. We sent an invitation to those chosen experts asking if they were willing to participate in the survey and then research questionnaire for those who agreed to take part.

For the analysis of qualitative data collected from experts, we have applied the *Grounded Theory* approach and its associated data-coding canon [49]. Codes are used to categorize "*similar data chunk*" or in other words "*coding is analysis*" of qualitative data [50, p. 79]. According to the coding manual by Saldana [51, pp. 58–59] we applied the first cycle of coding to the initial analysis of raw qualitative data, and, the second cycle of coding was used to group similarly coded data in the first cycle. At the preliminary stage of analysis we employed descriptive coding to summarize in a short phrase the basic topic of a passage of qualitative data [51, p. 88]. Descriptive coding allowed us to categorize an inventory of topics and to prepare a tabular account as presented on Tables 5, 6, and 7. To develop major categories from the data, we used focused coding (in other terminology axial coding) in the second cycle [51, p. 218]. This approach allowed us to reduce the number of initial codes and combine them into conceptual categories related to the TOE framework.

4   Research Findings

4.1   Findings of Theorization Process

Results of the theoretical investigation based on literature review present Table 3.

Table 3. Fitting of BPM CSFs and TOE factors based on literature review

TOE context	BPM CSFs	TOE factors for BPM
Technological context	Information technology, Development of service-oriented business applications and adapting the IT infrastructure, IS support	Complexity/Satisfaction with existing systems/Technology readiness
Organizational context	Top management support, Management involvement, Leadership	Top management support
	Strategic alignment, Alignment of processes to organizational goals	Perceived strategic benefits
	Governance, Clearly defined process owners, Appointment of process owners	Extent of coordination
	Methods, Methodology	Organizational readiness
	Project management, Change Management, Ability to implement the proposed changes	Organizational readiness
	Performance measurement, Measurement and control	Performance measurement
	People, Level of employee's specialization, Training and empowerment of employees, Employee motivation	Employees knowledge
	Culture, Communication, Teamwork, Social Networks	Culture conducive to organizational changes
Environmental context		Perceived environmental pressure

In the key stage of the process, as a result of the subsequent deduction, we combined factors of the same meaning, while reducing their number. For example, the key success factor of strategic alignment shows that the organization can indicate the impact of processes on the implementation of strategic objectives. Thus, this factor allows an assessment of the expected costs and benefits of BPM implementation. Factors matching the concept in the framework of the TOE are: perceived benefits, perceived costs, perceived barriers. These factors can all be measured with the help of a factor *"perceived strategic benefits of using BPM"*.

4.2   Findings of Eliciting Experts Knowledge

We have distinguished four groups of BPM experts: consultants from companies implementing BPM solutions, BPM professionals within the private and public sector organizations actively involved in organizational units responsible for BPM, e.g. in process competence centers, and, BPM researchers from the academia conducting research and publishing on BPM (professors and adjunct professors).

Invitations to take part in the study were sent to 45 experts, along with an explanation of the nature of the study, 41 of whom agreed to be involved (91%). We received completed forms from 37 experts (response rate 90%). Table 4 presents the characteristics of the research participants. The survey was conducted in Poland from mid-September to mid-November 2018.

Table 4. Experts' sample characteristics

Type of expert	Invited	Agreed	No. of participants	Response rate	Years of experience in BPM		
					Min	Max	Average
BPM Consultants	20	18	17	94%	10	20	18
BPM Professionals - private sector	9	9	7	77%	6	17	12
BPM Professionals - public sector	6	6	6	100%	2	25	11
Researchers of BPM	10	8	7	88%	8	15	12
Total	45	41	37	90%			

We posted the following open question to the participating experts: *"What factors may contribute to the success or failure of BPM in an organization before a decision is made to adopt this management concept? With each factor indicated, please add whether it favors the success or failure of BPM"*. We received 296 individuals items for BPM success and 227 for BPM failure. After clearing data from items that were too general (e.g. 'sector') or related to BPM CSFs, which could only be identified at the stage of project implementation (e.g. too lengthy process modeling time) we obtained 278 items for success and 194 for failure.

These raw data has been coded in the first cycle using descriptive coding that allowed us to sum up the number of responses obtained for initial grouped factors. Focused coding in the second cycle made it possible to group similar preliminary factors and assign them to the categories predefined in the literature. The success predictors and failure predictors were compiled in rows in the cases of opposing factors (antonyms). The occurrence of such codes has the effect of strengthening the given factor, e.g. "Top management support" is a success predictor, and "Lack of top management support" is a predictor of failure.

The results are grouped according to the three contexts of the TOE framework. Table 5 presents technological BPM adoption factors, where the findings obtained based on experts knowledge is consistent with the results of literature research.

Table 5. Technological BPM adoption factors based on experts opinion

Descriptive coding Success predictors	No. of responses	Descriptive coding Failure predictors	No. of responses	Focused coding
Organization needs to implement/modify an Enterprise System	12	The impossibility of implementing an Enterprise System	2	Satisfaction with existing systems
BPMS/BPA/iBPMS tools are used in organization	7	Incorrect use of BPMS tools	5	Complexity
Needed ICT resources are available in organization	3	Lack of availability of needed ICT resources in organization	6	Technology readiness
Organization develops service-oriented business applications	2			
IT supports Business	2			

The organizational context of BPM adoption in the opinion of experts turned out to be the most extensive and received much more responses than technological and environmental ones (Table 6). This proves that the most factors predicting the success or failure of BPM are contained within the organization. The results indicate that in addition to the factors explored in the literature studies, the "Leadership" factor and "Employee competency and commitment" remain very important for BPM experts.

Table 6. Organizational BPM adoption factors based on experts opinion

Descriptive coding	No. of responses	Descriptive coding	No. of responses	Focused coding
Success predictors		Failure predictors		
Top management support	18	Lack of top management support	12	Top management commitment
Top management has experience in the application of BPM	13	Lack of top management's experience in the application of BPM	13	
Top management understands the essence of organizational change	12	Lack of understanding of the essence of organizational change by top management	28	
Top management knows and understands the business case	11	Business case is not understandable	6	
High degree of consensus in the top management	2	Low degree of consensus in the top management	3	Leadership
		Lack of stable top management decisions	6	
		Rotation on managerial positions	10	
		Authoritarian leadership	3	
Change is related to strategy	10			Perceived strategic benefits
Consistency of strategy and activities	4			
Long-term strategy	1	No long-term strategic planning	4	
Specific goals of the change	6			
Awareness of financial benefits from the change	9			
Established rules for cooperation and responsibilities	10	No established rules for cooperation and responsibility	6	Extent of coordination
Mutual trust and confidence	9	Lack of mutual trust and confidence	3	
		Internal conflicts	2	
		Silos management	12	
Dedicated teams to implement changes	10	Lack of dedicated team to implement changes	4	
Incentive system related to the implementation of changes	10			
Competent employees to implement change	21	Lack of competent employees to implement change	17	Employee competency and commitment
Commitment of employees to change	17	Lack of employee commitment to change	3	
Implementation team has experience in the application of BPM	3			
Organizational culture conducive to open communication	14	Lack of organizational culture conducive to open communication	7	Organizational culture and communication

(continued)

Table 6. (*continued*)

Descriptive coding Success predictors	No. of responses	Descriptive coding Failure predictors	No. of responses	Focused coding
Organization performs measurements	7	No performance measurement	3	Performance measurement
		Lack of good practices	2	Organizational readiness
		Lack of financial resources	3	
Employees are aware of the essence of organizational change	9	The resistance against organizational change	12	
Organization uses other process-based concepts, e.g. ISO, lean	10	Failed implementation of other process-based concepts	7	
Effective change management methods	16	No effective change management methods	12	
Quick wins	2	Lack of quick wins	2	
Organization manages knowledge	4			
Organization uses continuous improvement	5			
Organization manages risk	3			

In the context of the environment, the experts drew attention to two main aspects of pressure from the environment: resulting from new regulations and legal conditions as well as pressure from the competitors, customers and suppliers (Table 7). The results obtained, based on expert opinion, is consistent with the results of literature studies, although the experts emphasized the importance of changes or stability of regulation and legal conditions.

Table 7. Environmental BPM adoption factors based on experts opinion

Descriptive coding Success predictors	No. of responses	Descriptive coding Failure predictors	No. of responses	Focused coding
The need to adapt the organization to new regulations and legal requirements	7			Regulatory and legal pressure
Friendly and stable regulatory and legal environment	2	Frequent changes of regulations and legal requirements	2	
Pressure from the competition	3			Market pressure
Pressure from suppliers	2			
Pressure from customers	2			

5 Discussion

5.1 Technological Context of BPM Adoption

Technological factors of BPM adoption can refer to the information technologies that are dedicated to modeling, analysis, simulation, automation, and process management in general. "Complexity", defined as "the degree to which an innovation is perceived as relatively difficult to understand and use" [52, p. 257] is considered as one of the fundamental factors that adversely affect adoption in many past IT adoption studies [38, 39]. Based on results of the BPM software adoption study [36], we suggest the same relationship for BPM in general, i.e. that the complexity of a BPM system and notation has a negative effect on the BPM adoption.

The adoption of BPM can also be affected by other relationships between processes and information technology (IT), such as the adoption of ERP systems, where a process-driven approach is commonly used in system implementations [18, 20]. Reference [37] note that the satisfaction level with existing IT systems plays a significant role in the shaping of motivations to change. Satisfaction with existing processes that are automated in ERP systems may discourage organizational changes. According to the knowledge of the experts the need to implement or modify an Enterprise System (such as ERP) can predict a successful BPM adoption. Satisfaction with service delivery processes through IT and general readiness of Information Technologies in an organization helps the adoption of BPM. This claim results not only from the experts knowledge, but also from the task-technology fit theory which describes the role of technology in BPM [22]. The task-technology fit is defined as *"the degree to which an organization's information systems functionality and services meet the information needs of the task"* [53, p. 93]. The lack of appropriate systems thus makes it impossible to perform tasks and processes in accordance with the BPM concept.

Thus, the next technological factor concerns the technology readiness: the higher the technological factor the more positive the impact on BPM adoption. However, satisfaction with existing systems has a negative effect on the BPM adoption. The more an organization is satisfied with its systems, the less it wants to change the processes to which it is accustomed.

5.2 Organizational Context of BPM Adoption

The TOE organizational context refers to the characteristics, structures, processes, and resources of an organization that may constrain or facilitate the adoption of innovation [37, 38]. The first factor takes into consideration the perceived strategic benefits of BPM. Awareness of benefits such as efficiency, effectiveness, and agility [54] can be a basic driver of a decision to adopt. Therefore, the hypothesis is formulated as follows: perceived benefits of using BPM have a positive effect on the BPM adoption.

Top management support is one of the most commonly mentioned CSFs, not only for BPM, but also for all organizational change projects. This is confirmed by both literature studies and experts knowledge in our study. It seems that *"commitment"* carries more weight than merely support, and can also include active engagement with understanding change based on experience. Effective decisions, monitoring and promoting acceptance of the project, and general change of management from the top, are crucial for a successful BPM adoption [17, 25]. The supporting role of top management in the previous change projects can be also a positive predictor for BPM adoption. Therefore, top management commitment has a positive effect on BPM adoption.

Organizational readiness is defined in research on innovation adoption as "the availability of the needed organizational resources for adoption" [32, 38, 55, p. 467]. Of particular importance is the perceived assessment by managers on the financial resources held by the organization and the organizational competence to undertake the adoption. The experience of the organization (competences at the organizational level) from the application of other management concepts, especially those based on processes, seem to also be of importance. This viewpoint confirms studies on BPM CSFs [25, 29] and theory of dynamic capabilities that "help a firm to adjust its resource mix" for continuous improvement [22]. The following statement is therefore suggested: organizational readiness has a positive effect on BPM adoption.

Coordination mechanisms can take the form of "processes, roles, or structural arrangements [...] as teams, informal linking roles, like those of change agents" [35, 56]. This factor seems highly important in the context of the development of BPM governance that establishes appropriate and transparent roles and responsibilities for BPM [28]. The resulting factor is the extent of coordination. The use of a coordination mechanism can have a positive effect on BPM adoption.

Performance measurement does not exist in previous studies using the TOE framework. However, the need to measure the effectiveness of the organization and its processes, and the inclusion of process performance measurement for continuous process improvement, are essential to the high level of BPM adoption and organizational maturity [22, 29]. The need for performance measurement results from strategic considerations and fosters the adoption of BPM. This result in the identification of the factor investigating the use of performance measurement, what can have a positive effect on BPM adoption.

Factors regarding organizational culture and communication have not been mentioned so far in research using the TOE framework. Probably because it was difficult to measure the impact of this factor in the context of adopting new technologies and innovations. However, in the area of BPM research there are strong arguments in the work of Hribar and Mendling [5] indicating the type of organizational culture that creates an environment for BPM. The results of these tests will allow to build an appropriate measurement instrument and thus to include the cultural factor in the BPM adoption model. BPM's adoption is very strongly linked to cultural and communication aspects [5, 28, 45] thus we believe that this factor must be included in the model.

The conclusion of the knowledge elicited by the experts indicates that among the significant organizational factors are also factors related to human resources, both in terms of leadership and employees. Both, authoritarian and unstable leadership adversely affects the targeting, motivating and inspiring of employees during the implementation of the change. Conversely, the key to success can be the skillful organization of competent employees' resources to implement change.

5.3 Environmental Context of BPM Adoption

BPM adoption can be the result of pressure exerted on an enterprise by its environment or external circumstances. Pressure can be exerted by business partners, competitors or government policies [1, 42]. A study of McCormack and Johnson [57] indicates that BPM maturity in a least advanced organization determines the level of cooperation and adaptation of inter-organizational processes. External conditions can also force the adoption of BPM in an organization, when, for example, the improvement and development of internal processes is forced upon it as the result of feedback from customers and suppliers [1, 27, 30].

In summary, perceived market pressure can have a positive effect on BPM adoption. Interestingly, some experts believe that a stable regulatory and legal environment favors the adoption of BPM, and some take the opposite view: new regulations and new legal requirements enforce the adoption of BPM. The direction of this influence should be determined using a measuring instrument in the adoption model in future studies of the adoption model.

6 Conclusion and Contribution

In this research we explored the factors that create environments receptive or unreceptive to BPM adoption and use. Factors have been identified within the TOE framework and grouped by the technological, organizational and environmental context.

Two methodological approaches to qualitative analyzes: one based on the literature review and the second based on experts knowledge allowed us to achieve our research aim and to answer the three research questions. This research paper presents initial steps for BPM model development. Figure 2 presents the proposed conceptual model for BPM adoption based on the identified list of factors.

The results of the proposed research could contribute to the development of a consistent theoretical model that would include the various factors influencing the successful adoption of BPM and thus contribute to the theory development. The methodological approach utilizing the TOE framework as the basis of the adoption model is novel in BPM research. The proposed initial list of BPM adoption factors may provide the foundation for further research. This list can be developed and modified using other data sources and types of research mentioned in the section about future research. The exploration of BPM adoption factors can contribute to the development of both individuals and entire organizations, and in both the public and private sectors. For individual employees and managers, it will be possible to raise awareness of BPM and identify gaps in competency delaying the adoption of BPM. At an organizational level, the model will help streamline organizational planning and resource development in all areas of the TOE framework. Knowledge about factors influencing successful BPM adoption can help predict the effects of BPM application in organizations that are less mature. A high level of BPM adoption allows an increase in the efficiency of processes carried out for citizens in the public and customers in the private sector, thus benefiting a country as a whole. Moreover, in practical aspects, the proposed study is the first step towards the development of a measuring instrument allowing the assessment of an organization's readiness to adopt BPM.

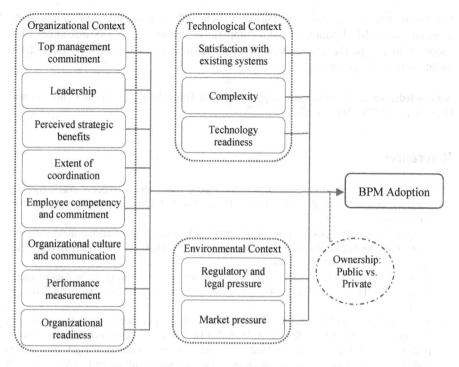

Fig. 2. Proposed conceptual BPM adoption model.

Practical applications of BPM in the public sector are still uncommon compared to the private sector [2]. However, many studies indicate the need to seek solutions that have been used in the management of profit-based organizations [1]. Thus, a BPM adoption model should also examine if the factors affecting BPM adoption differ between sectors, and if an ownership aspects affect BPM adoption.

7 Future Research

The initial identification of BPM adoption factors presented in this research is the basis for the development of the adoption model. However, as such factors have not yet been investigated, further studies are needed to verify the initial proposed list of factors. Subsequent studies should be of qualitative and quantitative research. Subsequent Delphi study rounds are planned to select and revise the most important factors. We plan to use a qualitative study with the aim of developing relevant hypotheses for future quantitative research on the phenomena. Mixed research methods are considered the most suitable in examining organizations that adopted BPM within the real-life context. Thus, to develop BPM adoption model we plan further research aims: to formulate and test research hypothesis based on qualitative research. The planned research process, after formulating hypotheses, involves the construction of a measuring instrument, the collection of empirical data, and, the conducting of appropriate statistical analyses to test the sample and hypotheses. This approach will facilitate the exploration of the determinants of BPM adoption and a comparative analysis of factors that affect BPM adoption in the public and private sectors. To develop a model to explain BPM adoption is our target aim.

Acknowledgments. This work was supported by the Polish National Science Centre, Poland, Grant No. 2017/27/B/HS4/01734.

References

1. Gabryelczyk, R., Roztocki, N.: Business process management success framework for transition economies. Inf. Syst. Manag. **35**(3), 234–253 (2018). https://doi.org/10.1080/10580530.2018.1477299
2. Houy, C., Fettke, P., Loos, P.: Empirical research in business process management – analysis of an emerging field of research. Bus. Process Manag. J. **16**(4), 619–661 (2010). https://doi.org/10.1108/14637151011065946
3. vom Brocke, J., Zelt, S., Schmiedel, T.: On the role of context in business process management. Int. J. Inf. Manag. **36**(3), 486–495 (2016). https://doi.org/10.1016/j.ijinfomgt.2015.10.002
4. Swenson, K.D., von Rosing, M.: Phase 4: what is business process management? In: von Rosing, M., von Scheel, H., Scheer, A.-W. (eds.) The Complete Business Process Handbook. Body of Knowledge from Process Modeling to BPM. Morgan Kaufmann, Burlington (2015)
5. Hribar, B., Mendling, J.: The correlation of organizational culture and success of BPM adoption. In: Proceedings of the European Conference on Information Systems (ECIS), Israel, Tel Aviv (2014). http://aisel.aisnet.org/ecis2014/proceedings/track06/2
6. Malinova, M., Mendling, J.: A qualitative research perspective on BPM adoption and the pitfalls of business process modeling. In: La Rosa, M., Soffer, P. (eds.) BPM 2012. LNBIP, vol. 132, pp. 77–88. Springer, Heidelberg (2013). https://doi.org/10.1007/978-3-642-36285-9_10
7. Reijers, H.A.: Implementing BPM systems: the role of process orientation. Bus. Process Manag. J. **12**(4), 389–409 (2006). https://doi.org/10.1108/14637150610678041
8. Jabareen, Y.: Building a conceptual framework: philosophy, definitions, and procedure. Int. J. Qual. Methods **8**(4), 49–62 (2009). https://doi.org/10.1177/160940690900800406
9. Webster, J., Watson, R.T.: Analyzing the past to prepare for the future: writing a literature review. MIS Q. **26**, xiii–xxiii (2002)
10. Hasson, F., Keeney, S., McKenna, H.: Research guidelines for the Delphi survey technique. J. Adv. Nur. **32**(4), 1008–1015 (2000)
11. Baker, J.: The technology-organization-environment framework. In: Dwivedi, Y.K., Wade, M.R., Schneberger, S.L. (eds.) Information Systems Theory, pp. 231–245. Springer, New York (2012). https://doi.org/10.1007/978-1-4419-6108-2_12
12. Tornatzky, L.G., Fleischer, M.: The Processes of Technological Innovation. Lexington Books, Lanham (1990)
13. Shapira, Z.: I've got a theory paper—do you?: conceptual, empirical, and theoretical contributions to knowledge in the organizational sciences. Organ. Sci. **22**(5), 1312–1321 (2011). https://doi.org/10.1287/orsc.1100.0636

14. Schmiedel, T., vom Brocke, J.: Business process management: potentials and challenges of driving innovation. In: vom Brocke, J., Schmiedel, T. (eds.) BPM - Driving Innovation in a Digital World. MP, pp. 3–15. Springer, Cham (2015). https://doi.org/10.1007/978-3-319-14430-6_1

15. Recker, J.: Evidence-Based business process management: using digital opportunities to drive organizational innovation. In: vom Brocke, J., Schmiedel, T. (eds.) BPM - Driving Innovation in a Digital World. MP, pp. 129–143. Springer, Cham (2015). https://doi.org/10.1007/978-3-319-14430-6_9

16. Tarafdar, M., Gordon, S.R.: Understanding the influence of information systems competencies on process innovation: a resource-based view. J. Strateg. Inf. Syst. 16(4), 353–392 (2007). https://doi.org/10.1016/j.jsis.2007.09.001

17. Al-Mudimigh, A.S.: The role and impact of business process management in enterprise systems implementation. Bus. Process Manag. J. 13(6), 866–874 (2007). https://doi.org/10.1108/14637150710834604

18. Gabryelczyk, R., Roztocki, N.: Effects of BPM on ERP adoption in the public sector. In: Proceedings of the 23rd Americas Conference on Information Systems (AMCIS), Boston, USA (2017). http://aisel.aisnet.org/amcis2017/AdvancesIS/Presentations/14/

19. Luftman, J.: Assessing business-IT alignment maturity. Commun. Assoc. Inf. Syst. 4(14) (2000). https://aisel.aisnet.org/cais/vol4/iss1/14/

20. Panayiotou, N.A., Gayialis, S.P., Evangelopoulos, N.P., Katimertzoglou, P.K.: A business process modeling-enabled requirements engineering framework for ERP implementation. Bus. Process Manag. J. 21(3), 628–664 (2015). https://doi.org/10.1108/BPMJ-06-2014-0051

21. Dwivedi, Y.K., Wade, M.R., Schneberger, S.L. (eds.): Information Systems Theory: Explaining and Predicting Our Digital Society, vol. 1. Springer, Heidelberg (2012). https://doi.org/10.1007/978-1-4419-6108-2

22. Trkman, P.: The critical success factors of business process management. Int. J. Inf. Manag. 30(2), 125–134 (2010). https://doi.org/10.1016/j.ijinfomgt.2009.07.003

23. Ram, J., Corkindale, D.: How 'critical' are the critical success factors (CSFs)?: examining the role of CSFs for ERP. Bus. Process Manag. J. 20(1), 151–174 (2014). https://doi.org/10.1108/BPMJ-11-2012-0127

24. Eikebrokk, T.R., Iden, J., Olsen, D.H., Opdahl, A.L.: Understanding the determinants of business process modelling in organisations. Bus. Process Manag. J. 17(4), 639–662 (2011). https://doi.org/10.1108/14637151111149465

25. Bai, C., Sarkis, J.: A grey-based DEMATEL model for evaluating business process management critical success factors. Int. J. Prod. Econ. 146(1), 281–292 (2013). https://doi.org/10.1016/j.ijpe.2013.07.011

26. Bandara, W., Alibabaei, A., Aghdasi, M.: Means of achieving business process management success factors. In: Proceedings of the 4th Mediterranean Conference on Information Systems. Athens University of Economics and Business, Athens (2009)

27. Buh, B., Kovacic, A., Stemberger, M.I.: Critical success sactors for different stages of business process management adoption – a case study. Econ. Res.-Ekonomska Istraživanja 28(1), 243–258 (2015). https://doi.org/10.1080/1331677X.2015.1041776

28. De Bruin, T., Rosemann M.: Towards a business process management maturity model. In: Proceedings of the Thirteenth European Conference on Information Systems (ECIS), Regensburg, Germany (2005)

29. Ravesteyn, P., Batenburg, R.: Surveying the critical success factors of BPM-systems implementation. Bus. Process Manag. J. 16(3), 492–507 (2010). https://doi.org/10.1108/14637151011049467

30. Skrinjar, R., Trkman, P.: Increasing process orientation with business process management: critical practices. Int. J. Inf. Manag. **33**(1), 48–60 (2013). https://doi.org/10.1016/j.ijinfomgt.2012.05.011

31. Oliveira, T., Martins, M.F.: Understanding e-business adoption across industries in European countries. Ind. Manag. Data Syst. **110**(9), 1337–1354 (2010). https://doi.org/10.1108/02635571011087428

32. Alshamaila, Y., Papagiannidis, S., Li, F.: Cloud computing adoption by SMEs in the north east of England: a multi-perspective framework. J. Enterp. Inf. Manag. **26**(3), 250–275 (2013). https://doi.org/10.1108/17410391311325225

33. Borgman, H.P., Bahli, B., Heier H., Schewski, F.: Cloudrise: exploring cloud computing adoption and governance with the TOE framework. In: Proceedings of the 46th Hawaii International Conference on System Sciences (HICSS), pp. 4425–4435. IEEE (2013)

34. Pan, M.J., Jang, W.Y.: Determinants of the adoption of enterprise resource planning within the technology-organization-environment framework: Taiwan's communications industry. J. Comput. Inf. Syst. **48**(3), 94–102 (2008)

35. Pudjianto, B., Zo, H., Ciganek, A.P., Rho, J.J.: Determinants of e-government assimilation in Indonesia: an empirical investigation using a TOE framework. Asia Pac. J. Inf. Syst. **21**(1), 49–80 (2011)

36. He, Y., Wang, W.: BPM software adoption in enterprises based on TOE framework and IS success model. Comput. Model. New Technol. **18**(12C), 195–200 (2014)

37. Chau, P.Y.K., Tam, K.Y.: Factors affecting the adoption of open systems: an exploratory study. MIS Q. **21**(1), 1–24 (1997)

38. Ismail, W., Ali, A.: Conceptual model for examining the factors that influence the likelihood of computerised accounting information system (CAIS) adoption among malaysian SME. Int. J. Inf. Technol. Bus. Manag. **15**(1), 122–151 (2013)

39. Ramdani, B., Kawalek, P., Lorenzo, O.: Predicting SMEs' adoption of enterprise systems. J. Enterp. Inf. Manag. **22**(1/2), 10–24 (2009). https://doi.org/10.1108/17410390910922796

40. Zhu, K., Kraemer, K.L., Dedrick, J.: Information technology payoff in e-business environments: an international perspective on value creation of e-business in the financial services industry. J. Manag. Inf. Syst. **21**(1), 17–54 (2004). https://doi.org/10.1080/07421222.2004.11045797

41. Zhu, K., Kraemer, K.L.: Post-adoption variations in usage and value of e-business by organizations: cross-country evidence from the retail industry. Inf. Syst. Res. **16**(1), 61–84 (2005)

42. Kuan, K.K., Chau, P.Y.: A perception-based model for EDI adoption in small businesses using a technology–organization–environment framework. Inf. Manag. **38**(8), 507–521 (2001). https://doi.org/10.1016/S0378-7206(01)00073-8

43. Zhu, K., Dong, S., Xu, S.X., Kraemer, K.L.: Innovation diffusion in global contexts: determinants of post-adoption digital transformation of European companies. Eur. J. Inf. Syst. **15**(6), 601–616 (2006). https://doi.org/10.1057/palgrave.ejis.3000650

44. Patton, M.Q.: Enhancing the quality and credibility of qualitative analysis. Health Serv. Res. **34**(5 Part II), 1189–1208 (1999)

45. Schmiedel, T., vom Brocke, J., Recker, J.: Which cultural values matter to business process management? Results from a global Delphi study. Bus. Process Manag. J. **19**(2), 292–317 (2013). https://doi.org/10.1108/14637151311308321

46. Cooper, H., Hedges, L.V.: Research synthesis as a scientific process. In: Cooper, H., Hedges, L.V., Valentine, J.C. (eds.) The Handbook of Research Synthesis and Meta-analysis. Russell Sage Foundation, New York City (2009)

47. Dalkey, N.C., Helmer, O.: An experimental application of the Delphi method to the use of experts. RAND Report RM-727, pp. 1–16 (1962)

48. Hoffman, R., Shadbolt, N.R., Burton, A.M., Klein, G.: Eliciting knowledge from experts: a methological analysis. Organ. Behav. Decis. Process. **62**(2), 129–158 (1995)
49. Corbin, J.M., Strauss, A.: Grounded theory research: procedures, canons, and evaluative criteria. Qual. Sociol. **13**(1), 3–21 (1990). https://doi.org/10.1007/BF00988593
50. Miles, M.B., Huberman, A.M., Saldana, J.: Qualitative Data Analysis: A Methods Sourcebook. Sage, Thousand Oaks (2014)
51. Saldana, J.: The Coding Manual for Qualitative Researchers, 2nd edn. Sage, Thousand Oaks (2013)
52. Rogers, E.M.: Diffusion of Innovations, 4th edn. Free Press, New York (2003)
53. Furneaux, B.: Task-technology fit theory: a survey and synopsis of the literature. In: Dwivedi, Y.K., Wade, M.R., Schneberger, S.L. (eds.) Information Systems Theory, pp. 87–106. Springer, New York (2012). https://doi.org/10.1007/978-1-4419-6108-2_5
54. Rudden, J.: Making the case for BPM: a benefits checklist. BPTrends (2007)
55. Iacovou, C.L., Benbasat, I., Dexter, A.S.: Electronic data interchange and small organizations: adoption and impact of technology. MIS Q. **19**(4), 465–485 (1995)
56. Chatterjee, D., Grewal, R., Sambamurthy, V.: Shaping up for e-commerce: institutional enablers of the organizational assimilation of web technologies. MIS Q. **26**(2), 65–89 (2002)
57. McCormack, K.P., Johnson, W.C.: Business Process Orientation: Gaining the e-Business Competitive Advantage. CRC Press, Boca Raton (2001)

Comparative Study of Different MCDA-Based Approaches in Sustainable Supplier Selection Problem

Artur Karczmarczyk[1] , Jarosław Wątróbski[2(✉)] , and Jarosław Jankowski[1]

[1] Faculty of Computer Science and Information Technology,
West Pomeranian University of Technology in Szczecin,
Żołnierska 49, 71-210 Szczecin, Poland
{artur.karczmarczyk,jaroslaw.jankowski}@zut.edu.pl
[2] Faculty of Economics and Management, University of Szczecin,
Mickewicza 64, 71-101 Szczecin, Poland
jwatrobski@wneiz.pl

Abstract. One of the crucial aspects of maintaining the business continuity of a company is the process of sustainable supplier selection. If the suppliers are chosen improperly, a slow-down or even a complete suspension of the operations within a company can occur. In this paper, a new unique approach is presented in which the classical MCDA paradigm is extended with aspects of temporal evaluation. In practical terms, three popular MCDA methods are used to evaluate suppliers based on data obtained from five temporal aggregation strategies. The combination of three MCDA methods (namely AHP, TOPSIS and COMET) allows to obtain a rank-reversal-free solution with a reference model and well defined hierarchical structure of the problem. Moreover, the rankings obtained from the MCDA methods are then aggregated to provide the Decision Maker a single ranking of suppliers. The effect of each temporal aggregation strategy on the eventual selection of the winning supplier is also studied.

Keywords: MCDA · Temporal aggregation · AHP · TOPSIS · COMET · PROMETHEE · Sustainable supplier selection

1 Introduction

The proper supplier selection has been the foundation of developing a competitive supply chain from the very beginning of the supply chain thinking [37]. This strategic decision can have a significant effect on the competitive advantage of a company, especially if an expansion to new markets is considered [8]. If decent suppliers are chosen, the operational costs can be decreased, as well as the company's overall productivity and effectiveness can be improved [16]. Furthermore, the appropriate arrangement of the supply base is vital for the logistics of materials and products, thus directly affecting the business continuity of the company [8].

© Springer Nature Switzerland AG 2019
E. Ziemba (Ed.): AITM 2018/ISM 2018, LNBIP 346, pp. 176–193, 2019.
https://doi.org/10.1007/978-3-030-15154-6_10

The increased integration between supply chain partners leads to supply chain efficiency, nevertheless, an over-dependence can result in propagation and amplification of disruptions [6]. The negative effects of failure to perform the supplier evaluation processes have been vastly studied. Over 20 years ago, Meade indicated that a wrong selection of suppliers could affect the processes within an organization negatively [27]. The succeeding studies expanded the negative consequences even further, over the complete integrated supply chain [17]. The negligence of the suppliers' evaluation process can lead to disruptions in the supply chain process or even to stopping the primary operations of a company [17].

Ever since the Internet and ICT (Information and Communication Technologies) was developed, the data processing efficiency has increased considerably. Consequently, it is now possible to monitor and evaluate the suppliers in an on-going and repeated manner. The data automatically collected by smart management information systems allows to perform a temporal-level evaluation of the suppliers, which creates new research areas. The aspect of the fluctuation of the suppliers' appraisal over time forms an interesting research problem. As an illustration, e-commerce businesses can have 30% more transactions in December than they have during summer [20]. In contrast, during the summer period, farming companies outsource work to suppliers to cope with the increased amount of work in the peak of the fruit picking season [15].

Within the last 20 years, the topic of the environment protection has been gaining increasing importance [45]. This increased environmental consciousness leads to the various stakeholders demanding for the companies to incorporate green practices into their daily operations [14,30]. Consequently, the criteria used to select suppliers in the previous decades [8] needed to be supplemented by criteria allowing to evaluate the GSCM (green supply chain management) practices [14,19].

Multi-criteria decision analysis (MCDA) methods have been successfully applied in such evaluation problems to find a "good" (but not optimal) "here and now" solutions. However, so far they rarely considered the temporal validity of the aggregated data or the partial evaluations. The authors attempted to address this problem in their prior work [47], where partial temporal evaluations were taken into account and in [25], where multiple MCDA methods were combined to provide a framework for dynamic sustainable supplier selection, taking into account the temporal aspects, the hierarchical structure of the decision problem, and exploring its full space, thus preventing the rank-reversal phenomenon. However, while solving all the aforementioned problems, the proposed approach produced multiple equally important rankings, rendering the actual decision making to be complex and problematic.

Therefore, the authors' contribution in this paper is to improve the approaches presented in [25,47] to facilitate the selection of a single best supplier based on the decision-maker's priorities regarding not only the temporal data aggregation method, but also the obtained ranking's hierarchical structure and rank-reversal resilience. In practical terms, the introduction of PROMETHEE II complete order analysis and the GAIA visual aid allowed to provide an approach in which the analyst can study how each of the data aggregation methods affects the final evaluation of each of the appraised suppliers.

The rest of this paper is organized as follows. Section 2 contains a literature review of the current state of the art. Section 3 presents the methodological framework. Section 4 contains empirical research and its results. The conclusions and future work directions are presented in Sect. 5.

2 Literature Review

The process of the supplier selection has considerable strategic importance for all of the involved parties. The literature analysis shows a wide range of theoretical and practical studies where the suppliers in the supply chain are evaluated and selected in various industry or trade areas [9,40].

Nowadays, the selection of sustainable suppliers has become a necessity. As a result of the increased awareness of the environmental issues, the competition between companies on the ground of providing green supply chain capabilities raises [1].

Companies tend to struggle with the eco-friendly supplier selection. However, this process can be facilitated by the advancements in the green supply chain management practice strategies [41]. A profound literature review of the approaches and analytical methods used in the evaluation process can be found in [42]. It is worth noting that the utilization of MCDA methods in their crisp, fuzzy and hybrid variants in such applications is becoming more popular.

The selection of sustainable suppliers is an important practical problem [40] while being the subject of many scientific studies [28]. The original essence of the supply chain [41] has been expanded by incorporating environmental factors into it. The evolution of the green SCM and green supplier terms towards sustainable SCM and sustainable supplier caused that the researchers' attention become wider to include a vast range of environmental and social factors [50]. The multi-criteria nature of the sustainable supplier selection problem caused that a number of methods from the MCDA family were used in this area [28,36]. The consideration of the current research trends caused that apart from the classic crisp versions of MCDA methods, their modern expansions based on the fuzzy-set theory are also widely used. On the other hand, the limitations of the individual MCDA methods often result in the fact that their usage for sustainable supplier selection problems is based on a comparative analysis of the results obtained by various methods or even combining several of them into a single decision process.

Table 1 contains selected applications of the MCDA methods in sustainable supplier selection. The literature review and applications presented in the table confirm a wide range of usage of MCDA methods in the considered problematic. It is worth noting that both American and European school methods have been applied there. Of course, the most popular methods include AHP [9,18,48], ANP [29,40] and TOPSIS [5,10,11,38]. Researchers, however, often try to combine

Table 1. MCDA methods application in the sustainable supplier selection problem

No.	Problem	M	P	W	V	T	Ref.
1	Choice of the global supplier for a manufacturing company	F. AHP	α	y	Fuzzy	n	[9]
2	Ranking of the suppliers	ANP	β	y	Crisp	n	[29]
3	Choice of supplier of electronic equipment	F. AHP	α	y	Fuzzy	n	[48]
4	Assessment of alternative suppliers for a business	F. ANP	β	y	Fuzzy	n	[40]
5	Choice of supplier	F. Promethee II	β	n	Fuzzy	y	[36]
6	Choice a new supplier of products for the telecommunications company	F. ANP, F. TOPSIS	α	y	Fuzzy	n	[28]
7	Choice of material supplier for key elements of new products	F. TOPSIS	β	y	Fuzzy	n	[10]
8	Choice of supplier for a key component in the production of automotive company	F. TOPSIS	α	y	Fuzzy	n	[5]
9	Selection of a strategic business partner in the logistics supply chain	F. AHP, F. TOPSIS	β	y	Fuzzy	n	[7]
10	Choice of supplier for local company	AHP, TOPSIS	β	y	Crisp	n	[39]
11	Choice of supplier	Promethee II	β	y	Crisp	y	[2]
12	Choice of the reserve supplier in order to ensure supplies	Electre I	β	y	Crisp	n	[12]
13	Choice of supplier for companies operating in the field of public roads and transport	Promethee II	β	y	Crisp	y	[13]
14	Choice of supplier for companies operating in the field of public roads and transport	Promethee I	β	y	Crisp	y	[13]
15	Choice of supplier for the manufacturer of the gear motor	F. AHP	β	y	Fuzzy	n	[3]
16	Supplier selection components for battery production	F. AHP, F. TOPSIS	α	y	Fuzzy	n	[43]
17	Supplier selection of metals for production of transmission for motorcycles	F. TOPSIS	β	y	Fuzzy	n	[23]
18	Supplier selection of metals for production of transmission for motorcycles	F. AHP	β	y	Fuzzy	n	[23]
19	Choice of supplier for a manufacturing company	F. TOPSIS	β	y	Fuzzy	n	[38]
20	Assessment of balanced supplier performance	F. TOPSIS	β	y	Fuzzy	n	[18]

Abbreviations: M – the used MCDA method; P – problematic; W – weights usage; V – performance values of the alternatives; T – thresholds usage; y – yes; n – no; α – choice; β – ranking

the advantages of these methods in a single common model, most commonly combining the preference modelling stage from the AHP method with generating the final ranking using TOPSIS [7, 23, 28, 39]. The emphasis in the research is also placed on the modeling of the imprecision of the measurement data itself.

The need to model the DM's preferences, including their natural under-specification, prompted researchers to use methods based on the outranking relationship [2,3,13,36] and, consequently, to use so-called pseudo-criteria instead of the real ones [2,13].

It is important to note, however, that the MCDA-based approaches indicated above produce a here-and-now assessment, based on criteria measurements collected for a single moment in time. In case of the supplier selection problem, the variability of each suppliers' evaluations in time should also be considered though. The prior efforts to provide the ability to aggregate measurements and evaluations collected over a period of time include the work of Banamar and De Smet [4], who extended the PROMETHEE II method to allow temporal evaluations, Sahin and Mohamed [34], who introduced a Spatial Temporal Decision framework based upon a combination of System Dynamics modelling, Geographical Information Systems modeling and multi-criteria analyses of stakeholders' views with the use of the AHP method or Zhu and Hipel [49], who used multiple stages grey target decision making method for vendor evaluation of a commercial airplane in China. In the authors' prior work, a framework extending the TOP-SIS method capabilities to evaluate and select green suppliers based on temporal analysis has been constructed in [46,47]. This approach was further extended in [25], where also AHP and COMET methods were integrated into the process, to allow taking into account the hierarchical structure of the decision problem, or the rank reversal problem. The latter approach however, due to the use of three separate MCDA methods considerably increased the complexity of deciding on the final best supplier from the set of obtained rankings. No easy step from having obtained separate rankings to the final decision was provided, nor was it studied how each temporal strategy or the decision makers' preference regarding the ranking methods affect the final choice. This forms an interesting research problem, to not only evaluate the sustainable suppliers from various scopes and over various temporal aggregation strategies, but also to study how each choice of the aggregation strategy or the decision maker's preference regarding the weight of hierarchical structure study, lack of rank-reversal, possibility to obtain a positive and negative ideal solutions affect the final selection of the supplier.

3   Methodological Framework

The selection of a sustainable supplier in the Green Supplier Chain Management is a complex problem that requires a proper approach. The popular MCDA-based approaches have some drawbacks. They are based on the classic MCDA paradigm, which assumes constancy of all of the elements of the decision support process. However, for the sustainable supplier evaluation process, taking into account its characteristics - its hierarchical structure as well as changeability of the appraisal elements in time - would be beneficial. Based on the above, the authors proposed in [25] using a complementary approach based on a precise mapping of the structure of the decision problem (derived from AHP), building

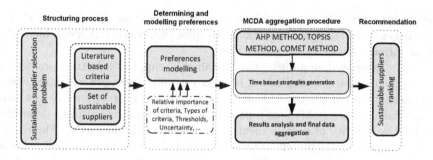

Fig. 1. Visual illustration of the proposed approach

a supplier reference model (TOPSIS), as well as minimizing the shortcomings of the two methods by incorporating the COMET method. The variable effect of each supplier appraisal in a period of time was also taken into account. Nonetheless, the approach did not provide an easy step from obtaining the rankings in the aforementioned MCDA methods and with various temporal aggregation strategies to the final decision on selection of the best supplier. The authors' contribution in this paper is to extend the prior approach [25] by providing the framework for selecting the best sustainable supplier based on the decision makers' preferences not only regarding individual evaluation criteria, but also regarding the actual selection process, i.e. the DM's preference regarding rank-reversal resistance, possibility to provide a reference model or take into account the decision problem hierarchical structure. Moreover, the means to study how these DM's preferences affected the final decision are provided. The framework is visually presented on Fig. 1 and is described in detail in the following subsections.

3.1 MCDA Foundations of the Proposed Framework

Since the selection of a sustainable supplier requires to take into account multiple performance and environmental criteria, it can be considered to be a multicriteria problem with a complex hierarchical structure. Rezaei et al. [31] provided a list of 23 supplier selection criteria most utilised in the periods 1966–1990 and 1990–2001, and combined them with 15 modern environmental criteria. However, such a vast set of criteria makes the evaluation difficult to perform. In our approach we address the following aspects:

A – the hierarchical structure of the sustainable supplier selection is well accounted-for;
B – the appraised sustainable suppliers can be referenced to a potential ideal and anti-ideal supplier;
C – the rank reversal probability is minimized.

The first one, A, is obtained by utilizing the Analytic Hierarchy Process (AHP) method to organize the evaluation criteria into a hierarchy. The AHP method by Saaty [33] is one of the most widely used and most well-known MCDA approaches. It is based on three main principles [26]: construction of a hierarchy, setting priorities and logical consistency.

In the proposed approach, the sustainable supplier selection problem is decomposed and structured into a hierarchy of objectives, criteria, sub-criteria and alternatives (suppliers). The utilized hierarchy of criteria from [25] was used. The decision maker (DM) uses a pairwise comparison mechanism to determine the relative priority of each element at each level of the hierarchy. The results of the comparison are presented on a scale of 1–9 in case of more preference or $\frac{1}{9} - 1$ in case of less preference. Such pairwise comparisons on each level of the hierarchy and their aggregation allow to indicate the overall preference of each of the suppliers based on the complete hierarchical evaluation criteria structure.

On the other hand, the aspect (B) was obtained by combining the TOPSIS method into the process. It is a popular MCDA decision-making technique, originally developed by Hwang and Yoon [22], which in the proposed approach allows to compare the relative distance of each of the evaluated suppliers to a potential ideal and anti-ideal one (PIS, positive ideal solution and NIS, negative ideal solution respectively). The best sustainable supplier should be as close as possible to the PIS, and as far as possible from the NIS. As a result of the TOPSIS method evaluation, each appraised supplier is described with its distance from PIS, NIS as well as with its relative closeness to the ideal solution (CC_i). The CC_i value is used here as the value of the utility function aggregating all evaluation criteria and, therefore, is used to produce the final ranking of suppliers.

Last, but not least, the aspect (C) is achieved by collating the aforementioned two methods with the Characteristic Objects METhod (COMET) [35]. This method allows to explore the complete space of possible solutions. The COMET method is based on the fuzzy sets theory. Characteristic objects are created and compared in it, instead of alternatives, in order to create a linguistic rule base. Each evaluated alternative is subsequently scored in a defuzzification process. As a result, since the full space of the decision problem has been studied with the characteristic objects, introduction of any new suppliers to the evaluation process would not affect the order of the prior-evaluated suppliers.

3.2   Temporal Aggregation of the Supplier Evaluation Results

Classically, the MCDA procedure requires the alternatives and criteria alike to be constant [21,32]. On the other hand, however, intuitively the criteria measurements collected closest to the time of evaluation are intuitively more valid than the ones collected in some other time. The criteria measurements from all periods can be aggregated using, for example, fuzzy sets theory or fuzzy numbers. However, this, by affecting the accuracy of the evaluation method input data, can oversimplify the model leading to the reduction of the decision support quality. Therefore, instead of aggregating the input data, the DM can perform a temporal aggregation of the outcomes produced by the evaluations produced in each period.

The temporal aggregation concept is based on the construction of a general utility function with an additional attribute called *forgetting*. Two possible types of forgetting strategies can be used:

TPEA
> Time Period Equal Aggregation – balanced impact of the individual ratings on the outcome of the assessment;

TDA
> Time Depreciated Aggregation – diminished significance of the historical data along with its increasing distance to the current period.

Regardless of the forgetting strategies chosen, the following formula allows to obtain the general utility of a supplier:

$$V(a^i) = \sum_{k=1}^{n} S_{ik} \cdot p(t_k) \tag{1}$$

where $V(a^i)$ means the general utility for the ith supplier on the basis of all n periods taken into account, S_{ik} denotes the utility of the ith supplier in period k and $p(t_k)$ stands for the significance of data for the k period in time t, based on the chosen forgetting strategy. S_{ik} is established in the previous step by the AHP, TOPSIS and COMET methods.

3.3   Final Aggregation of the Supplier Evaluation Results

Unfortunately, it needs to be noted that the $V(a^i)$ values obtained in Sect. 3.2 are dependent on the MCDA aggregation method and TPEA/TDA aggregation strategies chosen. In order to perform a comprehensive study, various methods and strategies should be used, resulting in multiple possible rankings of alternatives instead of a single one. In the empirical study in [25], the authors indicated the best supplier to be the one which appeared in all rankings within the best five ranks. Such intuitive approach would become very difficult, however, if multiple suppliers obtained similar appraisals in all rankings. Therefore, in the presented approach the authors extend their prior framework by introducing a subsequent MCDA decision-making step to produce the single final ranking of alternatives.

The final aggregation of the obtained rankings can be performed with the PROMETHEE II method and its GAIA visual module (Preference Ranking Organization METHod for Enrichment of Evaluations and Geometrical Analysis for Interactive Aid respectively). The family of PROMETHEE methods derives from both the American and European MCDA schools [44] by, on the one hand, being based on pairwise comparisons and outranking flows and, on the other hand, producing a complete ranking of the alternatives and assigning a single value of the utility function for each of them. Moreover, incorporation of the PROMETHEE's GAIA visual utility allows to study how each intermediate ranking based on various MCDA methods and various temporal aggregation strategies affects the final decision, i.e. which alternatives are supported or are in conflict with each of the methods [24].

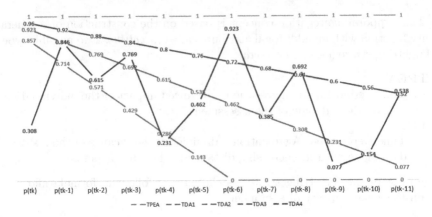

Fig. 2. Forgetting functions for TPEA, TDA1, TDA2, TDA3 and TDA4 strategies

4   Empirical Research

In the empirical study, the proposed approach was verified on a real company. On the basis of the monthly and yearly turnover, thirty suppliers were selected for the research. The suppliers were appraised based on the criteria resulting from a profound literature review made in [25]. Wherever automation was possible, the performance results of each supplier were obtained from ERP systems. In this manner, criteria such as delivery time, timeliness of deliveries or company's turnover were collected. The other criteria were obtained from surveys and expert judgment.

The criterial performance values were normalized and presented on a 5-point Likert scale. The utility values of each supplier were then obtained with the use of the AHP, TOPSIS and COMET methods. Five temporal aggregation strategies were used: TPEA, TDA1, TDA2, TDA3 and TDA4 (see Table 2 and Fig. 2).

The five temporal aggregation strategies require some explanation. In case of the simplest strategy, TPEA, the $p(t_k)$ value is always equal to 1, which means that the results from each evaluation period are equally important. In case of TDA1, TDA2 and TDA3 the forgetting function was spanning over 6, 12 and 24 months respectively. The forgetting function of the TDA4 strategy depended on the suppliers' turnover.

The results of the temporal evaluation of the suppliers based on the AHP, TOPSIS and COMET methods' partial evaluations are presented in Table 3. In order to ascertain brevity of the paper and its illustrative character, only five of the suppliers are presented in Table 3.

The correlation coefficient between the results obtained by each of the three methods and five temporal aggregation strategies are presented on Fig. 3. A high correlation between all rankings can be observed. However, it is clearly visible that, as intuition suggests, the highest correlation occurs between rankings

Table 2. Forgetting function parameters for TPEA, TDA1, TDA2, TDA3 and TDA4 strategies

Aggregation	TPEA	TDA1	TDA2	TDA3	TDA4
p(tk)	1	0.857	0.923	0.96	0.308
p(tk-1)	1	0.714	0.846	0.92	0.846
p(tk-2)	1	0.571	0.769	0.88	0.615
p(tk-3)	1	0.429	0.692	0.84	0.769
p(tk-4)	1	0.286	0.615	0.8	0.231
p(tk-5)	1	0.143	0.538	0.76	0.462
p(tk-6)	1	0	0.462	0.72	0.923
p(tk-7)	1	0	0.385	0.68	0.385
p(tk-8)	1	0	0.308	0.64	0.692
p(tk-9)	1	0	0.231	0.6	0.077
p(tk-10)	1	0	0.154	0.56	0.154
p(tk-11)	1	0	0.077	0.52	0.538

obtained with the same MCDA method. When the correlation between rankings produced by different methods are compared, AHP and TOPSIS methods are more correlated than any of these two methods with COMET. While AHP and TOPSIS operate locally exclusively on the evaluated suppliers, COMET uses the local information on the alternatives to explore the complete space of the decision problem, and hence the lower correlation values.

Although the usage of three separate MCDA methods allows to combine the best properties of these methods within the research, it also leads to a difficulty in the actual selection of the best supplier. The analysis of the temporal evaluation results from all three MCDA methods would allow to indicate the supplier A12 as the one appearing on the majority of the rankings within the top 5 suppliers, as it was shown in [25], however a more structured approach would be beneficial. Therefore, the authors extended the approach with an additional MCDA analysis step where the results from all rankings are aggregated into a single utility value. The utility function values from the AHP, TOPSIS and COMET methods are treated as criteria of the new decision problem. In the empirical study, the PROMETHEE method was used to aggregate the data, which allowed to consider the results from each temporal aggregation strategy separately, but also to group results from all temporal strategies under a single MCDA method group.

Such an approach allowed to obtain a single "good" solution instead of three sets of possible variants. In case of the evaluated set of 30 suppliers, regardless of the temporal aggregation strategy, the alternatives A5, A6, A9, A12 and A27 were always taking the first 5 ranks, however the order within the top-five

Table 3. Temporal evaluation of selected five of the suppliers based on the AHP, TOP-SIS and COMET methods and five temporal aggregation strategies: TPEA, TDA1, TDA2, TDA3 and TDA4.

Supplier	Supplier temp. evaluation ($V(a_i)$)					Supplier ranking in temp. evaluation				
Ai	TPEA	TDA1	TDA2	TDA3	TDA4	TPEA	TDA1	TDA2	TDA3	TDA4
AHP										
A1	0.3277	0.0825	0.1634	0.2422	0.1646	21	23	24	23	25
A2	0.3544	0.0891	0.1782	0.2628	0.177	15	17	16	15	16
A3	0.4262	0.1067	0.2123	0.315	0.2103	12	12	12	12	12
A4	0.3971	0.1001	0.1978	0.2934	0.1982	14	14	14	14	14
A12	0.5136	0.1257	0.2552	0.3792	0.2571	2	3	3	2	2
TOPSIS										
A1	7.4096	1.892	3.7341	5.4983	3.7436	15	17	17	16	16
A2	7.5508	1.9118	3.8349	5.6185	3.7822	13	16	13	13	14
A3	7.6704	1.9496	3.8679	5.6931	3.8418	11	14	12	12	13
A4	7.1932	1.802	3.5955	5.3224	3.5904	17	20	18	17	18
A12	9.0961	2.3101	4.6211	6.7691	4.5967	1	2	1	1	1
COMET										
A1	9.0881	2.329	4.5962	6.7523	4.6717	5	2	2	4	2
A2	8.9049	2.2777	4.5325	6.6312	4.5816	8	7	6	7	5
A3	8.6651	2.2267	4.3968	6.4456	4.4126	11	11	11	12	10
A4	8.9418	2.2138	4.4665	6.6146	4.5174	7	13	9	8	8
A12	9.1024	2.2848	4.5677	6.7444	4.5695	4	6	5	5	6

was varying depending on the temporal aggregation strategy chosen. Table 4 contains the rankings of the top five suppliers for the TPEA, TDA1, TDA2, TDA3 and TDA4, followed by data aggregated from all strategies combined. It can be observed that the supplier A12 proved to be best in all strategies but TDA1, where the supplier A6 slightly outranked it. On the other hand, the supplier A9 was ranked 5 in all strategies except TDA1, where it was ranked 3.

The usage of the PROMETHEE II method for the partial results aggregation also allows to analyze how individual methods support or oppose each supplier. Figure 4 contains a GAIA visual illustration of the evaluations produced by aggregating the AHP, TOPSIS and COMET results with equal weights, for TPEA, TDA1, TDA2, TDA3 and TDA4 temporal aggregation strategies, as well as with all strategies taken into consideration. The leading suppliers A5, A6, A9, A12 and A27 were marked in red. The analysis of Fig. 4 allows to observe the preference relations between the results obtained by each AHP method. It can be observed, that the AHP and COMET methods are not related in terms of

	TPEA-AHP	TDA1-AHP	TDA2-AHP	TDA3-AHP	TDA4-AHP	TPEA-TOPSIS	TDA1-TOPSIS	TDA2-TOPSIS	TDA3-TOPSIS	TDA4-TOPSIS	TPEA-COMET	TDA1-COMET	TDA2-COMET	TDA3-COMET	TDA4-COMET
TPEA-AHP	1.000	0.937	0.959	0.980	0.959	0.926	0.847	0.909	0.921	0.926	0.828	0.762	0.795	0.810	0.783
TDA1-AHP	0.937	1.000	0.986	0.975	0.947	0.875	0.902	0.913	0.899	0.895	0.762	0.788	0.772	0.774	0.737
TDA2-AHP	0.959	0.986	1.000	0.990	0.977	0.887	0.895	0.919	0.911	0.919	0.760	0.757	0.767	0.766	0.737
TDA3-AHP	0.980	0.975	0.990	1.000	0.977	0.904	0.877	0.920	0.919	0.927	0.794	0.771	0.792	0.794	0.769
TDA4-AHP	0.959	0.947	0.977	0.977	1.000	0.851	0.828	0.874	0.868	0.917	0.732	0.706	0.730	0.726	0.735
TPEA-TOPSIS	0.926	0.875	0.887	0.904	0.851	1.000	0.932	0.979	0.993	0.957	0.881	0.799	0.846	0.869	0.812
TDA1-TOPSIS	0.847	0.902	0.895	0.877	0.828	0.932	1.000	0.976	0.957	0.936	0.761	0.767	0.773	0.778	0.715
TDA2-TOPSIS	0.909	0.913	0.919	0.920	0.874	0.979	0.976	1.000	0.994	0.971	0.828	0.792	0.822	0.834	0.783
TDA3-TOPSIS	0.921	0.899	0.911	0.919	0.868	0.993	0.957	0.994	1.000	0.967	0.857	0.798	0.840	0.855	0.800
TDA4-TOPSIS	0.926	0.895	0.919	0.927	0.917	0.957	0.936	0.971	0.967	1.000	0.816	0.768	0.810	0.812	0.806
TPEA-COMET	0.828	0.762	0.760	0.794	0.732	0.881	0.761	0.828	0.857	0.816	1.000	0.930	0.975	0.993	0.960
TDA1-COMET	0.762	0.788	0.757	0.771	0.706	0.799	0.767	0.792	0.798	0.768	0.930	1.000	0.972	0.953	0.947
TDA2-COMET	0.795	0.772	0.767	0.792	0.730	0.846	0.773	0.822	0.840	0.810	0.975	0.972	1.000	0.989	0.978
TDA3-COMET	0.810	0.774	0.766	0.794	0.726	0.869	0.778	0.834	0.855	0.812	0.993	0.953	0.989	1.000	0.965
TDA4-COMET	0.783	0.737	0.737	0.769	0.735	0.812	0.715	0.783	0.800	0.806	0.960	0.947	0.978	0.965	1.000

Fig. 3. Correlation matrix between AHP, TOPSIS and COMET evaluations rankings based on TPEA, TDA1, TDA2, TDA3 and TDA4 forgetting strategies

preference, regardless of the temporal aggregation strategy. Figure 4a and c–e show a slight similarity of AHP and TOPSIS in terms of preference for most of the temporal aggregation strategies, however, in case of TDA1 (Fig. 4b) both these methods are very similar in terms of preference.

When all 30 alternatives are studied, it can be observed that all MCDA methods more or less support the five leading suppliers. Supplier A30, being very close to the centre of all charts on Fig. 4 is neither supported nor opposed by the rankings generated by any of the methods. Therefore, supplier A30 can be appraised as being mediocre. This can be confirmed by verifying its rank - 17 for TPEA, TDA2, TDA3, TDA4 and 19 for TDA1. A similar observation can be made for the supplier A1, which is ranked 15–16.

Last, but not least, the GAIA analysis can be used to study how each alternative is supported by each temporal aggregation strategy and each MCDA method. Figure 5 shows that the TPEA strategy supports the supplier A12 the most, whereas the TDA1 and TDA4 strategies are opposing it. The TPEA strategy is supported by the AHP and COMET methods, with the TOPSIS method being here neutral in terms of preference. The A12 alternative is also considerably supported by the TDA3 temporal aggregation strategy, whereas the TDA2 strategy is rather neutral in terms of A12 preference when compared to the remaining strategies.

Table 4. Temporal evaluation of the top 5 suppliers obtained with the PROMETHEE II method from partial AHP-, TOPSIS- and COMET-based results, based on TPEA, TDA1, TDA2, TDA3 and TDA4 strategies.

Rank	Supplier	Phi	Rank	Supplier	Phi	Rank	Supplier	Phi
TPEA			TDA1			TDA2		
1	A12	0.908	1	A6	0.8391	1	A12	0.8621
2	A6	0.8621	2	A12	0.8161	2	A6	0.8391
3	A27	0.8161	3	A9	0.7471	3	A27	0.7931
4	A5	0.7471	4	A27	0.7011	4	A5	0.7011
5	A9	0.7011	5	A5	0.6782	4	A9	0.7011
TDA3			TDA4			ALL		
1	A12	0.8851	1	A12	0.8621	1	A12	0.8667
2	A6	0.8621	2	A27	0.8391	2	A6	0.8391
3	A27	0.8161	3	A6	0.7931	3	A27	0.7931
4	A5	0.7471	4	A5	0.7701	4	A5	0.7287
5	A9	0.7011	5	A9	0.6552	5	A9	0.7011

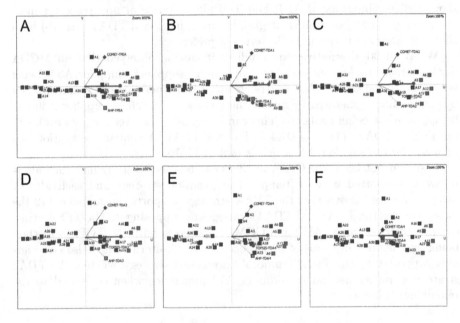

Fig. 4. Visual illustration of the evaluation produced by aggregating AHP, TOPSIS and COMET results with equal weights, for (A) TPEA, (B) TDA1, (C) TDA2, (D) TDA3, (E) TDA4, (F) all temporal aggregation strategies combined. (Color figure online)

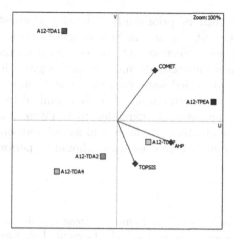

Fig. 5. Visual illustration of the support of the particular aggregation strategies and MCDA aggregation methods on the leading supplier A12.

5   Conclusions

The selection of sustainable suppliers is very important to the business continuity of each modern company. In case of a wrong choice, a non-negligible impediment or even a complete cease of operations of a company can be observed. Two tracks can be recognized in the current research. Firstly, a focus on the development of evaluation methods can be observed. Secondly, there is a focus on the sustainability factors of the green cities including both greening and human well-being.

The prior studies focused on evaluating the appraised suppliers based on their performance under environmental criteria. The approach presented in this paper presents the following authors' methodical contributions:

- usage of hybrid MCDA methods (AHP, TOPSIS, COMET) in order to avoid oversimplifying of the data aggregation, while avoiding rank reversal at the same time;
- combining multiple various functions of temporal data aggregation from various time periods under a single MCDA model;
- analysis and selection of data aggregation strategies from different periods of time in MCDA models based on statistical analysis and GAIA analysis of the obtained set of individual strategies.

At the same time, the practical contributions include the development of an approach to the evaluation and selection of sustainable supplier taking into account the specificity of the evaluated entity as well as the appropriate impact of the values of particular criteria from specified time periods on the evaluated supplier.

Compared to the authors' prior study [25], the performed research provides a framework for obtaining explicit and unambiguous decision support system for sustainable suppliers' selection, yet still derives from the best qualities of multiple MCDA evaluation methods and temporal aggregation strategies.

The research has identified some possible areas of improvement and future work directions. The presented empirical study is limited to a single case, however the framework can be easily extended to facilitate selection of suppliers based on different sustainable criteria as well as different domains of business. A further verification on divergent use cases should be performed.

References

1. Akman, G.: Evaluating suppliers to include green supplier development programs via fuzzy c-means and VIKOR methods. Comput. Ind. Eng. **86**, 69–82 (2015). https://doi.org/10.1016/j.cie.2014.10.013. http://www.sciencedirect.com/science/article/pii/S0360835214003441
2. Alencar, L., Almeida, A.: Supplier selection based on the PROMETHEE VI multicriteria method. In: Takahashi, R.H.C., Deb, K., Wanner, E.F., Greco, S. (eds.) EMO 2011. LNCS, vol. 6576, pp. 608–618. Springer, Heidelberg (2011). https://doi.org/10.1007/978-3-642-19893-9_42
3. Ayhan, M.B.: A fuzzy AHP approach for supplier selection problem: a case study in a Gear motor company. arXiv preprint arXiv:1311.2886 (2013)
4. Banamar, I., De Smet, Y.: An extension of PROMETHEE II to temporal evaluations CoDE-SMG-Technical report Series (2016). https://doi.org/10.1504/IJMCDM.2018.094371
5. Boran, F.E., Genç, S., Kurt, M., Akay, D.: A multi-criteria intuitionistic fuzzy group decision making for supplier selection with TOPSIS method. Expert Syst. Appl. **36**(8), 11363–11368 (2009). https://doi.org/10.1016/j.eswa.2009.03.039
6. Brandenburg, M., Govindan, K., Sarkis, J., Seuring, S.: Quantitative models for sustainable supply chain management: developments and directions. Eur. J. Oper. Res. **233**(2), 299–312 (2014). https://doi.org/10.1016/j.ejor.2013.09.032
7. Büyüközkan, G., Feyzioğlu, O., Nebol, E.: Selection of the strategic alliance partner in logistics value chain. Int. J. Prod. Econ. **113**(1), 148–158 (2008). https://doi.org/10.1016/j.ijpe.2007.01.016
8. Carter, C.R., Liane Easton, P.: Sustainable supply chain management: evolution and future directions. Int. J. Phys. Distrib. Logist. Manag. **41**(1), 46–62 (2011). https://doi.org/10.1108/09600031111101420
9. Chan, F.T., Kumar, N.: Global supplier development considering risk factors using fuzzy extended AHP-based approach. Omega **35**(4), 417–431 (2007)
10. Chen, C.T., Lin, C.T., Huang, S.F.: A fuzzy approach for supplier evaluation and selection in supply chain management. Int. J. Prod. Econ. **102**(2), 289–301 (2006). https://doi.org/10.1016/j.ijpe.2005.03.009
11. Chmielarz, W., Zborowski, M.: Scoring method versus TOPSIS method in the evaluation of E-banking services. In: 2018 Federated Conference on Computer Science and Information Systems (FedCSIS), pp. 683–689. IEEE (2018)
12. De Boer, L., van der Wegen, L., Telgen, J.: Outranking methods in support of supplier selection. Eur. J. Purchasing Supply Manag. **4**(2–3), 109–118 (1998). https://doi.org/10.1016/S0969-7012(97)00034-8

13. Dulmin, R., Mininno, V.: Supplier selection using a multi-criteria decision aid method. J. Purch. Supply Manag. **9**(4), 177–187 (2003). https://doi.org/10.1016/S1478-4092(03)00032-3

14. Eccles, R.G., Ioannou, I., Serafeim, G.: The impact of corporate sustainability on organizational processes and performance. Manag. Sci. **60**(11), 2835–2857 (2014). https://doi.org/10.1287/mnsc.2014.1984

15. Farm, B.: Broadwater Farm - Summer Fruit Picking - The Job and Pay. https://www.broadwaterfarm.biz/summer-fruit-picking-uk/

16. Gold, S., Seuring, S., Beske, P.: Sustainable supply chain management and inter-organizational resources: a literature review. Corp. Soc. Responsib. Environ. Manag. **17**(4), 230–245 (2010)

17. Golicic, S.L., Smith, C.D.: A meta-analysis of environmentally sustainable supply chain management practices and firm performance. J. Supply Chain Manag. **49**(2), 78–95 (2013). https://doi.org/10.1111/jscm.12006

18. Govindan, K., Khodaverdi, R., Jafarian, A.: A fuzzy multi criteria approach for measuring sustainability performance of a supplier based on triple bottom line approach. J. Clean. Prod. **47**, 345–354 (2013). https://doi.org/10.1016/j.jclepro.2012.04.014

19. Govindan, K., Rajendran, S., Sarkis, J., Murugesan, P.: Multi criteria decision making approaches for green supplier evaluation and selection: a literature review. J. Clean. Prod. **98**, 66–83 (2015). https://doi.org/10.1016/j.jclepro.2013.06.046

20. Grant, T.: 10 Ways to Drive E-Commerce Sales During Slow Online Shopping Months. https://www.infusionsoft.com/business-success-blog/sales/e-commerce/10-ways-to-drive-e-commerce-sales-during-slow-months

21. Guitouni, A., Martel, J.M.: Tentative guidelines to help choosing an appropriate MCDA method. Eur. J. Oper. Res. **109**(2), 501–521 (1998). https://doi.org/10.1016/S0377-2217(98)00073-3. http://www.sciencedirect.com/science/article/pii/S0377221798000733

22. Hwang, C.L., Lai, Y.J., Liu, T.Y.: A new approach for multiple objective decision making. Comput. Oper. Res. **20**(8), 889–899 (1993). https://doi.org/10.1016/0305-0548(93)90109-V. http://www.sciencedirect.com/science/article/pii/030505489390109V

23. Junior, F.R.L., Osiro, L., Carpinetti, L.C.R.: A comparison between Fuzzy AHP and Fuzzy TOPSIS methods to supplier selection. Appl. Soft Comput. **21**, 194–209 (2014). https://doi.org/10.1016/j.asoc.2014.03.014

24. Karczmarczyk, A., Jankowski, J., Wątróbski, J.: Multi-criteria decision support for planning and evaluation of performance of viral marketing campaigns in social networks. PLOS ONE **13**(12), 1–32 (2018). https://doi.org/10.1371/journal.pone.0209372

25. Karczmarczyk, A., Wątróbski, J., Ladorucki, G., Jankowski, J.: MCDA-based approach to sustainable supplier selection. In: 2018 Federated Conference on Computer Science and Information Systems (FedCSIS), pp. 769–778. IEEE (2018)

26. Macharis, C., Springael, J., De Brucker, K., Verbeke, A.: PROMETHEE and AHP: the design of operational synergies in multicriteria analysis: strengthening PROMETHEE with ideas of AHP. Eur. J. Oper. Res. **153**(2), 307–317 (2004). https://doi.org/10.1016/S0377-2217(03)00153-X. http://www.sciencedirect.com/science/article/pii/S037722170300153X

27. Meade, L., Sarkis, J.: Strategic analysis of logistics and supply chain management systems using the analytical network process. Transp. Res. Part E: Logist. Transp. Rev. **34**(3), 201–215 (1998). https://doi.org/10.1016/S1366-5545(98)00012-X. http://www.sciencedirect.com/science/article/pii/S136655459800012X

28. Önüt, S., Kara, S.S., Işik, E.: Long term supplier selection using a combined fuzzy MCDM approach: a case study for a telecommunication company. Expert Syst. Appl. **36**(2), 3887–3895 (2009). https://doi.org/10.1016/j.eswa.2008.02.045

29. Palanisamy, P., Abdul Zubar, H.: Hybrid MCDM approach for vendor ranking. J. Manuf. Technol. Manag. **24**(6), 905–928 (2013). https://doi.org/10.1108/JMTM-02-2012-0015

30. Piwowarski, M., Miłaszewicz, D., Łatuszyńska, M., Borawski, M., Nermend, K.: Application of the vector measure construction method and technique for order preference by similarity ideal solution for the analysis of the dynamics of changes in the poverty levels in the European union countries. Sustainability **10**(8), 2858 (2018). https://doi.org/10.3390/su10082858

31. Rezaei, J., Nispeling, T., Sarkis, J., Tavasszy, L.: A supplier selection life cycle approach integrating traditional and environmental criteria using the best worst method. J. Clean. Prod. **135**, 577–588 (2016). https://doi.org/10.1016/j.jclepro.2016.06.125. http://www.sciencedirect.com/science/article/pii/S0959652616308022

32. Roy, B., Vanderpooten, D.: The European school of MCDA: emergence, basic features and current works. J. Multi-criteria Decis. Anal. **5**(1), 22–38 (1996). https://doi.org/10.1002/(SICI)1099-1360(199603)5:1⟨22::AID-MCDA93⟩3.0.CO;2-F

33. Saaty, T.L.: Decision making with the analytic hierarchy process. Int. J. Serv. Sci. **1**(1), 83–98 (2008). https://doi.org/10.1504/IJSSci.2008.01759

34. Sahin, O., Mohamed, S.: A spatial temporal decision framework for adaptation to sea level rise. Environ. Model. Softw. **46**, 129–141 (2013). https://doi.org/10.1016/j.envsoft.2013.03.004. http://linkinghub.elsevier.com/retrieve/pii/S1364815213000558

35. Sałabun, W.: The characteristic objects method: a new distance-based approach to multicriteria decision-making problems. J. Multi-criteria Decis. Anal. **22**(1–2), 37–50 (2015). https://doi.org/10.1002/mcda.1525

36. Senvar, O., Tuzkaya, G., Kahraman, C.: Multi criteria supplier selection using fuzzy PROMETHEE method. In: Kahraman, C., Öztayşi, B. (eds.) Supply Chain Management Under Fuzziness. SFSC, vol. 313, pp. 21–34. Springer, Heidelberg (2014). https://doi.org/10.1007/978-3-642-53939-8_2

37. Seuring, S., Müller, M.: From a literature review to a conceptual framework for sustainable supply chain management. J. Clean. Prod. **16**(15), 1699–1710 (2008). https://doi.org/10.1016/j.jclepro.2008.04.020

38. Sevkli, M., Zaim, S., Turkyilmaz, A., Satir, M.: An application of fuzzy TOP-SIS method for supplier selection. In: 2010 IEEE International Conference on Fuzzy Systems (FUZZ), pp. 1–7. IEEE (2010). https://doi.org/10.1109/FUZZY.2010.5584006

39. Shyur, H.J., Shih, H.S.: A hybrid MCDM model for strategic vendor selection. Math. Comput. Model. **44**(7–8), 749–761 (2006). https://doi.org/10.1016/j.mcm.2005.04.018

40. Tseng, M.L., Chiang, J.H., Lan, L.W.: Selection of optimal supplier in supply chain management strategy with analytic network process and choquet integral. Comput. Ind. Eng. **57**(1), 330–340 (2009). https://doi.org/10.1016/j.cie.2008.12.001

41. Uppala, A.K., Ranka, R., Thakkar, J.J., Kumar, M.V., Agrawal, S.: Selection of green suppliers based on GSCM practices: using fuzzy MCDM approach in an electronics company. In: Handbook of Research on Fuzzy and Rough Set Theory in Organizational Decision Making, pp. 355–375 (2017). https://doi.org/10.4018/978-1-5225-1008-6.ch016. https://www.igi-global.com/chapter/selection-of-green-suppliers-based-on-gscm-practices/169495

42. Wang, C.H.: Using quality function deployment to conduct vendor assessment and supplier recommendation for business-intelligence systems. Comput. Ind. Eng. **84**, 24–31 (2015). https://doi.org/10.1016/j.cie.2014.10.005. http://www.sciencedirect.com/science/article/pii/S0360835214003362

43. Wang, J.W., Cheng, C.H., Huang, K.C.: Fuzzy hierarchical TOPSIS for supplier selection. Appl. Soft Comput. **9**(1), 377–386 (2009). https://doi.org/10.1016/j.asoc.2008.04.014

44. Wątróbski, J., Jankowski, J., Ziemba, P., Karczmarczyk, A., Zioło, M.: Generalised framework for multi-criteria method selection. Omega (2018). https://doi.org/10.1016/j.omega.2018.07.004

45. Wątróbski, J., Ziemba, E., Karczmarczyk, A., Jankowski, J.: An index to measure the sustainable information society: the Polish households case. Sustainability **10**(9), 3223 (2018)

46. Wątróbski, J., Sałabun, W.: Green supplier selection framework based on multi-criteria decision-analysis approach. In: Setchi, R., Howlett, R.J., Liu, Y., Theobald, P. (eds.) Sustainable Design and Manufacturing 2016. SIST, vol. 52, pp. 361–371. Springer, Cham (2016). https://doi.org/10.1007/978-3-319-32098-4_31

47. Wątróbski, J., Sałabun, W., Ladorucki, G.: The temporal supplier evaluation model based on multicriteria decision analysis methods. In: Nguyen, N.T., Tojo, S., Nguyen, L.M., Trawiński, B. (eds.) ACIIDS 2017. LNCS (LNAI), vol. 10191, pp. 432–442. Springer, Cham (2017). https://doi.org/10.1007/978-3-319-54472-4_41

48. Yang, J.L., Chiu, H.N., Tzeng, G.H., Yeh, R.H.: Vendor selection by integrated fuzzy MCDM techniques with independent and interdependent relationships. Inf. Sci. **178**(21), 4166–4183 (2008). https://doi.org/10.1016/j.ins.2008.06.003

49. Zhu, J., Hipel, K.W.: Multiple stages grey target decision making method with incomplete weight based on multi-granularity linguistic label. Inf. Sci. **212**, 15–32 (2012). https://doi.org/10.1016/j.ins.2012.05.011. http://linkinghub.elsevier.com/retrieve/pii/S0020025512003556

50. Ziemba, E.: The ICT adoption in government units in the context of the sustainable information society. In: 2018 Federated Conference on Computer Science and Information Systems (FedCSIS), pp. 725–733. IEEE (2018). https://doi.org/10.15439/2018F116

Approach to IS Solution Design and Instantiation for Practice-Oriented Research – A Design Science Research Perspective

Matthias Walter[✉]

Chair of Information Systems, esp. IS in Manufacturing and Commerce,
TU Dresden, Dresden, Germany
matthias.walter3@tu-dresden.de

Abstract. In the context of our long-term research project following design science research methodology, this paper contributes a methodical approach to design and instantiate an information system for evaluation in practice-oriented research. Based on previous research on improving information system support for early product-cost optimization in the discrete manufacturing industry, we present and discuss our methodical approach to derive prototypes based on an evaluated requirements model, identified implementation challenges, and elaborated solution use cases. The objective of the outlined approach comprising different working steps is to derive an interactive user interface prototype that is feasible for further artifact evaluation within a range of institutional contexts. Together with experts from the practice of software engineering, we iterated through these working steps to determine the approach's feasibility to instantiate our solution design. The paper at hand provides descriptive as well as visual examples for each of these working steps to improve the approach's comprehensibility. Beyond providing lessons learned from the application of our approach in the context of our research project for other projects, we also share results from an initial evaluation for a prototype instantiated with the outlined approach to underline and discuss the approach's applicability.

Keywords: Product-cost optimization · Product costing ·
Design science research · Enterprise systems · Artifact instantiation

1 Introduction

In times of globalization, demand rises for agility, innovation, and quality. Furthermore, shortened product life cycles and an amplified variety of product models have increased pressure on product manufacturers [1]. To keep up with the global competition under these conditions, optimizing product costs throughout a product's life cycle has become a major driver for success [2]. To ensure the long-lasting economic success of products in the upcoming decades, manufacturers have been attempting to optimize product costs for the overall product life cycle. This is especially true for the discrete manufacturing industry, where products like cars, trucks, airplanes, and high-tech machinery are assembled out of up to 100,000 globally sourced components [3].

© Springer Nature Switzerland AG 2019
E. Ziemba (Ed.): AITM 2018/ISM 2018, LNBIP 346, pp. 194–213, 2019.
https://doi.org/10.1007/978-3-030-15154-6_11

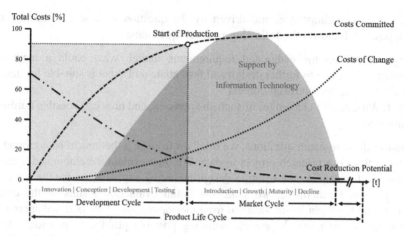

Fig. 1. Cost commitments and reduction potential along product life cycle [3, 4]

Figure 1 describes the cost situation in the life cycle of such products. Surprisingly, 90% of all product costs are determined before production starts, i.e., in the phase of product development. Linking this fact to the idea of product-cost optimization to ensure economic success, it becomes obvious that product development phases offer the most potential to optimize product costs. But, despite this immense potential, there is a lack of information system (IS) support for product-cost optimization during product development [3, 5, 6].

Due to the demand for new solutions to improve the IS support for early product-cost optimization within the industry [3, 6], we initiated a long-term research project framed by a design science research (DSR) approach [7]. This research project aims for improving IS support for product-cost optimization in product development and, therefore, aiding the industry in making use of the cost optimization potential during product development (Fig. 1). After the evaluation of solution requirements and implementation challenges based on a research collaboration with companies from the discrete manufacturing industry, we now aim to design possible solutions to improve the IS support for early product-cost optimization. In order to exploit the full potential of our industry research collaboration, it is recommended to evaluate such artifacts in their natural setting [8]. For this purpose, it is necessary to instantiate a potential solution design so that it can be evaluated by industry experts in their respective contexts. The question is: How can this be done?

This is where the paper at hand comes in. As an extension of Walter's [9] paper, we would like to depict and discuss our methodical approach for designing and instantiating an IS in the form of a mockup-based user interface (UI) prototype. Although DSR is generally gaining popularity in IS research [10], there are only a few research contributions that provide guidance for the design of at least partially instantiated artifacts in the context of DSR [11]. Further literature analyses have shown that most of the designed artifacts in DSR research are of type, method, or model [10] and can, therefore, provide only limited guidance for our practice-oriented research project. To counteract this circumstance, and driven by the question of how to elaborate such prototypes, we focus on the following research questions:

- **RQ1**: Based on the elaborated requirements model, what could a methodical approach look like to further design and instantiate an IS that is suitable for iterative evaluations in an industrial context?
- **RQ2**: What are the challenges of such an approach, and how can possible hurdles be mitigated?

To answer these research questions, we briefly introduce a theoretical background and the results from our research project to date. We then explain the elaborated approach to design and instantiate the solution design including explanations for the individual working steps. Furthermore, we share the initial evaluation results of the derived prototype and highlight lessons learned from the application of the outlined approach in the context of our research project, including possible pitfalls, to provide valuable insights for other researchers. Finally, the paper concludes with a discussion of research results.

2 Theoretical Background

Although there are IS available that aim at supporting product-cost calculation during product development in general [12], a lack of functionality and the demand for enhancements was identified in 2008 [5]. Building on this research, we further identified missing support for early product-cost optimization in the discrete manufacturing industry and highlighted resulting drawbacks [3, 6]. To counteract these drawbacks and improve IS support in early product-cost optimization, certain challenges must be addressed by a potential IS solution.

Beyond the product complexity in the discrete manufacturing industry itself, manufacturers are confronted with a high degree of data uncertainty during product development [13]. This is due to two reasons: One is the variety of alternatives for developing and producing a certain product (e.g., different product design, different production processes, material selection and their sourcing, and alternative production plants). Second is the fact that product-cost optimization aims to estimate and optimize future costs. In the case of the discrete manufacturing industry, the product life cycle for which costs must be estimated may span several decades (including product development and spare part supply) for products like automobiles and special-purpose machinery. These extended life cycles make it impossible to exactly determine future costs such as labor and energy costs as well as raw material prices [3].

As a result of this complexity and uncertainty, but also as a result of the organizational structure of product development including several internal and external stakeholders (e.g., product developers, production process engineers, production planers, cost controllers, and purchasers), product-cost optimization measures such as make-or-buy decisions, evaluation of alternative product concepts and production processes, and optimization of logistic costs are derived in a rather unpredictable context based on deliberations of these stakeholders and their collaboration [3]. Such deliberations do not follow fixed processes or best-practice patterns but originate from an evolving knowledge base along the product development phase and therefore result in dynamic, context-driven processes. Such processes can be classified as types of emergent knowledge process, as argued in our requirements elaboration [1]. Hence, potential solutions must support dynamically changing processes with a bandwidth of deliberations and tradeoffs based on complex, evolving, expert knowledge bases within the organization itself but also including external stakeholders like customers and suppliers [14].

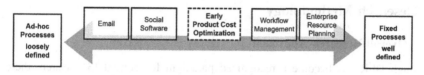

Fig. 2. Degree of process specification [1, 15]

With this justificatory knowledge in mind, developing potential solutions becomes a challenge: First of all, it is important to determine the right degree of process support for experts using the IS without being too restrictive in limiting their capabilities while carrying out product-cost optimization throughout their organization (Fig. 2). In addition, following the argument in Baskerville [8] and Böhringer [15], the developed solutions must be evaluated in the specific environment of their application. In our case, this requires an evaluation where business experts apply our solution design as support for their specific product-cost optimization processes and use cases (see Walter et al. [6] for examples) within their respective working contexts.

Due to the strong tie of our research problem to user-oriented and organizational design risks, it is necessary to reflect whether available DSR methods and guidance are appropriate to design and instantiate such a solution in our research context. This is especially important since it has been revealed that DSR methods consider organizational intervention to be of lesser importance [16].

In theory, the DSR solution design and development process is described as a rather individual and creative engineering process [11, 17]. Though there are general approaches available in the literature describing this process, the lack of guidance for artifact design in IS literature is evident [11]. Moreover, Riemer and Seidel [18] argued for further development of specific methods aimed at the co-constitutional character of user contexts and institutional environments. Such co-constitutional aspects can be approached in multiple ways. Sein et al. [19] criticized the strong sequencing of DSR, which separates developing artifacts from evaluating artifacts. To overcome this separation, action design research (ADR) has been recommended as a DSR method to closely link development to evaluation [19]. Further recommendations have been proposed in the literature [20]. Based on a comparative analysis of DSR with the constructive research approach, Piirainen and Gonzalez [20] highlighted the potential to improve DSR methods by developing best practices for collaborative development.

Beyond seeking such processual guidance for designing and instantiating a potential solution design for early product-cost optimization within the DSR discourse, it is worth examining how IS prototypes are being used in practice. One area of regular prototype development and evaluation is agile software development (e.g., rapid prototyping) [21]. One specific example within the area of development research is mockup-driven development [22]. This approach makes use of UI prototypes (mockups) to receive early and continuous feedback to guide modeling and, thus, align further application development. This coincides with the intention to use ADR [19] as a method to combine development and evaluation of artifacts into iterative steps.

3 Research Methodology

3.1 Overall Research Approach

Although DSR has become a recognized paradigm for current IS research, there is often disagreement about the value of research outcomes due to the multitude of processes, artifact types, and perspectives regarding grounding theory. To create a common understanding and to manage readers' expectations as a basis for the present work, we first classify our long-term research project according to the five DSR prototype genres proposed in Peffers et al. [23].

Therefore, we first highlight the overall aim of our research project, which is to improve the lack of IS support in early product-cost optimization and thus to counteract a problem evident in research literature [5, 24] as well as in industry [6]. One objective derived from this practice-related problem focusses on the elaboration of a solution design that is explicitly applicable (esp. for industrial practice). For this reason, our research project follows a design science research methodology (DSRM) [7] that is positioned as a DSR genre in Peffers et al. [23].

Due to the practical relevance of the research problem and the demand for new IS approaches within the industry [3, 6], we initiated a research collaboration with the software company SAP SE and other international companies from the discrete manufacturing industry. This research collaboration with partners from industry is particularly important for designing and evaluating potential solution designs in our research domain, because product costing carries a strong focus on expert knowledge [6, 25]. Moreover, industrial practice is the most important source of information for cost optimization projects [26]. Therefore, the access to knowledge from practitioner communities is fundamental for our research [1] and should be considered with necessary thoroughness. At the same time, such collaboration ensures that our research is relevant to practice as argued in Rosemann and Vessey [27].

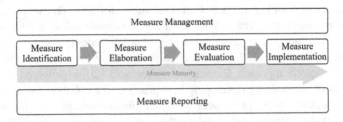

Fig. 3. Approach to support early product-cost optimization [1]

To establish a substantiated foundation for our long-term research activities, we elaborated and evaluated a requirements model that included 30 detailed requirements in combination with challenges for the implementation of potential solutions within the discrete manufacturing industry [1]. In addition, the knowledge exchange with domain experts helped us to gain a holistic understanding of applied product-cost optimization processes among different companies in this context [6]. This was essential to develop a rather abstract approach – with respect to emergent process characteristics and the degree of required process support (Sect. 2) – toward early product cost optimization, which has been agreed upon by industry experts (Fig. 3) [1].

3.2   Approach to Solution Design and Instantiation

In the context of the current state of our research project, the purpose of this paper is to draft and discuss a processual approach to designing and instantiating a potential solution design for future evaluation. Since our major objective is to develop an explicitly applicable solution, it is necessary to elaborate an approach that instantiates a solution design suitable for evaluation in industry. Such an instantiation is important to (a) enable the solution evaluation in its specific context of application resulting from the research domains' emergent process character (Sect. 2) and (b) be able to use evaluation criteria effectiveness and efficiency to assess our solution design as recommended in March and Smith [28].

Therefore, we developed a processual approach to developing a prototype using UI mockups. With this approach we would like to take advantage of the experiences that have been had with mockup-driven development approaches (Sect. 2) to build a bridge between our DSRM-based research project and the evaluating group of practitioners without research experience.

For the elaboration of this approach we considered the recommendation in Sonnenberg and vom Brocke [29] to aim for an evaluation in a naturalistic setting. Therefore, in the long run it is necessary to evaluate our solution design in the context of real problems with real users using a real system. In order to approach the dimension "real system" to the best extent possible even for the initial solution instantiation, the outlined approach must ensure the instantiation of a prototype that is able to depict real-world working processes.

As the elaborated solution approach to supporting early product-cost optimization (Fig. 3) provides support for the maturation of individual optimization measures (see Sect. 2 or [6] for examples) [1], our prototype development should be guided by such scenarios in which optimization measures mature from their identification through evaluation to implementation. This is important in particular as it aligns with the chosen DSR methodology since the process of designing an artifact always has its point of departure in the current world [18].

Therefore, we initiated our prototype development approach with a derivation of an example of product-cost optimization processes (Fig. 4). These process descriptions were then used to deduce different user scenarios, each representing one step in the exemplary optimization process. Such a user scenario describes the sequence of working tasks from the perspective of a specific expert user involved in the optimization processes (e.g., product cost controller, purchaser, engineer).

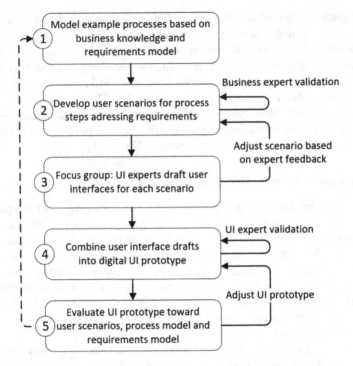

Fig. 4. Approach to transform requirements into UI prototype

Such user scenarios are designed in a way that they consider aspects of the previously evaluated requirements. This is important because we used these scenarios for a focus group with five UI experts from our research partner SAP SE who were not familiar with our research domain of product-cost optimization. Since the UI experts were not familiar with the optimization processes in the discrete manufacturing industry, we were able to validate and adjust our user scenarios in terms of comprehensibility. After the establishment of a common understanding, it was the task of the UI experts to transfer the user scenarios independently into UI drafts without further assistance. This was done using a paper-based approach.

Afterwards, each UI expert presented his UI drafts for each user scenario to the whole group. During this presentation, each focus group participant was encouraged to provide feedback for the different UI drafts. This feedback was helpful for us to then transfer the various paper-based designs into a digital "best-of-breed" UI prototype combining the most valuable concepts. This prototype was created with Balsamiq mockup software [30], which allows individual UI mockups (and their UI elements) to be linked together into an interactive prototype.

As the last step of this development approach, we internally evaluated the interactive UI prototype, first against our user scenarios and example processes and later against the evaluated requirements in detail. This iteration allowed us to adjust the prototype design and the user scenarios in advance to an evaluation with practitioners from the research domain.

This iterative approach to designing a rather mature prototype is necessary, because practitioners within the industry are usually limited in their buy-in to research activities (especially timewise) [31]. For this reason, it makes sense to integrate these important knowledge resources in less granular and well-prepared research increments that are feasible for practice-oriented evaluation to maintain collaboration motivation.

In order to prove that the outlined approach for our research project with the iterative concept is worthwhile and applicable, we have initiated a first evaluation for the outcome of its application: the UI prototype. In addition, this initial evaluation should provide results toward our research objective of improving early product-cost optimization in general. For this evaluation, four solution management experts from SAP SE responsible for product lifecycle management (PLM) in general and in particular for product life cycle cost management (PLCM) assessed our UI prototype. These four experts have an average professional experience of 23.5 years (with a minimum professional experience of 17 years), which is why we classify them as experts in our research domain. These experts were asked to perform a fictitious cost optimization scenario (make-or-buy analysis). We collected evaluation results with a questionnaire using a five-point Likert scale with options from one (strongly disagree) to five (strongly agree).

In the next section, we will discuss the single steps in the development approach (Fig. 4) in detail and support them with examples from our research project. Afterwards, we share the results of the initial prototype evaluation and provide lessons learned from the application of the elaborated instantiation approach (Fig. 4).

4   Research Findings

4.1   Processes Modeling (1) and User Scenario Design (2)

We first established an understanding of relevant cost-optimization approaches [6] and transformed these into exemplary process models. We started with a rather informal descriptive approach and later used model-based approaches to establish a basis for a collective understanding. In detail, we modeled the exemplary cost-optimization processes with BPMN 2.0 (Business Process Model and Notation) [32], which has been proven for its application in financial processes in Korczak et al. [33].

Due to the emergent process characteristics of our research domain (Sect. 2), process modeling is a challenge. This is because of emergent process adaptions in practice that can neither be foreseen nor fully defined by us; yet, at the same time, it is apparent that there is no chance to reach full process coverage. Therefore, we decided to transform those optimization approaches into process models that have been evaluated as the most relevant for early product-cost optimization within the discrete manufacturing industry (Table 1) [6].

Table 1. Top 5 optimization approaches (Scale 0–10 (Very important)) [6]

Optimization approach	Ø
Make-or-buy analysis	7.83
Material price optimization	7.78
Alternative concept and product designs	7.33
Alternative production plants	7.29
Alternative reference components, assemblies, materials, […]	7.06

It is important to emphasize that this set of modeled processes does not claim to be complete. Nevertheless, it provides valuable insights into where and how the support of practitioners needs to be improved.

Furthermore, process modeling helped us to identify the various process stakeholders. By differentiating between different user roles and their individual tasks within the optimization process, we were able to identify each business expert's contribution to carrying a cost optimization measure from a vague idea to its implementation in a product-cost calculation. Building on this, we derived specific user scenarios, each representing one step in the modeled optimization process. These user scenarios form a descriptive sequence of granular working tasks from the perspective of the specific user role. These user scenarios were then enriched by transforming evaluated requirements into dedicated user actions along the processual working tasks. This was done similarly to the approach of formulating user stories in agile software development to describe functional requirements [34].

User scenario: Create a new proposal for a make-or-buy analysis for a specific component in your product

The cross-functional "cost-optimization workshop" for the development of product "Pump P-100" is in progress. You have identified a target cost deviation for the component "Casing" in your current product-cost calculation. Together with experts from different specialties such as purchasing, engineering, and production planning, you have identified and discussed potential optimization measures. As product cost controller, Peter, it is your task to initiate the most promising optimization measure "Make-or-buy analysis for component Casing" for further evaluation.

To do so, the following working steps must be accomplished:

- Create the optimization measure for component "Casing" in your costing structure.
- Create an achievement plan for the measure. The product-cost calculation of "Pump P-100" is part of a customer quotation and, therefore, must be done by 2017-11-30.
- In order to reach the target costs, the measure must achieve savings of 300€. This targeted impact was agreed on during the cost optimization workshop. Maintain this targeted impact for the measure to enable further evaluations.
- Assign the responsibility for the next evaluation steps to user Joe from the purchasing department.

Fig. 5. User scenario to create a new optimization measure

Figure 5 shows a rather simple scenario from the beginning of the optimization process for a cost-optimization measure of type "make-or-buy analysis" (Table 1) that is being used in our prototype development. The scenario is written from the perspective of the product cost controller – who is responsible for the management of cost optimization measures at most companies [3] – and addresses requirements from our evaluated requirements model [1]. For example, we approach the requirement working toward a functionality that supports "target costing" during the identification of an optimization measure ("Identification," Fig. 3). In addition, we address requirements from the area of measure management ("Measure Management," Fig. 3). In detail, this is the basic requirement of a centralized solution to managing the optimization measure among product-cost calculations, the assignment of responsibilities, the ability to create achievement plans, and the need to link the measure to components in existing product-cost calculations. To prioritize requirements for our prototype, the requirements were not only validated for their general relevance but were prioritized on a scale from 0 (not important) to 10 (very important). Table 2 shows selected requirements and their evaluation results.

Table 2. Excerpt of the evaluated requirements model (Scale 0–10 (Very important)) [1]

	Ø	σ
Measure management		
Collect cost-optimization measures	7.78	1.72
Select measures for projects, calculations, [...]	8.06	1.43
Define responsibilities	6.78	2.44
Create achievement plans	7.06	2.29
Estimate measure impact	8.29	1.45
Measure identification		
Target costing	8.72	1.45

The user scenario in Fig. 5 implies that there is an IS for performing early product-cost calculation in place with which our prototype can integrate (Sect. 2). As identified in previous research, this is not always the case in practice [3]. Nonetheless, the elaborated implementation challenges in previous research demand an integrated approach to ensure artifact acceptance by the end-users [1]. Moreover, this scenario implication seems to be valid because such IS are available on the market [12], although their functionality cannot cover all requirements among the discrete manufacturing industry [6].

Based on the gamification concept known from agile software development [35], we have extended each user role in our exemplary optimization processes with the help of avatars (see Walter [9] for an example). This made it possible to present the user roles and their specific tasks in an easily understandable and transparent way, despite descriptive, mostly text-based, user scenarios.

4.2 Focus Groups with UI Experts (3)

The elaborated user scenarios build the foundation for the next step in our prototype development process. In contrast to software engineering practice where mockups are used to enrich descriptive requirements [36], our research focuses on the derivation of prescriptive design knowledge to improve IS support for emergent cost-optimization processes. Therefore, we decided to use the process of transforming requirements into visual mockups as an initial step to identify possible success criteria and design principles to support ex-post evaluations [37].

Due to our research collaboration with SAP SE, we had the chance to involve experts from the SAP Innovation Center Network for user interface design in business software [38]. In a focus group involving five senior experts, with more than seven years of work experience each, who have focused on UI conception and development, we first introduced the research topic driven by our problem identification [3]. Afterwards, we introduced the research approach (Fig. 4) and stated the objective of creating UI drafts aimed at the task fulfillment described in the set of user scenarios. As the last step of our introduction, we outlined the selected optimization process based on our BPMN models with the support of user role avatars.

Since the role of creativity in suggesting solutions was highlighted in the context of DSR in Offermann et al. [11], we chose a pure paper-based approach to initially draft UI proposals. Nevertheless, this deliberation was not made without intention: Research has shown that paper-based approaches have certain advantages over digital prototyping approaches. Paper-based prototypes are particularly preferable when different design solutions need to be negotiated and stakeholder feedback is considered important [39]. Since we planned to have open feedback discussions among experts and, moreover, wanted to combine different solutions into a "best-of-breed" UI prototype later in the process, the paper-based approach seemed more valuable from a research perspective.

To create the UI drafts, we iterated through the optimization process based on the user scenarios as an iteration increment. The user scenario was presented to the focus group followed by the opportunity to clarify issues regarding its comprehensibility. By challenging the comprehensibility with the experts, we were able to further enhance the user scenarios. After reaching a collective understanding of the user scenario, the experts were asked to draft the UI individually. To underpin our claim to exemplary action, selected results of this focus group session are presented in Fig. 6.

Fig. 6. Paper-based drafts implementing user scenario from Fig. 5

At the end of each iteration cycle, each focus group participant presented his UI draft for a specific user scenario, supported by an argument for the chosen design concept. Afterwards, the other participants could provide feedback and clarify open questions. In total, we derived 47 individual, paper-based UI design proposals for the optimization process of type "make-or-buy analysis" distributed over two separate sessions with a total session duration of five working hours. The challenge in the following working step is to combine these various drafts into an interactive prototype.

4.3 Elaboration (4) and Validation (5) of UI Prototype

To transform the various paper-based UI drafts into one interactive UI prototype that would be suitable for evaluation with industry experts, we combined the most promising (also taking into account UI expert feedback during the focus group session) drafts into digital mockups. We used the dedicated mockup software Balsamiq [30] to create an interactive UI prototype.

Such an interactive UI prototype consists of multiple mockups, each representing a certain UI screen (Fig. 7). The major advantage of such a digital prototype over a paper-based prototype is the ability to link the different mockups (UI screens and their elements such as buttons or text fields) to each other. The result is an interactive UI prototype that a user can click through similarly to a real, implemented application.

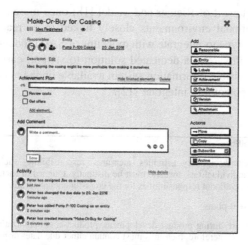

Fig. 7. Individual UI mockup for user scenario from Fig. 5

As was to be expected, not all expert UI drafts could be combined with each other. This was not due to specific UI elements or their arrangement on screens, but rather in terms of different conceptual approaches addressing user scenarios. With the help of the digital UI prototype, we can easily exchange a series of individual UI screens to provide alternative concepts for parallel evaluation. This is extremely helpful to simulate and evaluate different approaches toward process support (Sect. 2).

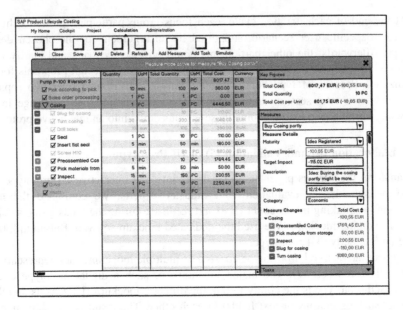

Fig. 8. UI prototype functionality integrated with SAP Product Lifecycle

To stress the argument of Riemer and Seidel [18] once more and, thus, enable an evaluation in institutional environments closely linked to a "real system" [29], we designed the UI prototype to integrate with mockups of SAP Product Lifecycle Costing (Fig. 8) [40]. This software is a dedicated solution to support early product-cost calculation and is one possible information system available on the market with which our solution design can potentially integrate [12].

Define responsibilities

Due to highly interdisciplinary activities, measures' responsibilities such as functional organizations or individual task owners, must be distinctly assigned to each measure. This ensures clear organizational responsibilities for the cross-functional optimization processes.

Create achievement plans

Due to time pressure during product development, product-cost optimization must be accomplished on time. Therefore, measures must contain either due dates or product development-related gates, enabling ongoing reporting.

Fig. 9. Exemplary descriptions for the evaluated requirements (Table 2) [1]

The further development of this UI prototype is linked to its internal evaluation. This internal evaluation uses three previously elaborated elements for evaluation: process models, user scenarios, and the requirements model, including a requirement description (Fig. 9). Initially, we verified that the prototype addressed the tasks outlined in the user scenarios. Furthermore, we checked whether the prototype implemented by the user scenarios still corresponded to the requirements description in the validated requirements model. Finally, the interactive prototype needed to support the task accomplishment as designed in the process models (Sect. 4.1).

4.4 Demonstration of Applicability and Lessons Learned

To demonstrate the applicability of the outlined approach, we asked business experts to click through the elaborated UI prototype on their own, following the underlying fictitious cost-optimization scenario (Sect. 3.2). It took up to 45 min per participant to complete the evaluation scenario. The results in Table 3 show that not only the elaborated prototype scenario with its processes (see Sect. 4.1) was rated as being realistic, but also that the elaborated prototype was perceived as being easy to use. Furthermore, the experts state that the solution design itself is useful to support product costing and enhances productivity as well as transparency.

Table 3. Results of initial prototype evaluation (Scale 0–5 (Strongly agree))

Evaluation criterion	Ø	σ
The scenario of the prototype test was realistic	4.3	0.4
The prototype is easy to use	4.0	0.0
The prototype is useful to support product costing	4.3	0.4
The prototype enhances productivity in product costing	3.8	0.4
The prototype enhances transparency in product costing	4.0	0.0

In addition to the demonstration of the approach's feasibility to design and instantiate a solution, we want to contribute lessons learned from the application of this approach for our research project. Although the approach with its examples from our research project seems easy to implement at first glance, there are still some hurdles to overcome. We want to show these in the following, as they can also be relevant for other researchers in similar research contexts.

During the focus group sessions with UI experts (Sect. 4.2), we underestimated the duration of the iteration duration per user scenario. Looking back, the time required for each scenario can be estimated to be one hour. Contrary to our expectations, the initial scenario explanation with subsequent questions about comprehensibility was very time consuming. This was mainly due to the UI expert's lack of knowledge in the specific research domain of early product-cost optimization and its application in practice. Due to the unexpected delay, we had to schedule a second appointment with the UI experts to finish the draft of the optimization process of type "make-or-buy" (Sect. 4.1). Due to time constraints, we had to consult another UI expert and, thus, employed initial ramp-up efforts once more. In order to counter such timing problems, sufficient time should be planned in advance.

From our perspective, there is a chance to speed up the drafting process. Our assumption of providing the user scenarios for each step of the process in terms of process comprehensibility led to a certain redundancy across several user scenarios (e.g., different user roles were accessing the collection of optimization measures in a similar way). By removing such redundant scenarios and, moreover, focusing on less self-explanatory scenarios, we could have been more efficient (without losing relevant findings for our solution design).

For the next prototype development, we aim at a focus group approach that further enhances the creativity of involved UI experts. Though our idea of a paper-based approach was appropriate in our research context to develop potential approaches to solving identified problems, we strongly believe that user scenarios provide too much guidance to elaborate ground-breaking findings. Nonetheless, the approach of drawing paper-based prototypes is less time consuming than drafting digital prototypes with dedicated software (Sect. 4.3).

In general, the approach of aiming at such interactive UI prototypes for evaluation is valuable for us. Instead of needing to implement a full-stack prototype, which, in addition, could have been limited by the extensibility options of available product costing software (Sect. 4.1), we could efficiently iterate through the development process to further enhance the prototype. This would simplify the testing and evaluation of several solutions in parallel. It would also motivate stakeholders to participate in the research (e.g., with new ideas or concepts), as development and its output would be progressing rapidly.

In addition, it should be mentioned that difficulties may arise when deriving and interpreting the process models and their user scenarios from the industry context into the research context. Therefore, we highly recommend evaluating the single process step results (Fig. 4), e.g., process models and user scenarios, with domain experts to prevent the derivation of (partly) incorrect scenarios. To easily communicate and evaluate such results, model-based approaches like BPMN 2.0 (Sect. 4.1) should be used to establish a collective understanding for all stakeholders.

Furthermore, it must be ensured that the transfer of research domain content to the UI experts has been successful. Though we thoroughly introduced our research domain, including the core of our problem identification [3, 6] and the approach to derive a UI prototype (Fig. 4), multiple questions for each scenario were raised. This was time consuming but necessary for a collective understanding. The transfer from paper-based UI drafts and their underlying conceptual ideas to the digital UI prototype involves similar transition difficulties that we recommend verifying with UI expert consultations, at least briefly, after the mockups have been created.

5   Discussion of Findings

First, the question must be asked of whether the outlined approach is a valid contribution to practice-oriented DSR since we utilize a variety of well-established elements and approaches from software engineering (e.g., paper-based prototypes and mockup-driven development). According to Vaishnavi and Kuechler [17], the development of tentative solution designs to solve identified problems is a rather pedestrian process in which no novelty beyond the state-of-the-art is required. Rather, the novelty should be part of the solution design itself. Following this argument, we do not state the outlined approach to design and instantiate a solution design as our research artifact, but as a valuable contribution to the scientific community for practice-oriented research.

This is especially true because, for example, the rare process guidance for artifact design has been criticized in Offermann et al. [11]. In detail, recent literature reviews have indicated only a small amount of IS research in the context of DSR that deals with the development of software-based artifacts [10]. This is underpinned in Riemer and Seidel [18], in which methods to enable IS researchers to become immersed into institutional environments are requested. As our approach results in UI prototypes for evaluation of solution designs in practical contexts, we are convinced that it is a valuable and engaging approach toward practice-oriented DSR.

What is indeed beneficial for our contextual prototyping are insights from works on ADR [19] as proposed in the context of DSR. Although we also rely on the knowledge of industry experts to design and validate potential solution designs, unlike the ADR approach, they are not part of our research team. Nonetheless, the strong interference with the practical context opens up room for discussion about the methodological rigor of our proposal to design a potential solution for further evaluation. As argued in Gallupe [41], there are certain conflicts in the discipline of IS research when it comes to the influence of methodical rigor. With this contribution, we want to respond to and later solve a practical problem that IS routine problem solving [42] has failed to address for many decades [3, 5, 25] and now must be tackled by IS research.

In this research context, due to the emergent character of product-cost optimization processes (Sect. 2), the major design risk of our solution design is related to organizational and user-oriented aspects (and not technical ones). For this reason, we pursue the "Human Risk & Effectiveness" evaluation strategy as recommend in FEDS-framework [37]. For this evaluation strategy, the presented approach helps us not only to design, but also to evaluate different solution designs by real users in their real contexts without the need to develop a real system. This required considerably less effort than regular software-based prototypes, but nonetheless helped us to gain the prescriptive design knowledge we were looking for to elaborate an objective-centered solution to improve early product-cost optimization. However, it must be pointed out that the evaluated prototype in the long run does not replace an evaluation with a "real system" to ultimately reach a naturalistic evaluation setting as recommended in Sonnenberg and vom Brocke [29].

What should be of further interest is the approach's applicability to instantiate a prototype that suits evaluation by practitioners. With the outlined approach, we were able to integrate our solution design with an existing information system and, thus, to address one major implementation challenge to improve IS support in early product-cost optimization [1]. At the same time, this enables us to evaluate the solution design in a range of different organizational contexts that are familiar with the information system with which we integrated. Furthermore, it can be inferred from the evaluation results (Table 3) that the approach could not only contribute to the derivation of a realistic evaluation scenario, but also that the resulting prototype was easy to use for domain experts without requiring further knowledge or instructions regarding our research project and its proposal for solution design. Moreover, the first evaluation (Table 3) shows a successful demonstration of the elaborated solution design for early product-cost optimization to enhance IS support for early product costing. Nonetheless, further in-depth prototype evaluations with real users are required to assess the effectiveness and efficiency of our solution design as recommended in March and Smith [28].

Beneficial for us in sharpening the understanding of our research problem were the iterative validations and adjustments during the approach's execution; furthermore, the approach enabled new and improved existing collaborations with research stakeholders. According to Jönsson and Lukka [43], participation has the potential to enrich descriptions of the research process as well as increase the understanding of the artifact and its instantiation, which also is important to reach our objective of general applicability. Though the participation of experts in our approach led to unexpected efforts (Sect. 4.4), we can confirm and highly recommend a broad participation – especially if it concerns participants from other disciplines. Hence, the presented approach has the potential to provide thought-provoking ideas, prevent tunnel vision among researchers, and strengthen research relevance [27].

Therefore, we are convinced that the presented approach can contribute to finding further answers to the research questions associated with our long-term research project. In addition, the concept to design the prototype iteratively improves result quality and, hence, helps to better use the already difficult-to-reach experts within the industry. However, researchers who want to adapt this approach for their research must bear in mind that some hurdles may arise, especially regarding the transitions between the individual steps of the approach in Fig. 4:

- Derivation of misguiding processes and user scenarios by the researchers
- Knowledge transfer to UI experts regarding the research domain and the objective to think beyond boundaries
- Transformation of UI drafts back into the research domain-oriented context.

To avoid such knowledge transition issues, validation and participation are key contributions to successfully instantiate an IS solution design in the form of a prototype that is applicable for practical evaluation.

6   Conclusion

Overall, we outlined our approach to developing an interactive mockup-based UI prototype based on an evaluated requirements model with 30 individual requirements in the context of our long-term research project. This research project follows a DSRM process [7] to improve early product-cost optimization in the discrete manufacturing industry. In conjunction with this practical problem and its emergent character [1], we need to design and propose an IS solution that can be evaluated in the context of institutional environments as part of an iterative evaluation strategy.

The outlined approach of designing and instantiating an IS solution in the form of a prototype has proven its value for us: Well-established techniques and state-of-the-art approaches from the software engineering discipline in combination with DSR approaches helped us to derive an easy-to-use prototype for further evaluation in practical contexts. In addition, the outlined approach improved research quality and strengthened relations with stakeholders with reasonable development efforts (compared to software-based prototypes). At the same time, the collaboration with research stakeholders avoided tunnel vision and ensured solution relevance.

Moreover, we addressed the evident need within the literature to provide further guidance for the design phase of DSR projects. The applicability of the outlined approach was proven in the context of our research project. To provide meaningful guidance to IS researchers in similar contexts, the presented approach was enriched with examples and lessons learned. By this, we hope to further encourage researchers in practice-oriented research and, at the same time, motivate industry experts to join scientific research projects to solve relevant problems.

Following our DSRM process model [7], we further concentrated on the improvement of our UI prototype and its ability to solve the problem identified in [3, 6]. The approach presented in this paper forms the basis for an appropriate solution design to improve IS support in early product-cost optimization. Therefore, the next step of our long-term research project is to further evaluate and adapt our solution with real users in real contexts.

References

1. Walter, M., Leyh, C., Strahringer, S.: Toward early product cost optimization: requirements for an integrated measure management approach. In: Drews, P., Funk, B., Niemeyer, P., Xie, L. (eds.) Proceedings of the Multikonferenz Wirtschaftsinformatik 2018 (MKWI 2018), pp. 2057–2068. Leuphana University Lüneburg, Lüneburg (2018)
2. Brinker, B.J.: Guide to Cost Management. Wiley, New York (2000)
3. Walter, M., Leyh, C.: Knocking on industry's door: product cost optimization in the early stages requires better software support. In: Proceedings of the IEEE 19th Conference on Business Informatics (CBI 2017), pp. 330–338. IEEE, Thessaloniki (2017). https://doi.org/10.1109/cbi.2017.33
4. Eigner, M., Stelzer, R.: Product Lifecycle Management: Ein Leitfaden für Product Development und Life Cycle Management, 2nd edn. Springer, Heidelberg (2009). https://doi.org/10.1007/b93672
5. Schicker, G., Mader, F., Bodendorf, F.: Product Lifecycle Cost Management (PLCM): Status quo, Trends und Entwicklungsperspektiven im PLCM – eine empirische Studie. In: Arbeitspapier Wirtschaftsinformatik II (2/2008). Universität Erlangen-Nürnberg, Nürnberg (2008)
6. Walter, M., Leyh, C., Strahringer, S.: Knocking on industry's door: needs in product-cost optimization in the early product life cycle stages. Complex Syst. Inf. Model. Q. (CSIMQ) 13, 43–60 (2017). https://doi.org/10.7250/csimq.2017-13.03
7. Peffers, K., Tuunanen, T., Rothenberger, M.A., Chatterjee, S.: A design science research methodology for information systems research. J. Manag. Inf. Syst. 24(3), 45–77 (2007). https://doi.org/10.2753/MIS0742-1222240302
8. Baskerville, R.: What design science is not. Eur. J. Inf. Syst. 17(5), 441–443 (2008). https://doi.org/10.1057/ejis.2008.45
9. Walter, M.: An approach to transforming requirements into evaluable UI design for contextual practice - a design science research perspective. In: Ganzha, M., Maciaszek, L., Paprzycki, M. (eds.) Proceedings of the 2018 Federated Conference on Computer Science and Information Systems (FedCSIS 2018). ACSIS, vol. 15, pp. 715–724. IEEE, Poznań (2018). https://doi.org/10.15439/2018f235

10. Thakurta, R., Müller, B., Ahlemann, F., Hoffmann, D.: The state of design – a comprehensive literature review to chart the design science research discourse. In: Proceedings of the 50th Hawaii International Conference on System Sciences (HICSS 2017), pp. 4685–4694. AIS, Waikoloa Village (2017). https://doi.org/10.24251/hicss.2017.571

11. Offermann, P., Levina, O., Schönherr, M., Bub, U.: Outline of a design science research process. In: Proceedings of the 4th International Conference on Design Science Research in Information Systems and Technology (DESRIST 2009), pp. 1–11. ACM, New York (2009). https://doi.org/10.1145/1555619.1555629

12. Voelker, S., Walter, M., Munkelt, T.: Improving product life-cycle cost management by the application of recommender systems. In: Drews, P., Funk, B., Niemeyer, P., Xie, L. (eds.) Proceedings of the Multikonferenz Wirtschaftsinformatik 2018 (MKWI 2018), pp. 2019–2030. Leuphana University Lüneburg, Lüneburg (2018)

13. Vosough, Z., Kammer, D., Keck, M., Groh, R.: Visualizing uncertainty in flow diagrams: a case study in product posting. In: Proceedings of the 10th International Symposium on Visual Information Communication and Interaction, Bangkok, pp. 1–8 (2017). https://doi.org/10.1145/3105971.3105972

14. Markus, M.L., Majchrzak, A., Gasser, L.: A design theory for systems that support emergent knowledge processes. MIS Q. 26(3), 179–212 (2002)

15. Böhringer, M.: Emergent case management for ad-hoc processes: a solution based on microblogging and activity streams. In: zur Muehlen, M., Su, J. (eds.) BPM 2010. LNBIP, vol. 66, pp. 384–395. Springer, Heidelberg (2011). https://doi.org/10.1007/978-3-642-20511-8_36

16. Cole, R., Purao, S., Rossi, M., Sein, M.K.: Being proactive: where action research meets design research. In: Avison, D., Galletta, D., DeGross, J.I. (eds.) Proceedings of 24th International Conference on Information Systems, Las Vegas, pp. 325–336 (2005)

17. Vaishnavi, V.K., Kuechler, W.: Design science research methods and patterns: innovating information and communication technology, 2nd edn. CRC Press, Boca Raton (2015). https://doi.org/10.1201/b18448

18. Riemer, K., Seidel, S.: Design and design research as contextual practice. Inf. Syst. E-Bus. Manag. 1(3), 331–334 (2013). https://doi.org/10.1007/s10257-013-0223-2

19. Sein, M.K., Henfridsson, O., Purao, S., Rossi, M., Lindgren, R.: Action design research. MIS Q. 35(1), 37–56 (2011). https://doi.org/10.2307/23043488

20. Piirainen, K.A., Gonzalez, R.A.: Seeking constructive synergy: design science and the constructive research approach. In: vom Brocke, J., Hekkala, R., Ram, S., Rossi, M. (eds.) DESRIST 2013. LNCS, vol. 7939, pp. 59–72. Springer, Heidelberg (2013). https://doi.org/10.1007/978-3-642-38827-9_5

21. Pranam, A.: Product Management Essentials: Tools and Techniques for Becoming an Effective Technical Product Manager. Apress, Berkeley (2018). https://doi.org/10.1007/978-1-4842-3303-0

22. Rivero, J.M., Grigera, J., Rossi, G., Luna, E.R., Montero, F., Gaedke, M.: Mockup-driven development: providing agile support for model-driven web engineering. Inf. Softw. Tech. 56(6), 670–687 (2014). https://doi.org/10.1016/j.infsof.2014.01.011

23. Peffers, K., Tuunanen, T., Niehaves, B.: Design science research genres: introduction to the special issue on exemplars and criteria for applicable design science research. Eur. J. Inf. Syst. 27(2), 129–139 (2018). https://doi.org/10.1080/0960085x.2018.1458066

24. Stark, J.: Product Lifecycle Management: Volume 1: 21st Century Paradigm for Product Realisation. DE, 3rd edn. Springer, Cham (2015). https://doi.org/10.1007/978-3-319-17440-2

25. Lück, D., Leyh C.: Integrated virtual cooperation in product costing in the discrete manufacturing industry: a problem identification. In: Proceedings of the Multikonferenz Wirtschaftsinformatik 2016 (MKWI 2016), pp. 279–290. Technische Universität Ilmenau, Ilmenau (2016)
26. Mörtl, M., Schmied, C.: Design for cost - a review of methods, tools and research directions. J. Indian Inst. Sci. **95**(4), 379–404 (2015)
27. Rosemann, M., Vessey, I.: Toward improving the relevance of information systems research to practice: the role of applicability checks. MIS Q. **32**(1), 1–22 (2008). https://doi.org/10.2307/25148826
28. March, S.T., Smith, G.F.: Design and natural science research on information technology. Decis. Support Syst. **15**(4), 251–266 (1995)
29. Sonnenberg, C., vom Brocke, J.: Evaluation patterns for design science research artefacts. In: Helfert, M., Donnellan, B. (eds.) EDSS 2011. CCIS, vol. 286, pp. 71–83. Springer, Heidelberg (2012). https://doi.org/10.1007/978-3-642-33681-2_7
30. Balsamiq: Rapid, effective and fun wireframing software. https://balsamiq.com. Accessed 19 Dec 2018
31. Österle, H., Otto, B.: Consortium research. Bus. Inf. Syst. Eng. **2**, 283–293 (2010). https://doi.org/10.1007/s12599-010-0119-3
32. Chinosi, M., Trombetta, A.: BPMN: an introduction to the standard. Comput. Stand. Inter. **34**(1), 124–134 (2012). https://doi.org/10.1016/j.csi.2011.06.002
33. Korczak, J., Dudycz, H., Nita, B., Oleksyk, P.: Semantic approach to financial knowledge specification - case of emergency policy workflow. In: Ziemba, E. (ed.) AITM/ISM-2017. LNBIP, vol. 311, pp. 24–40. Springer, Cham (2018). https://doi.org/10.1007/978-3-319-77721-4_2
34. Cohn, M.: User Stories Applied: For Agile Software Development. Addison-Wesley Professional, Boston (2004)
35. Lombriser, P., Dalpiaz, F., Lucassen, G., Brinkkemper, S.: Gamified requirements engineering: model and experimentation. In: Daneva, M., Pastor, O. (eds.) REFSQ 2016. LNCS, vol. 9619, pp. 171–187. Springer, Cham (2016). https://doi.org/10.1007/978-3-319-30282-9_12
36. Reggio, G., Leotta, M., Ricca, F.: A method for requirements capture and specification based on disciplined use cases and screen mockups. In: Abrahamsson, P., Corral, L., Oivo, M., Russo, B. (eds.) PROFES 2015. LNCS, vol. 9459, pp. 105–113. Springer, Cham (2015). https://doi.org/10.1007/978-3-319-26844-6_8
37. Venable, J., Pries-Heje, J., Baskerville, R.: FEDS: a framework for evaluation in design science research. Eur. J. Inf. Syst. **25**(1), 77–89 (2016). https://doi.org/10.1057/ejis.2014.36
38. SAP Innovation Center Network. https://icn.sap.com/home.html. Accessed 2 Dec 2018
39. Sefelin, R., Tscheligi, M., Giller, V.: Paper prototyping - what is it good for?: a comparison of paper- and computer-based low-fidelity prototyping. In: CHI 2003 Extended Abstracts on Human Factors in Computing Systems, pp. 778–779. ACM, Ft. Lauderdale (2003). https://doi.org/10.1145/765985.765986
40. SAP Product Lifecycle Costing. https://www.sap.com/products/product-lifecycle-costing.html. Accessed 15 Dec 2018
41. Gallupe, R.B.: The tyranny of methodologies in information systems research. SIGMIS Database **38**(3), 20–28 (2007). https://doi.org/10.1145/1278253.1278258
42. Gregor, S., Hevner, A.R.: Positioning and presenting design science research for maximum impact. MIS Q. **37**(2), 337–355 (2013). https://doi.org/10.25300/misq/2013/37.2.01
43. Jönsson, S., Lukka, K.: There and back again: doing interventionist research in management accounting. In: Chapman, C.S., Hopwood, A.G., Shields, H.G. (eds.) Handbook of Management Accounting Research, vol. 1, pp. 373–397. Elsevier (2006). https://doi.org/10.1016/s1751-3243(06)01015-7

Synthetic Indexes for a Sustainable Information Society: Measuring ICT Adoption and Sustainability in Polish Government Units

Ewa Ziemba[(✉)] [iD]

University of Economics in Katowice, 1 Maja 50, 40-287 Katowice, Poland
ewa.ziemba@ue.katowice.pl

Abstract. The paper is complementary with papers [1–3] which aims were to advance information society research by examining and understanding the information and communication technologies (ICT) adoption within government units in the context of the sustainable information society (SIS). In [4] the impact of ICT adoption on sustainability within government units was explored, whereas this paper extends these research findings by new insights into SIS measurement. The aim of this paper is to propose an approach to the measurement of two constructs shaping SIS, i.e. ICT adoption and sustainability within government units. ICT adoption is described by four sub-constructs, i.e. ICT outlay, information culture, ICT management, and ICT quality, whereas sustainability is composed of ecological, economic, socio-cultural, and political sustainability. This study employs a quantitative approach and, additionally, Hellwig's taxonomic measure of development is adopted for multivariate comparative analyses to evaluate ICT adoption and sustainability within government units. A value of the Hellwig's synthetic indicator can be in the interval [0, 1] where a higher value of the indicator means that the object is closer to the pattern. The survey questionnaires were used and data collected from 185 government units were analyzed. We proposed and calculated five synthetic indicators for measuring ICT adoption, i.e. ICT adoption index and sub-indexes of ICT outlay, information culture, ICT management, and ICT quality as well as five synthetic indexes for evaluating sustainability, i.e. sustainability index and sub-indexes of ecological, economic, socio-cultural, and political sustainability. The research revealed that the medium level of ICT adoption index, i.e. in the interval (0.34, 0.68], is in the largest share of examined government units (68.6%). With regard to sustainability, the medium level of sustainability index is in the interval (0.32, 0.64] and is characteristic for 71.2% of government units. Furthermore, the high levels of ICT adoption and sustainability indexes exceeding the value of 0.68 for ICT adoption and 0.64 for sustainability are indicated by 17.0% and 14.4% of government units respectively.

Keywords: ICT adoption · Sustainability · Sustainable public administration · Information society · Measurement · Government units · Public administration · Poland

© Springer Nature Switzerland AG 2019
E. Ziemba (Ed.): AITM 2018/ISM 2018, LNBIP 346, pp. 214–234, 2019.
https://doi.org/10.1007/978-3-030-15154-6_12

1 Introduction

The sustainable information society (SIS) is a new phase of information society development in which information and communication technologies (ICT) are becoming key enablers of sustainability [5–14]. Researchers and various organizations have explored the areas where the information society, sustainable development, and ICT come together, and identified some correlations between those concepts [15–21]. Overall, the SIS is a multidimensional concept encompassing ecological, economic, cultural, social, and political sustainability, all of which could be strongly influenced by adopting ICT by society stakeholders, mainly enterprises, households, and public administration [13, 14].

In general terms, enormous ICT potential for the SIS development can be approached from two angles: ICT as an industry and ICT as a tool [14]. As an industry, ICT have become a major economic driver in the hardware, software, telecommunications, and consulting services sectors. ICT as a tool can be used to transform and improve business, everyday life of people, and public governance. This study examines ICT used as a tool to revolutionize public administration and create sustainable public administration.

Some researchers have focused on the application of sustainability and sustainable development theories to public administration practice [22–25]. Bartle and Leuenberger [22] expressed that sustainability should be added as a major pillar of public administration in addition to others, i.e. economy, efficiency and effectiveness, reliability and predictability, openness and transparency, accountability, and social equity [26]. In response to challenges determined in the 2030 Agenda for Sustainable Development [27], a new list of public administration pillars was indicated; among which innovative and technology empowered governance is specified [28]. Innovations in public service delivery empowered by ICT allowed many governments to improve quality and affordability of public services, increase efficiency and effectiveness [11, 18, 21, 29]. This resulted in more openness, greater transparency, higher productivity, better performance and more sustainable services [30].

Following an extensive review of the literature, it can be stated that it did not uncover any deep studies providing objective assessment measures of SIS development in general, as well as with respect to ICT adoption and sustainability in public administration. Such measures and tools would help clarify areas that need further improvement and stimulate the progress of society towards SIS and public administration to sustainable public administration. In light of the above limitations, this paper focuses on exploring how the level of SIS can be evaluated. Its aim is to propose an approach to the evaluation of two constructs shaping SIS, i.e. ICT adoption and sustainability within government units.

The paper is structured as follows. Section 1 is an introduction to the subject. Section 2 states the theoretical background of ICT adoption, sustainability, and their measurement. Then research questions are posed. Section 3 describes the research methodology. Section 4 presents the research findings on the evaluation of ICT adoption and sustainability within government units. Section 5 provides the study's contributions, implications, and limitations as well as considerations for future investigative works.

2   Theoretical Background and Research Questions

2.1   ICT Adoption

ICT are defined as a diverse set of software and hardware, to perform together various functions of information creation, storing, processing, preservation and delivery, in a growing diversity of ways [31]. Based on Ross's and Vitale's study [32], the adoption of ICT is defined as ICT design, implementation, stabilization, and continuous improvement. It embraces the whole spectrum of activities from the period when government units justify the need for adopting ICT until the period when government units experience the full potential of ICT and derive benefits from them [4].

Based on a stream of research, Ziemba [4] advanced a model, which categorizes the adoption of ICT into four sub-constructs: ICT outlay (Out), information culture (Cul), ICT management (Man), and ICT quality (Qua). A detailed analysis allows for specifying primary variables which can be used to measure the identified sub-constructs and ICT adoption as a whole. These variables are presented in Table 1. The sub-construct of ICT outlay includes the government units' financial capabilities and expenditure on ICT adoption, as well as funding from the European Union funds. The information culture sub-construct embraces digital and socio-cultural competences of government units' employees and managers, constant improvement of these competences, personal mastery and creativity of employees, and incentive systems encouraging employees to adopt ICT. The ICT management sub-construct comprises the alignment between information society strategy and ICT adoption, top management support for ICT projects, as well as the adoption of newest management concepts and standard ICT solutions developed at the national level. It also includes the implementation of legal regulations associated with ICT adoption, regulations on ICT and information security and protection. The ICT quality sub-construct consists of the quality, interoperability, and security of back- and front-office information systems, quality of hardware, maturity of e-public services, and the adoption of electronic document management system, electronic delivery box, as well as ERP and BI systems. The construct asserted that the four sub-constructs were interrelated and critical to the design of the ICT adoption within government units in the context of the SIS.

2.2   Sustainability

Multiple linkages between government and sustainable development have been set out in the 2030 Agenda for Sustainable Development [27]. The main goal was formulated to promote peaceful and inclusive societies for sustainable development, provide access to justice for all and build effective, accountable and inclusive government units at all levels.

The conceptualization and operationalization of sustainability is based in this paper on the definition of sustainable development [33]. According to Schauer [11], sustainable development has four dimensions which are ecological, social, economic and cultural sustainability. Fuchs's [34] conceptualization of sustainability in the information society resonates with the Schauer's approach. He examined five dimensions of sustainability, i.e. ecological sustainability (enhancement of the natural environment),

Table 1. Sub-constructs and primary variables of ICT adoption and sustainability constructs in the context of government units (Source: [4])

Primary variables of the ICT adoption construct				Primary variables of the sustainability construct	
Out1	Financial capabilities	Man18	Management concepts adoption	Ecl1	Sustainability in ICT
Out2	Expenditure on ICT	Man19	Information security regulations	Ecl2	Sustainability by ICT
Out3	Funding acquired from the European funds	Man20	ICT regulations	Eco3	Reducing cost
Cul4	Managers' ICT competences	Man21	ICT public project	Eco4	Developing and increasing in the number and maturity of e-public services
Cul5	Employees' ICT competences	Man22	Adoption of standard ICT solutions developed at the national level	Eco5	Increasing effective and efficient management and decision-making
Cul6	Managers' permanent education	Man23	Competitive ICT market	Eco6	Increasing efficiency and effectiveness of customer service
Cul7	Employees' permanent education	Qua24	ICT infrastructure quality	Eco7	Increasing transparency of operations and employee responsibility
Cul8	Employees' personal mastery	Qua25	Back-office system quality	Eco8	Increasing efficiency and effectiveness of work organization
Cul9	Managers' socio-cultural competences	Qua26	Front-office system quality	Eco9	Increasing satisfaction with public services
Cul10	Employees' socio-cultural competences	Qua27	Interoperability of back- and front-office system	Soc10	Improving competences

(continued)

Table 1. (*continued*)

Primary variables of the ICT adoption construct				Primary variables of the sustainability construct	
Cul11	Employees' creativity	Qua28	Back-office system security	Soc11	Improving working environment
Cul12	Incentive systems	Qua29	Front-office system security	Soc12	Increasing safety of society members
Man13	Alignment between information society strategy and ICT adoption	Qua30	E-public service maturity	Soc13	Reducing social exclusion
Man14	Supporting management models with ICT	Qua31	ERP system adoption	Pol14	Increasing e-democracy
Man15	ICT management procedure	Qua32	EDMS (electronic document management system) adoption	Pol15	Increasing and facilitating access to public services
Man16	ICT project team	Qua33	Adoption of an electronic delivery box	–	–
Man17	Top management support	Qua34	BI (business intelligence) system adoption	–	–

technological sustainability (usability of technologies), economic sustainability (wealth for all), political sustainability (participation), and cultural sustainability (wisdom). It is therefore expected that sustainability within government units comprises four kinds of sustainability: ecological, economic, socio-culture, and political. Such an approach was verified and confirmed by Ziemba [4].

Ecological sustainability (Ecl) is the ability of government units to maintain rates of renewable resource harvest, pollution creation, and non-renewable resource depletion by means of conservation and proper use of air, water, and land resources [35, 36]. Economic sustainability (Eco) means that the government units gain competitive edge, reduce costs, organize work in a better and more efficient way, increase the number and maturity of public services delivered electronically, and boost government sharehold-ers' value by adopting sustainable practices and improved public decision-making [18, 19, 36]. Socio-cultural sustainability (Soc) is based on the socio-cultural aspects that need to be sustained, e.g. trust, common meaning, diversity, capacity for learning and capacity for self-organization [37]. It is seen as dependent on social networks, making community contributions, creating a sense of place and offering community stability and security [38]. Political sustainability (Pol) rests on the basic values of democracy and partnership relations between government units and other SIS stakeholders. It is related to government openness, transparency and responsiveness, as well as democratic public decision-making [39]. Table 1 presents the description of all specified sustainability sub-constructs and variables measuring them.

2.3   Measurement of ICT Adoption and Sustainability

Based on SIS theory and the previous research [1–4] two constructs should be embraced in the measurement of SIS, i.e. ICT adoption and sustainability. In addition, various benchmarks of information society [30, 41] employ two approaches to the quantitative description of such a society. The first one comprises the list of indicators characterizing information society, whereas the other one is connected with the so-called synthetic indexes (synthetic indicators) which are based on the chosen set of indicators.

A set of indicators and synthetic indexes for measuring information society can be found in works of many organizations, e.g. Eurostat, ITU (International Telecommunication Union), OECD, World Bank, WEF (World Economic Forum), and IDC (International Data Corporation) [42]. The best known measurement synthetic indexes are the ICT Development Index (IDI) worked out by ITU and Networked Readiness Index (NRI) of the authorship of the WEF. The IDI is a composite index combining eleven indicators on ICT access, use and skills, and it is based on the three-stage model for information society development, i.e. readiness, intensity, and impact [40]. The NRI is composed of four sub-indexes described by fifty-four indicators: an environment sub-index, a readiness sub-index, a usage sub-index, an impact sub-index [43]. Furthermore, E-Government Development Index (EGDI) gauges the application of ICT within government (e-government) in the three most important dimensions, namely the scope and quality of online services, the status of the development of telecommunication infrastructure, and the inherent human capital [44]. EGDI is a composite index which embraces these three indices that can be extracted and analyzed independently. According to the 2030 Agenda for Sustainable Development [27], the multiple linkages to sustainability have been included and analyzed in EGDI in 2018. Selected or proxy themes related to e-government and sustainable development have been analyzed, for example, open government data, e-participation, mobile-government and whole-of-government approach. However, the measurement is fragmentary and does not embrace the all sustainable imperatives and whole of ICT adoption approach mentioned above.

Various sets of indicators for measuring sustainability exist already and it seems that constantly new ones are being developed. Kerk and Manuel [45] created a comprehensive Sustainable Society Index embracing 22 indicators grouped into five categories: personal development, clean environment, well-balanced society, sustainable use of resources, and sustainable world. Panda et al. [46] developed a composite Urban Social Sustainability Index for assessing the social sustainable development by Urban India. It includes 27 indicators under seven themes, i.e. demography, education, health, equity, housing, poverty, and safety themes.

After analyzing indexes for measuring ICT adoption and sustainability, the overall conclusion is that none of the existing indexes seems to fit the SIS needs completely. In other words, not a one gives a comprehensive and good insight into all relevant issues of SIS in a transparent, simple and easily understandable way, showing at a glance to what extent an information society is sustainable or not and to what extant ICT adoption is used for achieving sustainability. So, new indexes have to be developed, based on a set of indicators in accordance with the nature of SIS, the essence of which is ecological, economic, cultural, social, and political sustainability strongly influenced by adopting ICT within public administration. They should allow us to examine how governments can use e-government and ICT to build sustainable and resilient societies.

2.4 Research Questions

As mentioned above, it was observed that there is a research gap in the existing body of knowledge related to measuring ICT adoption and sustainability within government units using multidimensional statistical methods and based on synthetic indexes of development. In order to bridge the gap this study proposes an approach to the evaluation of ICT adoption and sustainability within government units and focuses on addressing the following questions:

Q1: What synthetic indexes may be used to evaluate ICT adoption within government units?
Q2: What is the level of ICT adoption within Polish government units?
Q3: What synthetic indexes may be used to evaluate sustainability within government units?
Q4: What is the level of sustainability within Polish government units?

3 Research Methodology

3.1 Research Instrument

The Likert-type instrument (questionnaire) was developed that consisted of two SIS constructs: ICT adoption and sustainability. The task of respondents was to assess the primary variables describing:

- The four sub-constructs of the ICT adoption construct, i.e. ICT Outlay (Out), information culture (Cul), ICT management (Man), and ICT quality (Qua) (Table 1). The respondents answered the question: *Using a scale of 1 to 5, state to what extent do you agree that the following situations and phenomena result in the efficient and effective ICT adoption within your government unit?* The scale's descriptions were: 5 – strongly agree, 4 – rather agree, 3 – neither agree nor disagree, 2 – rather disagree, 1 – strongly disagree; and
- The four sub-constructs of the sustainability construct, i.e. ecological (Ecl), economic (Eco), socio-cultural (Soc), and political sustainability (Pol) (see Table 1). The respondents answered the question: *Using a scale of 1 to 5, evaluate the following benefits for your government unit resulting from the efficient and effective*

ICT adoption? The scale's descriptions were: 5 – strongly large, 4 – rather large, 3 – neither large nor disagree, 2 – rather small, 1 – strongly small.

3.2   Research Subjects and Procedure

In April 2016, a pilot study was conducted to verify the draft of a survey questionnaire. Seven experts participated in the pilot study, i.e. five researchers from an information society and business informatics, and two employees of the Silesian Centre of Information Society in Katowice (ŚCSI). ŚCSI is a government unit that is responsible for information society development in the Silesian Province in Poland. Finishing touches were put into the questionnaire, especially of a formal and technical nature. No substantive amendments were required.

The study examined government units from the Silesian Province in Poland. The region was chosen due to its continuous and creative transformations related to restructuring and reducing the role of heavy industry in the development of research and science, supporting innovation, using know-how and transferring new technologies, as well as increasing importance of services. In response to the changing socio-economic and technological environment intensive work on the development of the information society has been carried out in the region for several years. The subsequent development strategies of the information society assumed that the potential of the region, especially in the design, provision and use of advanced ICT would be increased [47]. All this means that the results of this research can be reflected in innovative efforts to build a SIS in the region and, at the same time, constitute a modus operandi for other regions throughout the country and in other countries.

Selecting a sample is a fundamental element of a positivistic study [48]. A random sample was used for statistical consideration to provide representative data. A survey questionnaire was submitted to all 185 government units in the Silesian Province.

The subjects were advised that their participation in completing the survey was voluntary. At the same time, they were assured of anonymity and guaranteed that their responses would be kept confidential.

3.3   Data Collection

Having applied the Computer Assisted Web Interview and employed the ŚCSI platform, the survey questionnaire was uploaded to the website. The data were collected between 30 May 2016 and 15 July 2016. After screening the responses and excluding outliers, there was a final sample of 118 usable, correct, and complete responses. It means that 64% of all government units from the Silesian Province completed their responses fairly, in all respects. The sample ensured that the error margin for the 95% confidence interval was 5%.

Table 2 provides details about government units' size, and their participation in SKEAP project. This project was carried out by the municipal and district authorities of the Silesian Province in 2005–2008. The project's result was the Electronic Communication System for Public Administration called SEKAP [49]. It enables government units to provide e-public services at different levels of maturity to all society stakeholders. It could be presumed that the government units which participated in SEKAP more skillfully entered into ICT adoption than those which did not.

Table 2. Analysis of government units profiles (N = 118)

Characteristics	Frequency	Percentage
Number of employees		
Less than 50 (small)	51	43.22%
50 and above (large)	67	56.78%
SEKAP partner		
Yes	91	77.12%
No	27	22.88%

3.4   Data Analysis

The data were stored in Microsoft Excel format. Using Statistica package and Microsoft Excel, the collected data were analyzed in two stages. The first stage evaluated ICT adoption and sustainability within Polish government units, whereas the other stage classified the analyzed government units into clusters according to their levels of ICT adoption and sustainability.

In the first stage, the calculations were performed on the basis of Hellwig's taxonomic measure of development also known as Hellwig's synthetic indicator of development [50] which has been adopted for multivariate comparative analyses [51]. This measure is one of classical methods of linear ordering of multivariate objects. It determines the Euclidean distance of each multivariate object from the development pattern (reference object, pattern object) [52, 53].

The procedure of determining Hellwig's synthetic indicator of development is as follows:

1. Selection of diagnostic variables based on substantive and statistical reasons, and gathering of relevant statistics data.
2. Standardization (normalization) of diagnostic variables x_{ij} according to the following formula:

$$z_{ij} = \frac{x_{ij} - \bar{x}_J}{S(x_j)}$$

where:

i – the number of objects (respondents);
j – the number of variables;
$\bar{x}_J$ – the mean value of the variable j;
$S(x_j)$ – the standard deviation of the variable j; and
z_{ij} – the standardized (normalized) value of the variable j for the object i (x_{ij}).

3. Determination of the object with the best (highest) values of the diagnostic variables – (the reference object, development pattern) on the basis of the following formula:

$$z_{0j} = \max_i \{z_{ij}\}$$

where:

z_{0j} – the standardized maximum value of the variable z_{ij} when the variable is a stimulant – the so-called pattern (reference).

4. Calculation of the Euclidean distance d_{i0} of each object from the constructed pattern:

$$d_{i0} = \left[\sum_{j=1}^{m} \left(z_{ij} - z_{0j} \right)^2 \right]^{\frac{1}{2}}$$

5. Determination of the value of the Hellwig's synthetic indicator of development d_i for the object i according to the following formula:

$$d_i = 1 - \frac{d_{i0}}{d_0}$$

where:

d_{i0} – the Euclidean distance of the object from the reference object;
d_0 – the distance of the object from the pattern determined in accordance with the following formula to normalize d_i in the interval [0, 1]:

$$d_0 = \bar{d}_0 + 3SD(d_0)$$

where:

$SD(d_0)$ – the standard deviation of d_0; and
$\bar{d}_0$ – the average distance between objects and the development determined in accordance with the following formulas:

$$\bar{d}_0 = \frac{1}{n} \sum_{i=1}^{n} d_{i0}$$

$$SD(d_0) = \left[\frac{1}{n} \sum_{i=1}^{n} \left(d_{i0} - \bar{d}_0 \right)^2 \right]^{\frac{1}{2}}$$

The values of the synthetic indicator d_i are in the interval [0, 1] and a higher value of the indicator means that the object is closer to the pattern. The closer the value of a given object to the reference object is, the higher the level of development.

Additionally, Kruskal-Wallis one-way analysis of variance and Dunn's multiple comparison tests were used to determine if there were statistically significant differences between distributions of d_i for the ICT adoption sub-constructs and sustainability sub-constructs in the examined government units.

In the other stage, implementation of cluster analysis resulted in grouping of the analyzed subjects – government units – into three clusters according to the levels of ICT adoption and sustainability. Two measures: arithmetic mean $\bar{d}$ and standard deviation $SD(d)$ of values d_i were used for this purpose:

$$\bar{d} = \frac{1}{n}\sum_{i=1}^{n} d_i; \quad SD(d) = \left[\frac{1}{n}\sum_{i=1}^{n}(d_i - \bar{d})^2\right]^{\frac{1}{2}}$$

The following groups (classes) of government units according to their ICT adoption and sustainability development were defined [50]:

- Group 1 with the highest level of synthetic indicator of development (high level of ICT adoption/sustainability) embraces government units at a distance from the pattern exceeding $\bar{d} + SD(d)$:

$$d_i > \bar{d} + SD(d)$$

- Group 2 with the medium level of synthetic indicator of development (medium level of ICT adoption/sustainability) embraces government units at a distance from the pattern ranking in the interval $(\bar{d} - SD(d), \bar{d} + SD(d)]$:

$$\bar{d} - SD(d) < d_i \leq \bar{d} + SD(d)$$

- Group 3 with the lowest level of synthetic indicator of development (low level of ICT adoption/sustainability) embraces government units at a distance from the pattern not exceeding $\bar{d} - SD(d)$:

$$d_i \leq \bar{d} - SD(d)$$

We determined means of d_i as an indicator of development level and after that found a structure of development groups.

4   Research Findings

The statistical analyses enabled the differentiation of government units in terms of their levels of ICT adoption and sustainability. A generalized comparison of the levels of ICT adoption and sustainability is followed by a description of the situation of three analyzed development groups in terms of sub-constructs of ICT adoption and sustainability.

4.1 ICT Adoption Indexes

The following research questions were posed regarding ICT adoption within government units:

Q1: What synthetic indexes may be used to evaluate ICT adoption within government units?

Q2: What is the level of ICT adoption within Polish government units?

The ICT adoption construct includes 34 variables divided into four sub-constructs, i.e. ICT outlay (Out), information culture (Cul), ICT management (Man), and ICT quality (Qua) (Table 1). Therefore, in order to answer these two questions the following Hellwig's synthetic indicators of ICT adoption were determined and calculated:

- Index of ICT adoption – ICT;
- Sub-index of ICT outlay – ICT(Out);
- Sub-index of information culture – ICT(Cul);
- Sub-index of ICT management – ICT(Man); and
- Sub-index of ICT quality – ICT(Qua).

Table 3 contains the value of such an index and sub-indexes of ICT adoption for Polish examined government units.

Table 3. Synthetic indicators of ICT adoption within Polish government units determined by Hellwig's method

Index/ sub-index	Value of index/ sub-index	Standard deviation	Group 1	Group 2	Group 3
ICT	0.51	0.17	17.0%	68.6%	14.4%
ICT(Out)	0.61	0.20	11.9%	70.3%	17.8%
ICT(Cul)	0.49	0.16	19.5%	64.4%	16.1%
ICT(Man)	0.51	0.17	15.3%	68.6%	16.1%
ICT(Qua)	0.44	0.15	17.8%	62.7%	19.5%

The value of ICT index is 0.51 (Table 3) which means that the level of ICT adoption within Polish examined government units is distant from the pattern by 0.49. The 2nd group of ICT adoption development – the group with the medium level of ICT adoption – comprises the largest share of examined government units (68.6%). The highest and lowest levels of ICT adoption are specific for a smaller and similar number of government units, 17.0% and 14.4% of government units respectively. In addition, 85.6% of government units are characterized by medium and high levels of ICT adoption.

The values of the ICT adoption sub-indexes are in the interval [0.44, 0.61] which means that the levels of ICT outlay, information culture, ICT management, and ICT quality are similar distant from the pattern by 0.39, 0.51, 0.49, 0.56 respectively. In addition, it was proved that ICT adoption within government units was differentiated for ICT outlay, information culture, ICT management, and ICT quality. The result of the Kruskal-Wallis test was as follows: (H(3, N = 472) = 44.286 and p = 0.000). The differences in the levels of these sub-constructs were examined using the Dunn *post hoc* test. The obtained results of pairwise comparisons confirmed the statistically significant higher value of ICT outlay and the statistically significant lower value of ICT quality. Furthermore, not significant differences were indicated between the level of information culture and the level of ICT management.

For all the ICT sub-constructs, the 2nd group of ICT adoption development is predominant, while the respective shares of government units in groups 1st and 3rd are similar and much smaller than in the 2nd group. The largest number of examined government units is in the 1st and 2nd groups combined. In general, the highest percentages of government units are in the 1st and 2nd groups of information culture and ICT management (83.9% of government units). Medium and high levels of ICT outlay and ICT quality are indicated in a slightly smaller percentage of government units, 82.2% and 80.5% of government units respectively. Figure 1 presents the structure of the ICT adoption groups by ICT adoption sub-constructs.

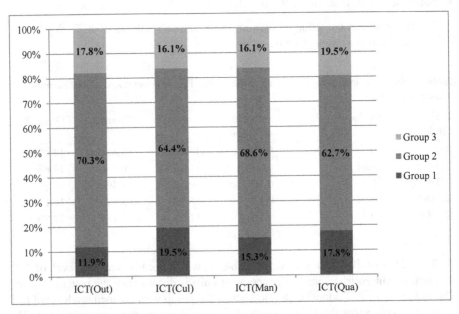

Fig. 1. Percentage of government units in the groups of ICT adoption.

4.2 Sustainability Indexes

The following research questions were posed regarding sustainability within government units:

Q1: What synthetic indexes may be used to evaluate sustainability within government units?

Q2: What is the level of sustainability within Polish government units?

The sustainability construct includes 14 variables divided into four sub-constructs, i.e. ecological (Ecl), economic (Eco), socio-cultural (Soc), and political sustainability (Pol) (Table 1). Therefore, in order to answer these two questions the following Hellwig's synthetic indicators of sustainability were determined and calculated:

- Index of sustainability – SIS;
- Sub-index of ecological sustainability – SIS(Ecl);
- Sub-index of economic sustainability – SIS(Eco);
- Sub-index of socio-cultural sustainability – SIS(Soc); and
- Sub-index of political sustainability – SIS(Pol).

Table 4 contains the value of such an index and sub-indexes of sustainability for Polish government units.

Table 4. Synthetic indicators of sustainability within Polish government units determined by Hellwig's method

Index/ sub-index	Value of index/ sub-index	Standard deviation	Group 1	Group 2	Group 3
SIS	0.48	0.16	14.4%	71.2%	14.4%
SIS(Ecl)	0.51	0.17	8.5%	68.6%	22.9%
SIS(Eco)	0.49	0.16	15.3%	66.1%	18.6%
SIS(Soc)	0.50	0.17	20.3%	62.7%	17.0%
SIS(Pol)	0.55	0.18	25.4%	61.0%	13.6%

The value of SIS index is 0.48 (Table 4) which means that the level of sustainability in the Polish examined government units is distant from the pattern by 0.52. The 2nd group of sustainability – the group with the medium level of sustainability – comprises the largest share of government units (71.2%). The highest and lowest levels of sustainability are specific for a smaller and the same share of government units – 14.4%. In addition, 85.6% of government units are characterized by medium and high levels of sustainability.

The values of the sustainability sub-indexes are in the interval [0.49, 0.55] which means that the levels of ecological, economic, socio-culture, and political sustainabilities are similar distant from the pattern by 0.49, 0.51, 0.50, 0.45 respectively. In addition, it was proved that sustainability was not differentiated for ecological, economic, socio-cultural, and political sustainability. The result of the Kruskal-Wallis test was as follows: ($H(3, N = 472) = 5.128$ and $p = 0.163$).

For all SIS sub-constructs, the 2nd group of sustainability is predominant, while the respective shares of government units in the 1st and 3rd group are much smaller than in group 2nd. The largest number of examined government units is in the 1st and 2nd group combined. In general, the highest percentages of government units are in the 1st and 2nd group of political sustainability (86.4% of government units). A slightly smaller percentage of government units are characterized by medium and high levels of economic and socio-cultural sustainability, 81.4%, and 83.0% of government units respectively. The lowest percentages of government units are in the 1st and 2nd group of ecological sustainability (77.1% of government units). Figure 2 presents the structure of the sustainability groups by sustainability sub-constructs.

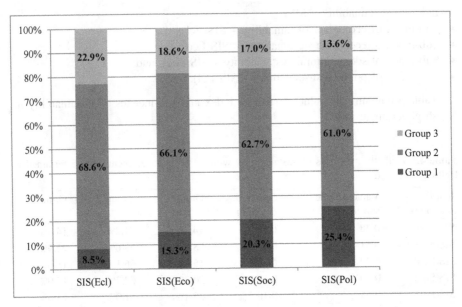

Fig. 2. Percentage of government units in the groups of sustainability.

4.3   ICT Adoption and Sustainability Levels

The results of the grouping of government units by their levels of ICT adoption and sustainability using Hellwig's method are shown in Fig. 3.

It has been found that the largest share of examined government units (68.6%) is at the medium level of ICT adoption, i.e. in the interval (0.34, 0.68] according to the index calculated based on Hellwig's method. The high level of this index exceeding value of 0.68 is characteristic for 16.9% of government units, whereas the low level of ICT adoption index not exceeding the value of 0.34 – for 14.4% of government units.

With regard to sustainability, the largest share of examined government units (71.2%) is also at the medium level, i.e. in the interval (0.32, 0.64] according to the index calculated based on Hellwig's method. The high level of sustainability exceeding value of 0.64 is characteristic for 14.4% of government units. Furthermore, the low level of sustainability index not exceeding the value of 0.32 is characteristic for the same percentage of government units (14.4%).

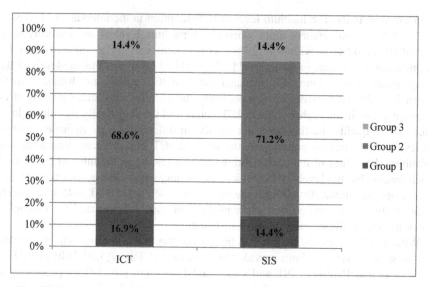

Fig. 3. Percentage of government units in the groups of ICT adoption and sustainability.

5 Conclusions

5.1 Research Contribution

This work contributes to the existing research on the SIS, especially the evaluation of ICT adoption and sustainability within government units by:

- proposing synthetic indexes of ICT adoption determined by Hellwig's method and indicating the level of ICT adoption within government units, separated into the levels of ICT outlay, information culture, ICT management, and ICT quality; and
- proposing synthetic indexes of sustainability resulting from ICT adoption determined by Hellwig's method and indicating the level of sustainability within government units, separated into the levels of ecological, economic, socio-cultural, and political sustainability.

The new indexes have been developed, based on a set of indicators in accordance with the nature of SIS, the essence of which is sustainability strongly influenced by adopting ICT within government units. The synthetic indicators of ecological, economic, socio-culture and political sustainability are used to describe and assess the level of sustainability within government units. With regard to the adoption of ICT, it embraces the whole spectrum of activities from the period when government units justify the need for adopting ICT until the period when government units experience the full potential of ICT and derive benefits from them. Therefore, the synthetic indicators of outlay on ICT, information culture, ICT management, and ICT quality are used to describe and evaluate ICT adoption.

According to the indexes calculated based on Hellwig's method, this study indicated that ICT adoption and sustainability are at the medium levels in the largest share of government units. The medium level of ICT adoption in the interval (0.34, 0.68] is within 68.6% of government units, whereas the medium level of sustainability in the interval (0.32, 0.64] is within 71.2% of government units. The values of the ICT adoption sub-indexes are in the interval [0.44, 0.61] which means that the levels of ICT outlay, information culture, ICT management, and ICT quality are distant from the pattern by 0.39, 0.51, 0.49, 0.56 respectively. In addition, this study confirmed the statistically significant higher value of ICT outlay and the statistically significant lower value of ICT quality. Furthermore, not significant differences were indicated between the level of information culture and the level of ICT management. Regarding sustainability, the values of the sustainability sub-indexes are in the interval [0.49, 0.55] which means that the levels of ecological, economic, socio-culture, and political sustainabilities are similar distant from the pattern by 0.49, 0.51, 0.50, 0.45 respectively. Additionally, it was proved that sustainability was not differentiated for ecological, economic, socio-cultural, and political sustainability.

With regard to the existing research findings on the SIS, it is reasonable to conclude that this study expands findings provided by Schauer [11], Fuchs [5, 6], Hilty et al. [8, 9], Guillemette and Paré [18, 19], and Curry and Donnellan [16, 17] by presenting an approach to the measurement of ICT adoption and sustainability levels within government units. The proposed approach also adds new insights into the measurement of ICT adoption and sustainability within government units that is employed in EGDI in [44]. It analyses a whole spectrum of ICT adoption and various kinds of sustainability strongly influenced by such an adoption.

The research outputs are also complementary with findings related to the measurement of ICT adoption and sustainability within enterprises [3]. Generally speaking, ICT adoption and sustainability within government units are at the lower level than within enterprises. The values of ICT adoption and sustainability synthetic sub-indicators are also at the lower lever within government unit related to the values of such sub-indicators within enterprises.

5.2   Implications for Research and Practice

The research findings can be used by scholars to improve and expand the research on the SIS. Researchers may use the proposed synthetic indicators to do similar analyses with different sample groups in other countries, and many comparisons between different countries can be drawn. Furthermore, the proposed methodology constitutes a very comprehensive basis for identifying the levels of ICT adoption and sustainability, but researchers may develop, verify and improve this methodology and its implementation. For example, sub-constructs and primary variables of ICT adoption and sustainability constructs may be improved in such a way that measurement of ICT adoption and sustainability will allow to gain a more precise view of SIS.

This study offers several implications for government units. They may find the results appealing and useful in enhancing the adoption of ICT, experiencing the full potential of ICT and deriving various benefits from ICT adoption like ecological, economic, socio-cultural, and political. In addition, this study recommends some guidelines for measuring ICT adoption and the benefits resulting from ICT adoption. Furthermore, the findings can help government units develop sound ICT adoption plans and receive funding from the European Union that set itself a target of implementing the 2030 Agenda for Sustainable Development [27].

It should be emphasized that this research can be largely useful for the transition economies in Central and Eastern Europe. This is because the countries are similar with regard to analogous geopolitical situation, their joint history, traditions, culture and values, quality of ICT infrastructure, as well as building democratic state structures and a free-market economy, and participating in the European integration process.

5.3 Limitations and Future Works

As with many other studies, this study has its limitations. First, the ICT adoption and sustainability constructs are new constructs that have yet to be further explored and exposed to repeated empirical validation. Second, the sample included Polish government units only, especially from the Silesian Province. The study sample precludes statistical generalization of the results from Silesian government units to Polish government units. Finally, the research subjects were limited to government units and it is therefore only the viewpoint of government units toward ICT adoption for achieving sustainability. Caution should be taken when generalizing the findings to the SIS.

Additional research must be performed to better understand the SIS, ICT adoption and sustainability construct, and the levels of ICT adoption and sustainability. First, further validation of the levels of ICT adoption and sustainability should be carried out for a larger sample comprising government units from different Polish provinces. Second, research on the measurement of ICT adoption and sustainability in households should be conducted, because households are, besides enterprises and government units, the main stakeholders of SIS [13].

Acknowledgement. I wish to express my sincere gratitude to my friend Maria Jadamus-Hacura for helping with statistical analysis.

References

1. Ziemba, E.: The contribution of ICT adoption to the sustainable information society. J. Comput. Inform. Syst. **59**, 116–126 (2017). https://doi.org/10.1080/08874417.2017.1312635
2. Ziemba, E.: The ICT adoption in enterprises in the context of the sustainable information society. In: Ganzha, M., Maciaszek, L., Paprzycki M. (eds.) Proceedings of the 2017 Federated Conference on Computer Science and Information Systems FedCSIS, 3–6 September 2017, pp. 1031–1038. Czech Technical University in Prague, Prague (2017). http://dx.doi.org/10.15439/2017F89
3. Ziemba, E.: Synthetic indexes for a sustainable information society: measuring ICT adoption and sustainability in Polish enterprises. In: Ziemba, E. (ed.) AITM/ISM-2017. LNBIP, vol. 311, pp. 151–169. Springer, Cham (2018). https://doi.org/10.1007/978-3-319-77721-4_9
4. Ziemba, E.: The ICT adoption in government units in the context of the sustainable information society. In: Ganzha, M., Maciaszek, L., Paprzycki M. (eds.) Proceedings of the 2018 Federated Conference on Computer Science and Information Systems FedCSIS, 9–12 September 2018, pp. 725–733. Adam Mickiewicz University Poznan, Poland (2018). https://doi.org/10.15439/2018F116

5. Fuchs, Ch.: Sustainable information society as ideology (part I). Inf. Tarsadalom **9**(2), 7–19 (2009)
6. Fuchs, Ch.: Sustainable information society as ideology (part II). Inf. Tarsadalom **9**(3), 27–52 (2009)
7. Fuchs, Ch.: Theoretical foundations of defining the participatory, co-operative, sustainable information society. Inf. Comm. Soc. **13**(1), 23–47 (2010). https://doi.org/10.1080/13691180902801585
8. Hilty, L.M., Aebischer, B.: ICT for sustainability: an emerging research field. Adv. Intell. Syst. Comput. **310**, 1–34 (2015). https://doi.org/10.1007/978-3-319-09228-7_1
9. Hilty, L.M., Hercheui, M.D.: ICT and sustainable development. In: Berleur, J., Hercheui, M. D., Hilty, L.M. (eds.) CIP/HCC-2010. IAICT, vol. 328, pp. 227–235. Springer, Heidelberg (2010). https://doi.org/10.1007/978-3-642-15479-9_22
10. Houghton, John W.: ICT and the environment in developing countries: a review of opportunities and developments. In: Berleur, J., Hercheui, M.D., Hilty, Lorenz M. (eds.) CIP/HCC-2010. IAICT, vol. 328, pp. 236–247. Springer, Heidelberg (2010). https://doi.org/10.1007/978-3-642-15479-9_23
11. Schauer, T.: The sustainable information society – vision and risks. The Club of Rome – European Support Centre, Vienna (2003)
12. Servaes, J., Carpentier, N. (eds.): Towards a Sustainable Information Society. Deconstructing WSIS. Intellect, Portland (2006)
13. Ziemba, E.: The holistic and systems approach to a sustainable information society. J. Comput. Inform. Syst. **54**(1), 106–116 (2013). https://doi.org/10.1080/08874417.2013.11645676
14. Ziemba, E. (ed.): Towards a Sustainable Information Society: People, Business and Public Administration Perspectives. Cambridge Scholars Publishing, Newcastle upon Tyne (2016)
15. Avgerou, C.: Discourses on ICT and development. Inf. Technol. Int. Dev. **6**(3), 1–18 (2010)
16. Curry, E., Donnellan, B.: Understanding the maturity of sustainable ICT. In: vom Brocke, J., Seidel, S., Recker, J. (eds.) Green Business Process Management – Towards the Sustainable Enterprise, pp. 203–216. Springer, Heidelberg (2012). https://doi.org/10.1007/978-3-642-27488-6_12
17. Donnellan, B., Sheridan, C., Curry, E.: A capability maturity framework for sustainable information and communication technology. IT Prof. **13**(1), 33–40 (2011). https://doi.org/10.1109/MITP.2011.2
18. Guillemette, M.G., Paré, G.: Toward a new theory of the contribution of the IT function in organizations. MIS Q. **36**(2), 529–551 (2012)
19. Guillemette, M.G., Paré, G.: Transformation of the information technology function in organizations: a case study in the manufacturing sector. Can. J. Adm. Sci. **29**, 177–190 (2012). https://doi.org/10.1002/cjas.224
20. Seidel, S., Recker, J., vom Brocke, J.: Sensemaking and sustainable practicing: functional affordances of information systems in green transformations. MIS Q. **37**(4), 1275–1299 (2013)
21. Watson, R.T., Boudreau, M.C., Chen, A.J., Huber, M.: Green IS: building sustainable business practices. In: Watson, R.T. (ed.) Information Systems, pp. 247–261. Global Text Project, Athens (2008)
22. Bartle, J.R., Leuenberger, D.Z.: Sustainable Development for Public Administration. M.E. Sharpe, New York (2009)
23. McDonald, W.: Sustainable development and public administration: challenges and innovation in citizen engagement. Rev. Pub. Adm. Manag. **5**(2), 219 (2017). https://doi.org/10.4172/2315-7844.1000219

24. Parrado, S., Löffler, E.: Towards sustainable public administration. National Agency for the Evaluation of Public Policies and Quality of Services, Madrid (2010). http://www.eupan.eu/files/repository/Final_Report_on_Measuring_Sustainability.pdf. Accessed 4 Jan 2019
25. Radu, L.: How to develop sustainable public administration reforms. Transylv. Rev. Adm. Sci. **44E**, 180–195 (2015)
26. Svara, J.H., Brunet, J.R.: Social equity is a pillar of public administration. J. Public Aff. Educ. **11**(3), 253–258 (2005). https://doi.org/10.1080/15236803.2005.12001398
27. United Nations: Transforming Our World: The 2030 Agenda for Sustainable Development. A/RES/70/1 (2015). https://sustainabledevelopment.un.org/content/documents/21252030%20Agenda%20for%20Sustainable%20Development%20web.pdf. Accessed 4 Jan 2019
28. United Nations: Compendium of innovative practices in public governance and administration for sustainable development. Division for Public Administration and Development Management, Department of Economic and Social Affairs (2016). https://publicadministration.un.org/publications/content/PDFs/Compendium%20Public%20Governance%20and%20Administration%20for%20Sustainable%20Development.pdf. Accessed 4 Jan 2019
29. Jurado-González, J., Gómez-Barroso, J.L.: What became of the information society and development? Assessing the information society's relevance in the context of an economic crisis. Inf. Technol. Dev. **22**(3), 436–463 (2016). https://doi.org/10.1080/02681102.2016.1155143
30. Palvia, P., Baqir, N., Nemati, H.: ICT for socio-economic development: a citizens' perspective. Inf. Manag. **55**, 160–176 (2018). https://doi.org/10.1016/j.im.2017.05.003
31. Nord, J.H., Riggio, M.T., Paliszkiewicz, J.: Social and economic development through information and communications technologies: Italy. J. Comput. Inf. Syst. **57**(3), 278–285 (2017). https://doi.org/10.1080/08874417.2016.1213621
32. Ross, J.W., Vitale, M.R.: The ERP revolution: surviving vs thriving. Inf. Syst. Front. **2**(2), 233–241 (2000). https://doi.org/10.1023/A:1026500224101
33. Sachs, J.D.: The Age of Sustainable Development. Columbia University Press, New York (2015)
34. Fuchs, C.: Sustainability and the information society. In: Berleur, J., Nurminen, M.I., Impagliazzo, J. (eds.) HCC 2006. IIFIP, vol. 223, pp. 219–230. Springer, Boston, MA (2006). https://doi.org/10.1007/978-0-387-37876-3_18
35. Nicolette, J., Burr, S., Rockel, M.: A practical approach for demonstrating environmental sustainability and stewardship through a net ecosystem service analysis. Sustainability **5**, 2152–2177 (2013). https://doi.org/10.3390/su5052152
36. Nyström, T., Mustaquim, M.M.: Finding sustainability indicators for information system assessment. In: Proceedings of the 19th International Academic Mindtrek Conference, Tampere, 22–24 September 2015, pp. 106–113 (2015). https://doi.org/10.1145/2818187.2818278
37. Missimer, M., Robèrt, K.H., Broman, G.: A strategic approach to social sustainability. part 2: a principle-based definitions. J. Clean. Prod. **149**(1), 42–52 (2017). https://doi.org/10.1016/j.jclepro.2016.04.059
38. Khan, R.: How frugal innovation promotes social sustainability. Sustainability **8**(10), 1034 (2016). https://doi.org/10.3390/su8101034
39. Ngwenya, B.: Realigning governance: from e-government to e-democracy for social and economic development. In: Bwalya, K.J., Mutula, S. (eds.) Digital Solutions for Contemporary Democracy and Government, pp. 21–45. IGI Global, Hershey (2015). https://doi.org/10.4018/978-1-4666-8430-0.ch002
40. ITU: International Telecommunication Union. Measuring the Information Society Report 2016. International Telecommunication Union, Geneva (2016)

41. Information Economy Report 2017: Digitalization, Trade, and Development. United Nations Conference on Trade and Development UNCTAD (2017)

42. Ziemba, E., Żelazny, R.: Measuring the information society in Poland – dilemmas and a quantified image. In: Ganzha, M., Maciaszek, L., Paprzycki M. (eds.) Proceedings of the 2018 Federated Conference on Computer Science and Information Systems FedCSIS, 9–12 September 2018, pp. 1185–1192. AGH University of Science and Technology, Cracow (2013)

43. Bilbao-Osorio, B., Dutta, S., Lanvin, B. (eds.) The Global Information Technology Report 2014. Rewards and Risks of Big Data. World Economic Forum, Geneva (2014)

44. United Nations: E-government Survey 2018. Gearing e-government to support transformation towards sustainable and resilient societies. United Nations, New York (2018). https://www.unescap.org/sites/default/files/E-Government%20Survey%202018_FINAL.pdf. Accessed 24 Dec 2018

45. Van de Kerk, G., Manuel, A.R.: A comprehensive index for a sustainable society: the SSI—the sustainable society index. Ecol. Econ. **66**, 228–242 (2008). https://doi.org/10.1016/j.ecolecon.2008.01.029

46. Panda, S., Chakraborty, M., Misra, S.K.: Assessment of social sustainable development in urban India by a composite index. Int. J. Sustain. Built Environ. **5**, 435–450 (2016). https://doi.org/10.1016/j.ijsbe.2016.08.001

47. ŚCSI: Strategia rozwoju społeczeństwa informacyjnego województwa śląskiego do roku 2015 [Strategy of information society development in Upper Silesia region]. Śląskie Centrum Społeczeństwa Informacyjnego, Katowice (2009). http://www.e-slask.pl/article/strategia_rozwoju_spoleczenstwa_informacyjnego_wojewodztwa_slaskiego_do_roku_2015. Accessed 12 June 2016

48. Collis, J., Hussey, R.: Business Research: A Practical Guide for Undergraduate and Postgraduate Students. Palgrave Macmillan, New York (2003)

49. Ziemba, E., Papaj, T.: A pragmatic approach to e-government maturity in Poland – implementation and usage of SEKAP. In: Ferrari, E., Castelnovo, W. (eds.) Proceedings of 13th European Conference on eGovernment ECEG, 13–14 June 2013, pp. 560–570. University of Insubria, Como (2013)

50. Hellwig, Z.: Zastosowanie metody taksono micznej do typologicznego podziału krajów ze względu na poziom rozwoju oraz zasoby i strukturę wykwalifikowanych kadr (The application of the taxonomic method to the typological division of a countries due to their level of development, resources and structure of qualified personnel – in Polish. Przegląd Statystyczny **4**, 307–326 (1968)

51. Hwang, C.L., Yoon, K.: Multiple Attribute Decision-Making Methods and Applications. Springer, Heidelberg (1981). https://doi.org/10.1007/978-3-642-48318-9

52. Kaczmarczyk, P.: Application of the linear ordering methods in the voivodships research in the field of social media usage in enterprises in the period 2014–2017. J. Econ. Manag. **33** (3), 39–62 (2018). https://doi.org/10.22367/jem.2018.33.03

53. Bolibok, P., Żukowski, M.: The impact of inequalities in regional economic development on disparities in spatial distribution of cashless payment infrastructure in Poland. J. Econ. Manag. **21**(3), 173–188 (2015)

Author Index

Printed in the United States
By Bookmasters